First Year, Worst Year

First Year, Worst Year

Coping with the unexpected death of our grown-up daughter

BARBARA A. WILSON AND MICHAEL WILSON

John Wiley & Sons, Ltd

Other Wiley Editorial Offices

John Wiley & Sons Inc., 111 River Street, Hoboken, NJ 07030, USA

Jossey-Bass, 989 Market Street, San Francisco, CA 94103-1741, USA

Wiley-VCH Verlag GmbH, Boschstr. 12, D-69469 Weinheim, Germany

John Wiley & Sons Australia Ltd, 33 Park Road, Milton, Queensland 4064, Australia

John Wiley & Sons (Asia) Pte Ltd, 2 Clementi Loop #02-01, Jin Xing Distripark, Singapore 129809

John Wiley & Sons Canada Ltd, 22 Worcester Road, Etobicoke, Ontario, Canada M9W 1L1

Wiley also publishes its books in a variety of electronic formats. Some content that appears in print may not be available in electronic books.

Library of Congress Cataloging-in-Publication Data

Wilson, Barbara A., 1941–
  First year, worst year : coping with the unexpected death of our
grown-up daughter / Barbara A. Wilson and Michael Wilson.
      p. cm.
  Includes bibliographical references.
  ISBN 0-470-09359-5 (pbk. : alk. paper)
  1. Bereavement–Psychological aspects. 2. Adult children–Death–
Psychological aspects. 3. Wilson, Sarah, d. 2000–Death and burial. 4.
Wilson, Barbara A., 1941- –Diaries. 5. Mothers–United States–Diaries. I.
Wilson, Michael, 1935-   II. Title.
  BF575.G7 W58 2004
  155.9′37–dc22

                                          2004007316

British Library Cataloguing in Publication Data

A catalogue record for this book is available from the British Library

ISBN 0-470-09359-5

Typeset in 10/12pt Bembo by Dobbie Typesetting Ltd, Tavistock, Devon
Printed and bound in Great Britain by TJ International, Padstow, Cornwall
This book is printed on acid-free paper responsibly manufactured from sustainable forestry
in which at least two trees are planted for each one used for paper production.

THIS IS A DIARY OF BEREAVEMENT
FOLLOWING THE DEATH IN PERU
ON MAY 12TH, 2000, OF
SARAH, A BELOVED DAUGHTER

A nobleman once asked a Chinese philosopher to grant his family a blessing. The famous scholar thought for a moment, then said "Grandfather dies, father dies, son dies". The nobleman was horrified, but the philosopher shrugged his shoulders. "What other way would you have it?" he said.
None.

(Reproduced from McCracken & Semel (eds), *A Broken Heart Still Beats*.)

Contents

Foreword

This remarkable diary is of the 'Worst Year' of their lives endured by Barbara and Mick Wilson after their adult daughter, Sarah, was drowned in Peru. It records the daily lives of two parents and their surviving children, struggling to make the terrible and exhausting journey from devastating, overwhelming grief, when the small light at the end of the dark tunnel can barely be glimpsed at all, through a more calm acceptance of the inevitable, to the stage of being able to resume their normal lives without it being a constant emotional struggle.

This does not mean, as my husband and I well know from the death of our 14-year-old twin son, Nicky, that the child you have lost has been forgotten and pushed to the back of your mind. Rather, it means that he or she has a constant place in the hearts and minds of the family circle and is able to be remembered and talked about frequently with pleasure as well as sadness.

Barbara and Mick rightly feel that other bereaved parents reading this diary may be helped to realise how much their early emotional turmoil is an unavoidable result of the tragedy they have suffered, but that there is (maybe unbelievably at first) light at the end of the long, dark tunnel, and they will be able to resume their more or less normal lives, slowly, with time.

The book will also appeal to the general reader with its examination of bereavement in general and its description of family life, work and travel that has to go on despite the loss of a loved child. There is also an account of Mick and Barbara's extraordinary expedition in the Peruvian mountains, led by the same guide who had tried to rescue their daughter. They climbed sometimes at 14,000 feet above sea level to the deepest canyon in the world, where they conducted their own ceremony in honour of Sarah who was last seen a year earlier at that point in the rapids of the River Cotahuasi.

There is an ancient Chinese poem that beautifully expresses the feelings of bereaved parents:

> He took his big candle
> And went into another room
> I cannot find:
> But I know he was here
> Because of all the happiness
> He left behind

Countess Mountbatten of Burma
March 2004

Acknowledgements

On a personal level our deepest thanks go to Carol, our rock and our strength during the first months of our bereavement, and also to Peter.

We also wish to thank The Compassionate Friends for their help and support during the worst year of our lives – particularly to Dinah Perkins (our first compassionate friend); Margaret and Jim Pringle and Joe and Iris Lawley; Julia Darling, Barbara's secretary, for her help in the early days and for typing the manuscript; Barbara's colleagues, Jonathan Evans, Agnes Shiel, Eve Greenfield, Hazel Emslie, Tom Manly, Narinder Kapur and Mike Kopelman for their generosity of spirit in troubled times; Ian Robertson for telling us about The Compassionate Friends; Anita Taub, Jill Winegardner and Stephanie Moore, friends of ours who knew and loved Sarah; Cindy, Sarah's best friend who was so devastated at the news; Fergus Gracey for laying flowers in South America on the "Day of the dead"; Jean Ferrandis for dedicating his playing of a Bartok song to Sarah; Jim Becker for his gift of "A broken heart still beats"; Audrey Holland who talked about her bereavement and was so helpful, and Audrey's dead son Ben; Hilary Green for reading an earlier draft and for her helpful comments and encouragement; Robin Green for her generous donations to The Compassionate Friends and The Oliver Zangwill Centre in memory of Sarah; Celia Geyer, Diana Youdale, Margaret Pringle, Jillian Tallon and Catharine Pointer, The Compassionate Friend's librarian for helping to track down people, prose and poems; Barbara Millar for her editing of the book; Vivien Ward at John Wiley & Sons Ltd for accepting the book; Deborah Egleton, also from Wiley, for helping us through the process of publishing; a big debt of gratitude is due to Countess Mountbatten for her introduction to the book; and finally, Anna and Matthew, Sarah's sister and brother, and Rosie and Francesca, Sarah's nieces, who will always have to live without this special person. Matthew also took many of the photographs for which we are also grateful.

The following acknowledgements are to people and publishers for permission to quote their work. For the story about the Chinese nobleman (see p. vi), "What kind of universe is this anyway?" by Mary Semel (see pp. 61–2) and "Fireflies" by David Morrell (see p. 63) reproduced from McCracken, A. and Semel, M. (eds) (1998) *A Broken Heart Still Beats* by permission of the Hazelden Foundation, copyright © 2000.

Terry Kettering's poem "The Elephant in the Room" (see pp. 69–70) reproduced from *Bereavement Magazine* (October 1989) by permission of Bereavement Publishing, Inc. (www.bereavementresources.com).

The extract from *Letter to a Younger Son* by Christopher Leach (see pp. 131–2), copyright © 1981 by Christopher Leach, reprinted by permission of Harcourt, Inc., and JM Dent, a division of The Orion Publishing Group.

"Stunning Pain" by Ann Finkbeiner (see pp. 62–3) reproduced from *After the Death of a Child* by Ann K. Finkbeiner (p. 4). Copyright © 1995 by Ann K. Finkbeiner. Reprinted with permission of The Free Press, a Division of Simon & Schuster Adult Publishing Group. All rights reserved.

The extract from *Paula* by Isabel Allende (see p. 112) reproduced by permission of HarperCollins Publishers Ltd. Copyright © 1994 by Isabel Allende. Translation copyright © 1995 by HarperCollins Publishers.

"Undo It, Take It Back" by Nessa Rapoport (see p. 113) reproduced from *A Woman's Book of Grieving* by Nessa Rapoport. Copyright © 1994 by Nessa Rapoport. Reprinted by permission of the author. All rights reserved.

"The Existence of Love" by Marjorie Pizer (see p. 113) reproduced from *Selected Poems, 1963–1983* by Marjorie Pizer (1984) by permission of the author.

"We miss you Sarah" (see p. 40) reproduced by permission of Brant (a mountain bike friend of Sarah's); his piece from the internet.

Photograph of Jean Ferrandis with his flute (plate section), copyright © Elise Hardy, Europeart, reproduced by permission.

The articles, "Woman dies in rafting holiday" and "Emotional Service Remembers 'Best person'", *The Mercury*, October 6th 2000 (see pp. 137–9) reproduced by permission of The Mercury Series.

"Obituary Sarah Jones" (see p. 139) reproduced by permission of *Global Adventure*.

"Being Lucky" by Patricia Lloyd (see pp. 166–7) reproduced by permission of the author.

"Twice the heartbreak" by Nigel Starmer-Smith (see pp. 167–71), which appeared in the *Sunday Telegraph* May 13th, 2001, reproduced by permission of The Telegraph Group Ltd.

"Rio Cotahuasi: The World's Deepest Canyon – Really!" by John Foss (see pp. 180–6) reproduced by permission of *South American Explorer* (article published in Spring 1996 edition).

Thanks to all of Sarah's friends who gave permission to include their speeches, letters and e-mails.

Thanks to Neil Storey at the British Embassy in Lima for permission to include the British Honorary Consul report.

Introduction

2003

The core of this book, the heart of it, is Barbara's journal, written in the year 2000, the year in which we lost our daughter in a white-water rafting accident. Sarah has never been found. Barbara has kept a daily diary for the past forty years and she kept it going, even during the very darkest of our days in that awful first and worst year. As a result of our experiences during the first year of bereavement, and our subsequent progress through grief in the next two years, we decided we would try to communicate our thoughts and feelings to others. While most people thankfully will never have to go through the mental and emotional agony of losing a child, they are nevertheless bombarded by images of grief through the popular press and television. As experienced grievers, we are of the opinion that this second-hand view is frequently superficial and can lead to equally superficial and automatic responses. So one of the driving forces behind this book is a desire to tell it as it is, to go beyond the nightmare imaginings of those whose only experience of the loss of a loved child is perhaps fuelled by media images.

We realised that the journal would make an impact on readers, but we also thought that the pain expressed in the journal throughout that first year needed building on so that some light through the darkness could be seen. People do not stay locked in grief unless they are made too ill by their losses. Most of us will pull through because there is no other alternative: life has to go on. We wanted to show that grieving people do change as time passes. So we have added additional material from our experiences during the third year after Sarah's death. The structure of the book is therefore as follows: each chapter starts with some reflections that both of us have put together during the year 2003, then proceeds to the 2000 journal, as we said, the 'heart' of the book. The final chapter breaks from this structure as it describes our 2001 journey to the Cotahuasi Valley in Peru, in mountains that at times reach 14,000 feet, and into the deepest canyon on earth, where our lovely Sarah is now laid to rest. We were taken there by the guide Pepe Lopez, who was on the original rafting expedition, and who was the last person on earth to see our Sarah as she drifted beyond his reach. We had to get there to say our final goodbyes.

We hope the reader will find other things in Barbara's journal that will excite his or her interest. Besides the main narrative dealing with grief, it also shows a mother and a family coming to terms with the world of work, and even the world of leisure, while at the same time carrying the awful burden of the loss of a child. The reader may be in for some shocks because our picture of bereavement includes accounts of times when we laughed, had fun, forgot our daughter, watched football on TV, argued over petty things. As we said, life in all its absurdity goes on even though you have been mentally and emotionally struck down by what you never wanted to happen. The book is also in some ways a travel document as Barbara continued to journey abroad during that first year, either to conferences or to trekking destinations. One of the ways Barbara coped with Sarah's death was through travel. The book also takes the reader to that wonderful country of Peru, and to what must be one of the strangest and most mysterious canyons in the world. We have included several prose extracts and poems that have helped or inspired us. A number of these pieces have been written by other parents who have lost a child. We also include an excellent description of the Cotahuasi River and its amazing canyon, written by an adventurous kayaker. The book finishes with our own journey to that extraordinary place, led by Pepe Lopez, the guide who had attempted to save Sarah from the dreadful rapids into which she was pitched on that fateful day of May 12th, 2000.

We shall switch from one narration to the other throughout this book, from the years 2003 and 2000 and on to 2001 in the final chapter. So the reader will be following two accounts: one is the less painful, reflective prose of a mother and father in the third year of their grieving; the other is the immediate, and at times shocking, blow-by-blow account of a mother's lamentations during the first awful year of the loss of a child. We hope the reader will learn something about grief, its nature and its progression from anguish to resolution; we hope you will learn something about our lovely daughter, Sarah, who died so violently on May 12th, 2000; we hope you will get to know the rest of the family; we hope you will learn something new about a most remote and beautiful part of Peru; and finally we hope you will be able to share our thoughts and feelings as we come through the darkest of times to a period of resolution.

We have, after three years, reached a stage when we can continue our lives reasonably normally. It is a period utterly different from the first year of our loss and, had we been told in those dark days that we would achieve such a degree of normalisation, we would have greeted the message with disbelief. How we have managed to get this far is part of our story. In it we shall offer our own reflections on bereavement and describe the tremendous support we have been given by friends and family; we shall show the reader how we learned to share our grief with fellow members of The Compassionate Friends (TCF). This is a club which is both terrible, because you can join only when you lose a child, and wonderful, because its members have, despite the most awful of losses, seemingly grown as human beings, exhibiting great dignity and warmth and providing the most exceptional empathy to those faced with the same agonising loss.

Although it is often said that people who face terrible personal deprivation such as the loss of a child frequently change their ways and 'become better people' we don't think this is a necessary adjunct of grief. Although the will to somehow be better people may be there, we think in our own case we frequently fall short of any noble aspirations, and resort to similar petty ways we exhibited before the death of Sarah: we still get angry, behave unfairly, are sometimes selfish, and are not always strong in our determination to be noble and perhaps highly principled. Nevertheless, we are very different people from those blissfully unaware parents who went about their daily lives not expecting the tragedy that was waiting round the corner. How are we different? We are not too sure? We hope such questions may be answered as our account develops. One thing is for certain, and that is that Sarah, our firstborn and blessed child was someone who was loved and respected by all the family. She was, despite her risk-taking and her somewhat eccentric attitude towards life, a most beautiful person, a loving daughter, and someone who lived her life to the full. She has always seemed to us to be without pettiness, without deceit or envy. She loved others fully with no questions asked, no demands made. It is hard to be without her but we write this book in honour of her and for her lovely sister and brother who share the views expressed in this introduction.

∽

CHAPTER ONE

There's terrible, terrible news

2000

MONDAY, MAY 15TH, 2000

It was nearly 3.00 p.m. I wanted to leave work early as my granddaughter, Rosie, had an orthodontist appointment at 4.30 in Bury St Edmunds. I was going to look after Rosie's little sister, Francesca, while my daughter, Anna, took Rosie to have a brace fitted on her teeth. My son, Matthew, was in Philadelphia and my older daughter, Sarah, was in Peru on a white-water rafting trip. Rosie and I were due to meet Sarah in Peru for a 10-day holiday later in the month.

I went into the next room to my colleague, Agnes, and said, "I'm leaving soon because of Rosie's orthodontist appointment." Agnes replied, "No you can't because Mick's on his way to meet you." My husband, Mick, had told me he had to go to Cambridge railway station that afternoon to meet an American visitor who was coming for a meeting with Mick and other publishing colleagues the following day. I said to Agnes, "No, Mick's not coming to see me, he's coming to Cambridge to meet an American guy at the station." Agnes said, "Well he phoned Eve." Eve was another colleague of ours. "What would he phone Eve for?" I said. Agnes would not say – she was being cagey, so I went to Eve's room and said, "Did Mick phone you?" "Yes." "Why?" A vague, noncommittal response came – "He's coming over, can't you wait for him?" I felt myself getting cross. I wanted to be home to look after Francesca and start the cooking. I phoned Mick's mobile number and was put through to the messaging service. I said, "Mick, I'm not waiting for you in Cambridge, I'll see you at home tonight." I locked up my room and went to leave but Agnes came out to stop me.

"Barbara, you can't go, there is a real problem and Mick is on his way to see you," said Agnes. "It's not Sarah and that bloody rafting?" I answered. She gave me a strange look – in retrospect I knew she was saying "Yes", but I didn't want to understand that so I said, "Maybe it's my cat, maybe my son-in-law has run over the cat." In my head I said, "Please let it be the cat, please let it be the cat." I love my cat Django but I knew I could live with his death. Never for a moment did I think, "Matthew (our son) has been shot in Philadelphia", even though 'Philly' is a dangerous city with lots of guns.

Another colleague, Tom, then came in and said, "Mick's on the phone – on my extension – and he sounds in a state." "Why doesn't Mick ring my extension?" I thought. I went into Tom's room and picked up the phone. Mick had heard my message and wanted to stop me leaving. He was crying and said, "Barbara, there's terrible, terrible news." I went cold and calm and said, "Is it Sarah?" "Yes," replied Mick. "Is she dead?" I asked. "We think so," said Mick, "she's missing and was last seen floating face down." "Well that's it," I replied. "I can't wait to see you," said Mick. I put the phone down and looked at Tom who said, "She's only missing." I was furious and said, "Tom, I'm not a fool." I went to Agnes and hugged her then paced up and down until Mick arrived.

I met Mick outside and we hugged each other crying together. He came in while I saw Agnes to tell her what parts of my schedule to cancel. I was quite calm and controlled then. There were meetings for the rest of the week and a talk I was giving for the Leonard Cheshire Homes up north on Friday. My secretary, Julia, was on leave that Monday but Agnes said she'd deal with everything. We left Mick's car in the car park and took my car home. On the way, Mick told me the story from his side.

He had been at work early that afternoon when his colleague, Denise, answered the phone. She said to Mick, "There's a Max Milligan for you." Mick's knees buckled. He knew there must be something wrong in Peru as there would be no other reason for Max Milligan to phone. Indeed we had only heard the name a few days earlier when Sarah had called from Cusco in Peru. She told us that she had met a guy called Max Milligan and had been on a mountain bike ride with him. Then this call. Mick took the phone and Max told him that there had been a terrible accident and Sarah was missing. He said he would give Mick a few minutes and would telephone again five minutes later. He did phone back and we learned that there were two rafts each with five people and a local guide. Sarah was on the first raft. The raft had been stuck in a 'hole', a hydraulic (I always see this in my mind as a whirlpool). The raft upended and all five fell out. The guide was able to remain on the raft. Four people were saved and Sarah was last seen floating face down. She had died on the Friday – May 12th – they had searched for two days but her body had not been found. At this stage we just heard the bare details. Mick telephoned our son in America and told him. He did not tell Anna as he thought she was at work and he did not have her number. He telephoned Eve to tell her to make sure I waited for him to arrive.

Sarah, Matthew and Anna were very close. There was less than three years in age between them and all of us kept in touch at least every two or three days. I had had an e-mail from Sarah on May 7th saying she would not be in touch for 12 days because she'd be in the wilds. I e-mailed her on the 7th saying "take care with the rafting", and again on the 11th to await her return. Matthew, thinking that Anna knew the awful news, telephoned her. She was really pleased to hear from him and then realised he was crying. She thought something had happened to him. When he told her about Sarah she kept saying, "Not my Sarah, not my Sarah", over and over. Matthew then wondered whether he had dreamt Mick's phone call.

On the way home from Cambridge we telephoned Anna and arranged for her and the two girls, Rosie and Francesca, to come to our house. We arrived home, shocked and weepy, although fewer tears flowed then than later. "Isn't it terrible?" I said to Anna. Anna was sobbing. Rosie, my granddaughter had always been close to Sarah, in fact Sarah had been present at Rosie's birth on Christmas Day, 1987, over 12 years earlier. That evening Rosie kept drawing pictures of Sarah and copying photographs of her. Francesca, who was four, was also attached to her auntie but she did not cry so much. She asked questions like – "We'll never see Sarah again will we?" We did not feel, however, that Francesca understood the finality of Sarah's death. None of us probably did at that stage.

My next job was to telephone my sister-in-law, Carol, who lives near Ipswich, about 25 minutes drive away. Carol is my best friend and one of the strengths of the family. Carol and her husband Peter were out but I left a message saying Sarah was missing, probably dead and to phone us.

Mick and I decided we had to get Matthew home as soon as possible. I telephoned Matt in Philadelphia and said I would try to get him a flight that night. By now it was about 6.00 p.m. in the UK and 1.00 p.m. in Philadelphia. I then called British Airways and said, "There has been an unexpected death in the family and I need to get my son home from Philadelphia to London this evening if possible." The British Airways staff member I spoke to was great. She said there was a seat available that evening for £106 (a very low price – was that because of the circumstances, I wonder? I will never know). She also said that Matthew would have to go to the ticket office in Philly and that she would tell the people in the office there what had happened so they would be kind to Matt. Such kindness from her and from the other good people at that time will not be forgotten. It meant so much to us then to know there were good people around. I phoned Matt to tell him what to do. He cried copiously. We were all crying frequently but I felt I had to sort things out as best I could, so I kept in control as much as possible.

Carol and Peter had, by now, heard the message and called to say they were on their way over. They arrived and Carol cooked something for us. I don't remember the details of the evening but we talked and talked and cried and cried. I remember feeling shocked at some point in the evening that I felt hungry. "How can you be hungry," I said to myself, "when your daughter has died?" But I was. I didn't eat much but I ate something.

Perhaps it was surprising that we did not hope that she would be found. At times I did – there were moments that day and the next when I thought that she might be washed up and found by some villagers. "Perhaps she'll be found with amnesia," I thought, "and they are trying to establish who she is." I always knew, though, that this was wishful thinking. The fact that she had been last seen face down, unconscious, and that the rafters had been searching for three days, told me that she was dead. Somehow we got through the evening. Anna, Rosie and Francesca went home, so did Carol and Peter, and eventually Mick and I went to bed.

We hardly slept. I managed an hour and Mick probably had the same. I felt so tired and wanted to sleep, but as soon as I came close, I jolted awake with the horror of it all. Eventually I slept but jolted awake again after an hour thinking, "Please let it not be true." Then the ghastly realisation that it was true. I said to Mick, "I need a cuddle." He obliged, we were both needing physical contact and held each other frequently in those early days.

One thing that made me feel particularly terrible was remembering the previous weekend. On Friday May 12th, the day Sarah died, I was giving a one-day workshop in Belgium. I came home that evening and got ready to go to Brighton the next day to attend a memorial service for Alan Parkin, a colleague who had died unexpectedly of a heart attack at the age of 49. I was, of course, totally unaware anything was amiss with Sarah. On Saturday May 13th, Mick and I drove down to Sussex University for the service. It was a beautiful sunny day and I was somewhat regretful that I could not sunbathe in the garden. During the afternoon I saw Alan Parkin's elderly mother crying. I said to another colleague, Narinder Kapur, "How terrible to outlive your children." Narinder said, "It's the worst thing." We stayed in Brighton that night and I went to a dinner with Alan's friends and colleagues. The next day we drove home after breakfast. During the drive I said to Mick, "Life is good at the moment. Work's going well. The kids are all sorted and we don't have to worry about money." Sarah was already dead and I had no idea! If there is any spiritual communication or life after death, or any of those things, then I would have known she was dead or would at least have had some sense of foreboding. She was my firstborn, most wanted, most treasured, most beloved daughter and I'd lost her. I always told her I couldn't live without her, she knew how much she was loved by her parents, her sister and her brother and she left us in such turmoil and despair.

TUESDAY, MAY 16TH, AND WEDNESDAY MAY 17TH, 2000

I was up before 3.00 a.m. and e-mailed my secretary, Julia, at 6.30 a.m. Julia was due back from leave that day. I wrote:

Dear Julia,

I don't know whether or not you have heard the terrible news but Sarah has drowned in a rafting accident in Peru. Five fell out of the raft and four managed to get to the safety lines. Sarah didn't. She seems to have lost consciousness in about 10 seconds. The others tried to get her but couldn't and she was last seen face down going down the river so we know there is no hope. This happened on Friday but we didn't know until yesterday afternoon. They are still searching for her body and will continue searching until tomorrow — it takes four days to get to the sea. The man at the Consulate thought that in accidents like this the bodies are hardly ever found and she will be listed as a missing person so we won't even get a death certificate or anything. It is just too too painful for all of us.

Julia please don't phone just yet as I can't bear it. You can e-mail if you want and please can you let Anita Taub and Stephanie Moore know as they were so fond of Sarah. Everyone loved her, she was so good. Matthew has just landed in London and will be home in a couple of hours. We are all totally devastated.

Love, Barbara

(We must have been in touch with the Consulate the previous day although I don't remember that happening.)

Matt landed early that morning and his cousin Simon, Carol's son, met him at Heathrow. They turned up later than they should as they were so busy talking and crying they missed the right exit from the M25. We feared for everyone at that time — if people were out of sight we thought something terrible had happened. Carol and Peter were there by 7.30 a.m. Matt came in and hugged everyone, crying all the time. He said he collected his ticket the night before. The staff in the British Airways office in Philadelphia were kind to him and said they knew he had had bad news. The stewardess on the flight gave him a row of three seats to himself. She found him some alcohol that he had asked for and said, "If there is anything you want let me know. If you want me to come and talk to you, let me know." Again neither Matt nor his father nor I have forgotten that.

He met Simon in the arrivals hall. Everyone around them was greeting someone with smiles, but Simon and Matthew hugged each other crying. Simon could have had little or no sleep in order to get to the airport on time. He wanted to do something helpful though and this was the most practical thing he could do.

I e-mailed Agnes to check she had cancelled everything.

Dear Agnes,

Things are pretty terrible here — lots of calls but no hard facts although they don't expect to find the body and so she'll be listed as a missing person and God knows what happens then as we can't get a death certificate and so on and so on. I can't cope with the phone very well at present and there are lots of practical calls to make and receive. I can cope with e-mails though so that's how people should get in touch at the moment. Thanks for your support yesterday.

Love, Barbara

I don't normally sign off 'love from' in e-mails to colleagues but that was what I wanted to do then. The family talked over and over about Sarah, how lovely she was, how stupid she was to go on such a trip. How angry we were with her for going on such a dangerous trip. By then we had been informed she had rafted on a grade 5 river, the most dangerous grade that it is possible to raft. Grade 1 is the easiest and grade 6 would be something like Niagara Falls. We knew she was rafting and that she had been rafting before in Bolivia the previous year, but we did not know she had chosen to go on this grade 5.

Anna, Rosie and Francesca came. Anna and I talked about the people we should telephone. We did not know the procedure. If someone dies in the United Kingdom, there is a procedure to follow and someone to tell you what to do. If you get a phone call from a foreign country, it is much more difficult. We had been in touch with the Consulate in Arequipa, the nearest city to the place where Sarah died and we had a call from the travel company that had organised Sarah's trip. This is a company run by two business partners and based in Peru. We were asked if we wanted them to arrange for a helicopter search for the body. I took the call and said, "Is it worth it?", thinking, "If they have been searching on the ground since Friday, how would a helicopter search help?" I was told it probably would be worth it and it would cost several thousand US dollars. We said to go ahead.

Another thing decided during these two days was that we all needed to go to Peru to see the people involved and the place where Sarah had died. Meanwhile Anna and I had other calls to make. Most of the Tuesday was taken up with calls. I telephoned the travel insurance firm. Sarah had taken out a special insurance for dangerous sports and I found a copy of the form. The woman I spoke to said, "It's probably a terrible mistake, people see someone in the water and think it's someone else." No doubt she thought she was being helpful but I was furious. She was no help whatsoever. Just as one remembers kindnesses with heightened awareness during grief, so one remembers crassness and stupidity in the same way. Because we were worried about the death certificate, I decided to telephone the Foreign Office. No one at all gave us any advice on how to proceed so I thought the Foreign Office would be a useful contact. I explained our daughter had died in Peru and was transferred to the South American section. The man there kept saying, "We cannot issue a death certificate without a body." I knew that! He'd told me several times. I wanted to know how long since the death we would have to wait until we were able to get a certificate of some sort. I did not succeed, however, in getting anything out of him except, "We cannot issue a death certificate without a body." We cried constantly even during the phone calls and it was so awful to come up against such incompetence. The next call was to the Registrar of Births, Deaths and Marriages in Bury St Edmunds. I explained the situation to the woman who answered the phone and, at least, she was kind enough. She said, "I've never been asked that question before. I'll try to find out." But time passed and nothing happened there.

We had been looking through Sarah's papers and came across the name of a firm of solicitors she had been dealing with. I telephoned them. Apparently they had only been involved in selling Sarah's flat a few months earlier. However, the woman I spoke to said she might be able to find out something about the procedure to follow when there is no death certificate. She phoned back later to say that a colleague of hers had known someone who fell from a yacht at sea and was never found. She said that we might be able to get an 'order of presumed death'. The witnesses to the accident should sign a statement before the British Consul and we should take this to a British coroner. She told us that we should get the British Embassy to organise this. I said this was the first concrete advice I'd had and thanked her very gratefully.

We had telephoned the British Embassy in Lima earlier and had been put through to a woman called Nicola Standen. She was kind and sensitive and said we should always ask for her when we telephoned. Nicola became our main lifeline for the next few days. I telephoned Nicola again after the call from the solicitor whose name I did not know. She said she would set the wheels in motion with one of the co-owners of the travel company. Nicola told me during the first call that they knew about the accident and that Sarah had been rafting on a grade 5 river and that the company had appeared to have taken all the right precautions and put the right safety procedures in place.

I had to cancel the flights to Peru that Rosie and I had arranged for May 28th. I had decided to have a 10-day holiday over there with Sarah and it was to have been my birthday present to Sarah who would have been 37 years old on June 11th. I e-mailed KLM to explain. I had booked the flights with my Flying Dutchman (Frequent Flyer) award points. I said in the e-mail that my daughter had died and we would no longer be going. KLM e-mailed back the following day to say my award points would be refunded. I also had to cancel a hotel I had booked in Lima and another in Cusco. The rest of the trip that I was to have taken had been organised by the company that Sarah went with. The people there now knew of course that we would not be making the original trip but an entirely different one.

By now e-mails, cards, letters and flowers were beginning to arrive. The first flowers delivered were from Mark and Celia, two mountain biking friends of Sarah's. On the accompanying card they said, "She was the sunshine in our lives." Needless to say, this made us weep more than ever. So did every e-mail, card and letter to arrive. Some of the correspondence that arrived on May 16th and 17th is included here to help sum up the events of the first days following the dreadful news. The first is from the mother of my very dear Brazilian friend, Anita.

May 16th, 2000, 10.30 a.m. *(to Julia Darling, my secretary)*

Dear Mrs. Darling,

My name is Vera Bobrow and I am Anita Taub's mother.
   This morning she sent me the awful news about the drowning of Sarah in Peru.

I have no words to express my feelings of sympathy for our dear Barbara in this moment of despair and loss. Please let her know that my heart aches for her pain and that I will be praying to God and asking Him to help dear Barbara stand this tragedy.

My family and I condole with Barbara and her family on her sweet daughter's death.

May God guide the family in this moment of distress.

Vera Bobrow

May 17th, 6.09 a.m. *(from me to Julia)*

Dear Julia,

It is still very bad here. Sarah hasn't been found. The helicopter search is over and there is one more day of the river search before they call it off. There is a woman at the British Embassy in Lima who has been very good. We heard the rafting was on a grade 5 river, the most dangerous so she should never have gone. The rest of the group were going to the Consulate in Arequipa yesterday to sign the statements. The guy in charge there is also supportive and of course everyone in the group is devastated too. We are all going out to Peru next week – probably Monday. We shall call in to the Embassy in Lima first, then go to Arequipa to collect the documents and visit the site to make our good-byes. After that we will go to Cusco to collect and decide on the fate of her belongings. Julia, it is so hard to live with this. People have phoned or e-mailed from all over the world. We shall have a big and splendid memorial service at some point in the summer. I can't make any decisions yet about our plans for the summer. I will go to the International Neuropsychology Society meeting in Brussels but I don't think I could do the two 2-day workshops in the USA. I know all the brochures have gone and it will be a mess but the thought of standing there for four days talking to strangers is awful. So can you let the people in Boston know and give them the reasons and my sincere apologies. Then can you get hold of Premier Travel who booked the flights with United Airlines and see if, in the circumstances, I can get a refund or at least a deferment until a later date. I was due to fly out on June 21st. I am sure Agnes is looking after the Dutch student. I know I have neglected her somewhat but I also know people will understand. Matthew, Anna and Rosie are all feeling terrible but so are people we never expected to feel so strongly. Why she felt the need for this high risk experience I don't know. It is such a waste and she was truly a wonderful person who gave so much to her family and friends.

Barbara

May 17th, 2000, 8.09 a.m. *(from Anita Taub to Barbara)*

Dear Barbara,

I have no words to comfort you. We are completely shocked, and I can imagine how you are feeling. We were all the family together yesterday and thought a lot on you and Sarah and prayed for you.

I am sure you know the great affection I have for you, and I am all the time thinking of you. Camila, Martha, Flavia and Angela are sending love to you. Dear Barbara, I am here for everything you need, no matter what. So do ring my mother if you need something in Peru, she knows people there. I didn't e-mail or called you because I don't want to disturb you.

Please take care of you, your lovely family, Francesca, Rosy. Sarah is in all of them.

Love, Anita

May 17th, 2000, 8.42 a.m. *(from Julia to Barbara)*

Dear Barbara,

I'm so sorry the helicopter search didn't find Sarah. I feel so devastated by this and can't get her or you, Mick and the family out of my mind. I know she was a wonderful person, not only from the way you always talked about her with so much love, but when I met her, albeit probably on only a dozen or so occasions, or spoke to her on the telephone – she was always so warm and friendly. Any words of comfort that I can try to give you just seem totally inadequate.

I will deal with everything here, so don't worry about that. I'll ring the Travel Agent as soon as they open at 9 am and let you know what she says.

Love, Julia

May 17th, 2000, 11.01 a.m. *(from Jon to Barbara)*

Barbara,

I tried to call a couple of times, but you are obviously having to sort out so many things and so I thought I would not interrupt, but email instead. I just wanted to let you know that I contacted Mark who has been in touch with Celia. She is working in Bahrain at the moment, until a week on Friday. She is devastated by the news, and Mark is flying out to Bahrain to be with her on Friday. Mark has also rung round many of the mountain bike people that he knows who knew Sarah. I have explained that if you are unable to have a funeral, that you will have some form of memorial for Sarah and it goes without saying that they want to be there. I said I would let Mark know when you have made plans. Sarah was obviously a very special person to them all.

I gather from Julia that you are going out to Peru next week. I know there is nothing that any of us can do to take away your pain, but so many of us desperately wish we could do that for you. If there is anything, anything at all, I can do in the meantime or while you are away do please let me know.

Jon

May 17th, 2000, 10.48 a.m. *(from Barbara to Anita)*

Dear Anita,

I want to thank you and your mother for your kind words. If I thought there was anything you could do in Peru I would ask for help but, Anita, I don't think there is anything to be done. We are in touch with the British Embassy in Peru and the Consulate in Arequipa. There is a woman at the Embassy called Nicola who has been very good, kind and sensible. It is such a terrible tragedy. We paid for a helicopter search yesterday but they could not find the body. There has been a river search going on since Friday, but nothing to report. They said the body would reach the sea in four days (that was yesterday) and also that bodies are rarely found in this particular river with this kind of accident. The problem now is a death certificate. We can't get one without the body so the people on the trip with her went to the consulate in Arequipa yesterday to sign statements so that she can be presumed dead. We then have to take the statements and a copy of the police report to a British coroner to see if they will accept this as evidence of death. Until then we can't get insurance or sort out her finances or her will. We cannot bury her without the body and I wanted to bury her in the churchyard opposite our house where my mother is buried. We will have a memorial service probably in September. She was so well known in the world of mountain biking that she has a huge number of friends. We will read some poems and play some of Sarah's favourite music and have a display of photographs and so forth. At the moment we are in great distress here as you can imagine. I cannot bear to think I will never see her again and never talk to her and laugh with her and take her to a restaurant. I loved her so much, so did her father, her sister, her brother and her niece Rosie. Francesca doesn't really understand although she knows we are all very unhappy.

We are going to Peru on Monday if I can arrange the flights. We will go first to the British Embassy in Lima and then to Arequipa to collect the signed statements and visit the site where she died. We will then go to Cusco to get her belongings. We will probably stay for a week – no longer. I know you care Anita and I am glad you got to know Sarah but at the moment nobody can help us with our grief. Please e-mail me if you want to. I can get my e-mails at home and check them regularly.

Love, Barbara

May 17th, 2000, 4.33 p.m. *(from Ian and Fiona)*

Dear Barbara,

I was just devastated to hear about Sarah. Fiona and my thoughts are with you, Mick, Anna and Matthew as you go through this nightmare. Words are useless, but I just want to say that we are with you in spirit. This is a most terrible thing to have to endure. I spoke briefly to Mick this morning, but I just wanted to say to you personally how heartbroken I am on your behalf. I am sure it must all seem so unreal to you at times.

Sarah was a special person – such a pure spirit in many ways. She was a credit to you and Mick. I hope you can take some small comfort in her specialness, and in the zest she showed for the rich life she had.

Our sincerest condolences, Barbara, to you, Mick, Anna and Matthew.

With love, Ian and Fiona

May 17th, 2000, 6.32 p.m. *(from Jill to Barbara)*

Dearest Barbara and Mick,

Words cannot express my horror and grief on learning the news of Sarah's loss. I am so grateful to Julia for writing and letting me know. I have been sitting here at my desk just absolutely stunned. I can just begin to imagine your feelings, and I do know that this loss changes your lives forever.

I have been thinking of South Africa and our trip to Robben Island. I am so glad that I had that recent time with Sarah. She was such a wonderful, strong young woman, and I will treasure those memories. She died as she lived, courageous and adventurous and loving nature.

Please know that I will be thinking of you all the time. If there is anything at all that I can do to be of help, please know that you can count on me – really, anything at all.

Know that around the world people will be holding you close and wishing you strength and courage as you begin coping with this most difficult of all losses.

I send you great love.

Jill

May 17th, 2000, 7.13 p.m. *(from Barbara to Ian Robertson)*

Thank you, Ian. Yes, we all know how special she was. We are all going to Peru on Monday to do all the various things we have to – and need to – do. There will probably be a memorial service in September. You and Fiona will be most welcome if you want to come.

Love to you all and treasure your three little ones.

Barbara

One thing I wanted to do on the Wednesday morning was go to the gym. Sarah had introduced me to the gym 15 months earlier when I wanted to get fit for a trip to Madagascar. Although I could not face work or telephone calls, I wanted the mindless, repetitive exercise, to try to exorcise some of the physical pain. The pain felt in the region of the heart was as if a horse had kicked me in the chest, it was a hard, solid, lump.

I went to the gym desperately hoping no one would speak to me. While on the exercise bike, the manager walked past and said, "All right?" My eyes filled with tears, I shook my head and said, "No." "What's wrong?" she said. I answered, "It's just too awful to speak about."

I finished the workout and thought I must say something to her. She was in the office talking to another instructor, Maxine. Both of them knew Sarah who was a regular gym-goer. I went in and told them sobbing all the while. They both coped, especially Maxine who told me her brother had died as a young man and she knew how badly her mother had taken it.

I went down to the changing rooms, had a shower and started getting dressed. An acquaintance with whom I had worked years ago in Oxford, started to speak to me. I cried even more and said, "My daughter's just drowned in Peru." "What on earth are you doing here then?" she said. "Well I have to do something," I answered. (In fact, over the next days, weeks and months I became obsessed with the gym.) Although I thought of Sarah non-stop while I was there, I could 'see' her in my mind's eye with her colourful shorts and intense involvement, I wanted to go through this pounding, thumping routine. I went again on the Thursday, Friday, Saturday and Sunday. I always cried and I do not know how many people noticed or saw me.

⌁

Chapter Two

Sarah lovely, Sarah happy

2003

Now that we have some distance between us – a three-year passage of time – our grief has changed. We are able to pull back from the horrors experienced in the immediacy of a family tragedy and gain some respite from our nightmare. As we said earlier, we are offering the reader two texts: one describing the anguish of the loss of a child in all the immediacy of the first and worst year; and one providing reflection and resolution that come with the passing of time. Why is our book taking this shape? We believe that the immediacy of grief has rarely if ever been presented to readers in such day-to-day detail as provided in Barbara's account. So we offer the journal. We also want to show that we have moved on from despair to a life that is again worth living to the full. We want to show the reader that we are picking up the pieces and that despite the worst kind of loss, the loss of one's child, we can still enjoy our daily living, can still make plans for the future, and can maintain a healthy interest in what is going on around us.

It is a hard thing for people to face up to the possibility of the loss of a child. Most describe it as a nightmare or beyond imagining. So we want to show them what it is like when you receive the phone call or the knock on the door, and what it is like for the next hours, days, weeks and months. We also want to stress that life goes on, has gone on for us and that there is a progression through grief. People do come out of despair, they are able to pull through the most awful times, and nothing, absolutely nothing is more awful than the death of one's child.

The reader may not know that Countess Mountbatten of Burma is the patron of TCF (The Compassionate Friends). In that role she has gained enormous respect from the membership and much affection from those who have met her. In a foreword she wrote to a book edited by Ena Mirren and The Compassionate Friends, entitled *Our Children*, she describes the loss of an elder twin son, a father, a mother-in-law and a local boy who ran the boat in which terrorists had placed and detonated a bomb. She wrote: "The intensity of the pain caused by the death of our twin, a particularly caring and loving child, dwarfed the pain of the loss of parents for my husband and me; so much so that I began to feel almost guilty that I could not mourn the death of my father properly, because he and I were particularly close. . . . In our case, the letters I truly valued were the few from people who understood that, to us, the real tragedy was the loss of Nicky, although most people seemed to think, understandably (because of Lord Mountbatten's standing in the Nation) more about my father's death."

We also know of a young mother who lost both her mother and four-year-old daughter in the same car accident. Over a year later the young woman was still consumed by grief for the loss of her child yet freely admitted that she had not begun to mourn the loss of her mother. Losing a spouse or a parent is not the same thing as losing a child. We can cope with death as a part of the natural order of things, but the loss of a child is all wrong, it is against nature and we cannot bear it.

For us in the past three years we have learned to mourn genuinely at the loss of young people in wars. Our attitude towards war of any kind has hardened almost into pacifism. The two world wars have come to mean much more to us in terms of the loss of young life. We were appalled too at the terrible loss of life when terrorists attacked the World Trade Centre on September 11th, 2001. Equally we are now dismayed and angered by the terrible loss of life amongst the Iraqi people by the terrible power of two of the mightiest nations in the world.

The violent end to young life is wrong, whether the person is an innocent worker going to her office at the World Trade Center, or a British soldier invading Iraq, or a young child killed in a US bombing raid on Baghdad. Who is to say that any one of these actions or re-actions is permissible or legitimate or divinely supported? Perhaps only in music and literature can we seem to get closest to the reality of a loss of life. William Shakespeare, for instance, is mentioned a number of times in this book. The fact that he lost more than one child in the plagues that hit Europe with such frequency in the sixteenth century shows in his deeply moving descriptions of parental grief. There is perhaps nothing more desperate than the anguished cry from King Lear as he carries his dead daughter onto the stage in the final act:

> . . . No, no, no life?
> Why should a dog, a horse, a rat have life,
> And thou no breath at all? Thou'lt come no more.
> Never, never, never, never, never.

2000

MAY 18TH TO 20TH

The calls seemed to go on and on. So did the tears, the constant talking about Sarah, the anger with her for doing such a stupid thing and putting us through such despair, the lack of sleep, the need to constantly hold each other and know each other's whereabouts. Mick went to see a neighbour without telling me and I was so sure he'd had a heart attack and died somewhere. He turned up OK.

Mick had decided he needed to work. He went in on Tuesday 16th, the day after we'd heard. Work for him proved to be a distraction. He had organised an international meeting in Bury St Edmunds for Tuesday May 16th. He was to have hosted it but several telephone calls on Monday 15th alerted his colleagues to Sarah's death. Mick felt he had to make an appearance on the Tuesday and attend at least part of the meeting. He went for lunch and said it had helped distract him from the horror of everything. He went into work for at least part of every day.

In contrast, Anna and I felt we never wanted to work again. I needed to be in contact with Julia who was telling the people who needed to know and dealing with as much of my work as she could. I did not want to go to work, however, and wondered if I should give it up completely. Until very recently I wanted to take early retirement but Mick was always against it. My first e-mail to Julia on May 18th at 5.48 a.m. was as follows:

Dear Julia,

We had a call from the owner of the travel company last night. He was on the raft and has been with the search party ever since. They had a day's rest yesterday as they were all so exhausted it wasn't safe to continue. However, the police rescue team and the owner's team are joining forces today to continue. They are all devastated. He said it has never happened to them before. The guides were appalled and one, Pepe Lopez (who has been on two previous trips with Sarah) dived in to try and swim to her but realised he wouldn't survive if he didn't get out. He was the last to see her and saw that Sarah was heading towards an area where the river went down under a pile of rocks. She might be trapped there. As the river waters are going down each day, they are still hoping to find the body. The company has a good reputation and is the one with best knowledge and experience of that river. I am sure they did everything possible. We have been told that she was in high spirits and had said that she was so pleased she had chosen that trip and chosen to go to Peru. All the villagers have been told. I asked if it would help to offer a reward and the owner said they have already done that.

We can't actually get to the site next week as it is a hard two-day trek to get there. Obviously Francesca couldn't manage that. We are going to the same river, though − further up. Even that is a 12-hour trip by road (and not a good road). They are a bit concerned about Francesca because of the altitude. It is very high. But we have to take her. She can't be left and we all need to be together at present.

Julia, I don't mind you giving out whatever information people ask for. There are no secrets and it is good to know that so many people care so deeply. Keep the e-mails coming − they are a solace at times. Fancy me saying that when I only learned to use them recently.

Love, Barbara

On May 17th and 18th I sorted out our trip to Peru. I did this through 'Journey Latin America'. I had to pay by credit card and had to phone the company to authorise such a large amount. I remember thinking how would poor people manage? They would not be able to go. How would most people cope with finding out what to do in these circumstances? Anna said that we were an educated and resourceful family yet we found it hard. Many people would have found it even harder. We booked six tickets for Mick, Anna, Matthew, Rosie, Francesca and me. We decided to leave on the afternoon of Sunday May 21st for Amsterdam with KLM and go on to Lima on Monday May 22nd.

We were in constant touch with the travel company that Sarah went with (we usually spoke to the co-owner) and with Nicola Standen at the British Embassy in Lima. I telephoned Lima every day at 3.00 p.m. which was 9.00 a.m. Peruvian time. Nicola was always gentle, kind and supportive. When I told the co-owner that Francesca was four years old, he said he was worried about her. I thought he was worried because there would be a 12-hour trip by van on dirt roads from Arequipa to Cotahuasi town (near to the river). I said, "Oh, she'll probably sleep." "It's not the travel," he replied, "but the altitude." We had not given a single thought to the altitude but I asked Anna to telephone her general practitioner to see if there was something we could take to give Francesca at high altitude. The reply was a blow to us all as I explained in my daily bulletin to Julia on May 19th.

> Dear Julia,
>
> On top of everything, we heard from the doctor yesterday that it would be very dangerous to take Francesca to the areas we are going to in Peru. Because the co-owner had said he was a bit worried about her in that altitude, Anna asked the doctor about medication. The doctor said she had never been asked this question before but would find out. She obviously went to some trouble contacting paediatricians and mountaineers. When she phoned back she said that children between two and five years shouldn't sleep above a certain height and children under two had to be at even lower height. Francesca could get very ill and could die. If she got ill we would have to get her down immediately and, of course, we can't do anything immediately in these conditions. So we cannot take her. Anna was so torn about whether to stay with Francesca or to come to talk to people who were with Sarah at the end, and she desperately wants to do that. I said she should decide by midday today. I think she will come. Francesca, who is furious about not coming, can stay in her own house with a friend of Anna's; and Carol and Peter (who she is close to) will help and take her out for tea and out at the weekend. If anything happened to us then Francesca is in deep trouble but Anna needs to come and it will make the trip easier.
>
> Julia, if there is anything that needs signing and someone could get here today then I don't mind doing it. I know I left you a whole pile of things when you were away.

We all slept a bit better last night. We were so exhausted yesterday. I woke up every hour but managed a total of 6 hours, which is the most I've had since last Sunday.

I can probably cope with one or two phone calls if there is a need. We are taking the girls to London tomorrow to see *The Lion King* and trying to be normal. We are staying up tomorrow evening, coming back Sunday morning and going to Stansted Sunday afternoon. Carol and Peter are taking us in two cars.

I'll be in touch on my return. We are hoping this trip will start to heal us all. Poor Anna and Matthew have taken it so badly and the poor owner of the travel company was originally being questioned for murder! He persuaded them otherwise though, thank goodness.

Love, Barbara

Anna did decide to come. She hated leaving Francesca and we all felt so vulnerable but she needed to see the place where Sarah had died. When we told Francesca she could not come because she might die, she became very angry saying, "I promise not to die." Anna said that although she wanted to take her, the doctor would not let her go. Francesca soon calmed down and said Anna's friend would be her mummy while we were away. The friend and her two children were sharing Anna's house at that time so we felt the disruption to Francesca would be minimal.

When I heard that Francesca could not come, I felt overwhelmed. I thought, "This is the last straw, I just cannot cope with anything else, I'm giving up." One cannot give up though, things have to be done, one has to consider other people and try to be strong for them. Rosie went back to school on Wednesday 17th. We felt she needed to be as normal as possible. She wanted to go back. People were kind to her and she was a special person for a few days. She continued to make drawings of Sarah and also to make little gifts to take to the river in Peru. Francesca was also back at nursery school. She was the least distressed. We felt uncomfortable about her seeing all the adults in the family crying constantly, but we also believed strongly that she needed to be included in the family grief and that she should talk about Sarah and be able to ask questions. Francesca's drawings at this time were of "ladies stepping into a river which was very cold". One day she said, "I'll never do cooking with Sarah any more, will I?" "No," we said, "Sarah has gone now."

Matthew had been looking through Sarah's music collection. The two of them had had similar tastes. Matt played us some of the things she had particularly liked. These included songs by Bob Dylan, The Waterboys, The Only Ones and others. We all wept heavily again. Mick and Matthew in particular were overwhelmed by the music. Matt's friends supported him, Mick was helped by work, Anna, Rosie and I supported each other. Francesca talked and drew but mostly was her usual self. Django, my cat, also changed his behaviour. He is an oriental short hair and, like other oriental cats, he is noisy, he meows a great deal and appears to be conversing with people. In the first few weeks after Sarah's death, however, when everyone he knew was crying, he became very silent. I do not remember him meowing at all and Mick and I commented on this. He became a quiet, subdued cat for several weeks. I said to him often, "Django, it should have been you who died." Mick said once, "He's too sensible to die." It was true, Django hides from cars and from strangers. He does not put himself in danger like Sarah.

This is an e-mail that came in on Friday May 19th, it was from one of Matthew's closest friends, Tracy.

> Dear Barbara and Mick,
>
> It is so difficult to know what to write, this is such a tragedy. I was so shocked when Matt told me and it was truly terrible to hear how much pain he was in and there was nothing I could do or say to make him feel any better. You don't expect to hear news like this, especially when I think of someone who was so young and energetic. It is devastating.
>
> I cannot begin to think how you must be feeling, the Wilsons so close. All I can think of to say are clumsy clichés – that time is a healer and that the pain the family are feeling now will diminish even though the loss remains. But I also feel that Sarah was doing what she loved, something that fulfilled her and what she was passionate about – and for however briefly she had realised her dream.
>
> The image and recollections I have of Sarah is of a girl very much alive, friendly, determined, caring and loving and that is the picture I keep.
>
> My deepest sympathies.
>
> Tracy

We had a letter from Sarah's best friend, Cindy. The two had been friends since they were eight years old and had met at primary school. Cindy wrote:

> I am so sorry that you're hurting and in so much pain.
>
> Thank you for including me – phoning me – especially Anna for having the capacity to care about how I might be in the middle of your grief.
>
> Sarah – such a unique, wonderful, good and special person. Everyone here was very touched by her – there's a great deal of sadness.
>
> I've enclosed some photos we took in a booth in 1976. I love these photos and I know Sarah did. It would be wonderful if you could take these to Peru and send them to her.
>
> I've also written a sort of letter – just a list of our favourite, repeatedly told memories really – but I'd also love it if she could take that with her. If there is anything I can do please say.
>
> Have a safe journey. Keep in touch. I love you, take care,
>
> Cindy

Another letter, one of many, came from an old friend of mine in Massachusetts, Kate Bernhardt. She said,

> I am so sorry to hear the news about Sarah. My heart is breaking for you both. I was always so impressed by Sarah − her honesty, her humour, her strength and her basic 'good'-ness, as well as by her obvious love for both of you.
>
> Barbara, you always told me that giving birth to your babies was the most thrilling moment of your life, which I failed to understand until I held my own baby in my arms. Of course, that moment soon passes, and then you have the job of raising those children. Sarah benefited from all that you both gave her. She was the kind of person who was completely engaged in life, and she got that enthusiastic spirit from you. I recall hearing about her passions − whether for bicycling, or for getting Barbara on the honours list, or for being an aunt for Rosie, or for being part of your business. I wish I could have known her better.
>
> I know that nothing I can say will ease your pain, but for myself I will always think of the courage, kindness and adventurousness, that Sarah brought to her life as a reminder to me that being a parent is all about giving your children as much of that spirit as you can, and then letting them go, even if they go places you'd rather they didn't. You did a fine, fine job with Sarah, and she will be missed by everyone who knew her, no matter how fleetingly.
>
> If it is at all possible, Ralph and I will come to the memorial service − it will be an outstanding tribute to a wonderful woman.
>
> With all my love,
>
> Kate

These and other letters, particularly from people who knew Sarah, were so important to us even though every one of them made us weep so much.

The ones who did not help much were those who sent cards or letters saying "thinking of you" or "I don't know what to say". We wanted communications that talked about Sarah, praised her, admired her, told us anecdotes about her. It is important to be personal. We know some people are embarrassed in the face of grief, one of our neighbours saw me at the bus stop waiting to collect Rosie from the school bus and she turned her back on me. She has never spoken to me since. She is a silly, ignorant woman who is thinking more of herself than of her bereaved neighbours.

Another person who infuriated me then was our general practitioner, a man who had always been awkward and ill-mannered. When Anna's very good GP had told us about the danger of Francesca travelling at altitude, she suggested we obtain some Diamox to help the rest of us. Anna and Rosie bought theirs. I telephoned our doctor's surgery to explain what we wanted and why. I told the receptionist who said she would tell the doctor who would probably telephone me. I thought the receptionist would have told him why I wanted the Diamox, that we were going to Peru because our daughter had died. She probably did tell him, but he did not let on. He said, "I gather you want to speak to me." I had to go through the story again. He could not even say he was sorry. He just told me to collect the Diamox from the pharmacy at the surgery. Not one word of sympathy or consolation.

I went to the pharmacy. Matthew drove me there. The pharmacist asked where we were going. I told her the story. She was sympathetic and said her brother had been killed in an aeroplane crash when he was 21 years old. He had been part of a rugby tour. His parents had paid for his ticket, the plane crashed and his body was never found. I was weeping for her tragedy and her parents. This was the first time I'd met someone who did not have a body to bury. I told her how unsympathetic the doctor had been. She said, "Oh, he's useless. His best friend died and he could not even telephone his friend's wife to say he was sorry. Why don't you change him?" "I thought you couldn't do that without a lot of trouble," I said. "Not any more," said this forthright woman, "there's a patients' charter now, you change him." I did after our return from Peru.

We had booked tickets to see *The Lion King* in London months before. We thought Rosie and Francesca would enjoy it. After Sarah's death we wondered if we should go, then decided we should, in an attempt to make life as normal as possible for our two granddaughters. We thought we should explain to people how we felt about Sarah and why we had decided to go to the theatre less than a week after hearing of Sarah's death. Two days after we heard, I spoke to German Berrios, who is originally from Peru, and a neuropsychiatrist and work colleague in Cambridge. German had lost his son at the age of 16, 20 years ago. I said, "Oh, you've been through this terrible pain too." He told me that we had to do all the normal things like eating and sleeping. He also said, "You learn to live with grief. You don't get over it and after 20 years we still feel pangs."

On May 20th Mick wrote a letter for the neighbours, some friends and family members:

Dear All,

Many thanks for your kind thoughts for us in what has been the worst week in our lives.

Sarah was the best person in the family and was dearly loved and treasured by all those lucky enough to have known her. We have had many communications from friends and relatives of Sarah's from around the world expressing their grief and fond memories. People who knew her when she was a childhood friend, a punk teenager, a skateboarder (for the

England team), a sailor (she was the secretary of Sussex University's sailing club), a mountain biker, a mountain bike journalist, the office administrator of a publishing company, and just a wonderful companion, have written to say how much she will be missed.

At home we are experiencing much pain: Sarah was the heart of the family from which all of us drew our strength. We don't have to tell those who knew her well how the light of her presence lit up every social event in which she was participating.

This weekend we will be taking our granddaughters, Rosie and Francesca, to see *The Lion King* in London. This trip has been planned for many months and we shall be able to delight in the company of the youngest generation of the family. Sarah was a fantastic auntie, and although Francesca, at the age of four, is a bit grumpy with us for being so tearful, Rosie, for whom Sarah was an idolised companion, is old enough to know the extent of her loss.

Sarah's body is still missing but the river level is dropping quickly at this time of the year so there is a small hope that she will be found. We have seen the written reports by her fellow rafters: the boat turned over and five fell into the water. All safety precautions had been taken and four of the five managed to grab hold of ropes or netting strung across the river. Accounts suggest that Sarah was injured and soon unconscious. Desperate attempts were made to rescue Sarah but to no avail. The Peruvian guide, Pepe, who knew Sarah well from two previous biking and rafting expeditions, risked his life at one stage when he instinctively jumped into the river to reach her but was beaten back by the rapids. When we are over in Peru we intend donating Sarah's bike, that she had bought specially for the trip, to Juan Carlos. She told us on her return from her last visit there that his bike was held together with bits of string so we know he could do with a new machine! For us, it will be good to know that the bike Sarah bought will be ridden round the Peruvian mountains she loved so much.

Anna, Matthew and Rosie are accompanying us to Peru as from Sunday and we shall be away for about eight days. Paul [Paul Vizor, Anna's ex-husband] will be looking after the house for us during that time. Although we won't be able to manage the two-day trek in the mountains to the place where Sarah was last seen, we shall be able to get to the river to say our goodbyes. If Sarah is not found it will simply add to her legend as a very special person who has returned to nature. She was always a risk taker. She died as she lived. She was a complete person in a way that most people are not. Although her life was short, it was full, exciting and, because of her remarkably good and forgiving nature, a life in which she was at peace with herself. Living for us now, without Sarah's love, is very hard indeed.

On the same day of the letter we received our itinerary from Peru.

Dear Family Wilson,

I have made the following arrangements for you:
22.5.00 Arrive KLM 741 18:15
The British Consul will meet you at the airplane and our agents in Lima
(AQP) have made arrangements for a minibus transfer to your Hotel. You
are booked into the Hotel Kamana.
23.5.00
The flight to Arequipa is at 06:00. So your transfer will be waiting
outside the Hotel at 04:00. It is quite early but it gives you more time in
Arequipa. Our agents will have your internal flight tickets and will check
you in and show you to the departure gate.
The flight number is:
AEROCONT 1113.
The owner of the travel company will meet you in Arequipa Airport and
transfer you to the hotel La Hosteria. You have a free day in Arequipa. If
you would like to meet the British Consul, he is available.
24.5.00
All-day journey to Cotahuasi village. It will take about 12 hours.
Overnight in a basic hostel. (We recommend you take sleeping bags
with you.)
25.5.00
Drive to the Rio Cotahuasi and maybe walk to Sipia Falls. The drive
takes $\frac{1}{2}$ hour so you will have a full day by the river. Overnight again in
Cotahuasi.
26.5.00
Journey back to Arequipa, 12 hours. Overnight hotel La Hosteria.
27.5.00
Transfer to the airport in Arequipa. $\frac{1}{2}$ hour flight to Cusco and transfer to
hotel Centenario. Hopefully you will meet Max Milligan.
28.5.00
Full day in Cusco.
29.5.00
Transfer to the airport and flight to Lima.
AVIANDINA 4144 09:00
Flight back to England in KLM 742 19.55

We had already been told to take five sleeping bags, a medical kit and various other
things. Between us we had two rather old sleeping bags so decided to buy five new
ones at Millets in Bury St Edmunds. We selected the bags, the medical kit and various
other things. As we went to pay, the assistant said, "Are you going on an expedition?"

We told her why we needed the equipment and she said, "We'll give you a 10% discount." That made us cry – once again we realised most people were good.

The day before *The Lion King* I arranged a hairdresser's appointment. I had not been out of the house since Monday afternoon and wondered how I would cope with this first trip. I decided I would not say anything about my family or anything personal. The hair stylist was from South America. Normally I would have told her my daughter was in Peru and told her of my various trips to South America. I didn't. I spoke about distant, non-emotional things, I did not cry. I felt as if I was recovering from an illness, a fever but I got through it even though I had not believed I could. As far as I know I seemed perfectly normal to the outside world even though my heart had broken.

On Saturday May 20th we drove to Cambridge and then took the train to London. Francesca loved the train. I think she enjoyed that as much as the show. We had lunch at an Italian restaurant and went to the theatre. Francesca was enthralled by the event. The effects were stunning. Rosie also enjoyed it although she was quiet. I was quietly weeping through much of the show. The old Lion King was able to save his son from danger and I was not able to save my daughter.

We met Matthew, Cindy and her partner Eleanor afterwards. Eleanor entertained the girls while Matt, Cindy, Mick and I talked about Sarah and cried.

We went home very downhearted. I knew in my head that the pain would ease in time, but I felt I now knew what people meant when they talk about a broken heart. How would I manage without my wonderful Sarah, my beloved, my angel, my travelling companion, my joy? I imagined at times that she was safe somewhere even though I knew that could not possibly be true. I kept seeing her smile and hearing her say, "Hi mum, do you want a coffee?" I thought of the day she left, May 3rd. I had returned from Brazil on April 30th, where I had been giving lectures and workshops. We had gone out that evening for a farewell dinner in Bury St Edmunds. Carol, Peter, Simon, Jo, Mick, Anna, Sarah and I were there. We had a great evening. Sarah said at the end, "See you all in November." She drove me into work on May 2nd as Mick needed my car. He had arranged to take Sarah to Stansted Airport on May 3rd. They had to leave at 5.00 a.m. The night before Sarah said, "I won't wake you up." "Oh yes," I said, "come and say goodbye." She came in to say goodbye at 4.50 a.m. She was tearful and hugged me. I said I'd see her on May 28th and if things got too bad, she was to get a ticket with her credit card and come home. She phoned later in the day to say her luggage hadn't arrived in Amsterdam, so they were going to put her on a later flight to Lima. The next day she telephoned in the evening to say she had arrived but her luggage had not. She was fed up. It turned up on Friday May 5th (exactly a week before she died). I spoke to her a couple of times between Friday and Sunday and sent several e-mails. She said in an e-mail to Anna that she was missing us but felt she had done the right thing. She left on Sunday May 7th for the trekking and rafting trip. That was the day I had the last e-mail from her.

Mick, Matthew and Anna were still very distressed. Matt said it should have been him that died. Anna said, "Mum, I'll try to be more like Sarah" (she meant more full of joy and optimism). I replied, "Sarah should have been more like you, more sensible, then she would not have died."

MAY 21ST–30TH, PERU

Carol and Peter took us to the airport on Sunday May 21st. Carol was still the main strength, cooking for us, hugging us, letting us cry, crying with us. Every family needs someone like Carol, particularly a family in such grief.

The flight to Lima, via Amsterdam, was tedious. It took $9\frac{1}{2}$ hours to Aruba, a stop there in a miserable airport waiting room and then another $3\frac{1}{2}$ hours to Lima. Throughout the flight we all had regular bouts of weeping and anguish. I saw a South American woman crying frequently and thought, "She's going home because someone has died." We hated hearing any bad news. We did not want anybody to be sad or unhappy. Anna managed to telephone Francesca from the plane. All was well at home.

On the second flight from Aruba to Lima, I was sitting next to Rosie. After the meal we put our seats back – or tried to. The two people behind said, "Oh no!" and pushed the seats forward. I turned round and said, "We've finished our meal, the plates have been cleared, it's OK to put the seats back", but they would not have it. They jammed their knees against the seats. Rosie was upset and wanted to sleep. I told the stewardess who said to the two people we were allowed to put our seats back, but they were unhappy with this and tried to prevent us as far as possible by pushing the seats forward every now and again.

Eventually the journey passed and we arrived in Lima. As we were walking along the corridor from the plane we saw a man holding a placard saying "The Wilson Family". We went up to him and he led us to Nicola Standen and a man from the Embassy. They took us through the diplomatic channel and out to a minibus that delivered us to our hotel, and then they waited while we checked in. They offered to take us out to dinner but we were all tired, particularly Rosie. Instead we ate in the hotel and went to bed. We did not learn anything new. Nicola was just as sympathetic and kind as she had been on the telephone.

The co-owner of the travel company had made the arrangements using the money I had paid for the planned 10-day trip with Sarah and Rosie at the end of May. We were collected by car early the next morning and taken to the airport. Nicola was there to help us through. The owner of the travel company, who had been the leader of Sarah's disastrous rafting expedition, met us in Arequipa. He took us to the hotel 'La Hosteria', a pretty hotel with a courtyard full of flowers and a terrace that had stunning views of the snow-capped Andes. Sarah had stayed there just a short while before, just prior to setting off on the trekking trip.

We joined the owner of the travel company in a lounge to go through the details of what had happened. It was unreal, we were jet-lagged. He was telling us that Sarah had seemed distressed when they saw her passing in the water. "Was she screaming?" asked Mick. "No." "Was she bleeding?" "No, she couldn't help herself, she couldn't catch hold of the safety lines, she must have been injured." We were told it was less than a minute, less than 30 seconds, less than 10 seconds before she lost consciousness. The story was not entirely consistent. We were told how much she was enjoying the holiday, she'd been very happy. The guide had gone down the route in a boat first and all seemed well. There were two rafts, each with five people plus a guide. Sarah was in the first raft with four men. All the crew had been asked whether they wanted to go and all had shouted, "Yes!" (peer pressure we thought, people can't show they are nervous at a time like this). We heard how the owner was in one of the rescue craft and had seen one guy go past, then Sarah, although he could not tell who was who then as they were all wearing wet suits and helmets. He went after and rescued the guy. We did not get a more complete picture until the following year when we went to the site with Pepe Lopez. Pepe was the guide in a rescue boat who saw Sarah going past and chased after her in the boat. He realised she was going too fast, so he landed and tried to reach her overland by cutting off a corner. He then dived in to try to reach her but was approaching more rapids so had to get out or he too would have died. Sarah floated on – by then she was face down although earlier, we were to learn, she had made eye contact with Pepe as she was swept past.

We went to see the British Consul in Arequipa to collect the official report of the accident as witnessed by the expedition team. He tried to be kind but we felt we had little in common. Here is the report, quoted in full:

ACCOUNT OF THE DISAPPEARANCE OF SARAH JONES* ON THE RIO COTAHUASI 12/5/00

During a commercial rafting expedition on the Rio Cotahuasi, organised by [name of the company], Sarah Jones fell from her raft in the region of Ninochaca and appeared to be knocked unconscious before disappearing from sight, despite all attempts to rescue her from the

---

*Jones is Sarah's married name as she was married to Gez Jones for ten years until they separated two years before she decided to make a new start in Peru. Gez would have figured in this book had he made contact with us or any of Sarah's and his mutual friends in the immediate time after her death. However, he did not make any such contacts and he could not bring himself to attend Sarah's memorial service. We were shocked at his non-appearance at the service and learned later that his sister had spent considerable time and effort trying to persuade him to attend, but to no avail. There has never been an explanation apart from his sister's, who indicated that Gez was too embarrassed to put in an appearance. This is a sad conclusion to what was, for eight years, a very happy marriage. Sarah loved Gez and, although he was several years younger than her, he grew up within that marriage and benefited professionally as well as humanly from his connection with her. Although Sarah was very unhappy about her separation from Gez in the last two years of her life, she remained brave and strong in her determination to remain vitally human: she never resorted to self-pity and continued to throw herself into mountain biking activities that she once shared with Gez. We always say that had she and Gez been able to have a baby they would still be together and she would not have looked for some other compensatory way of living by going to Peru. Despite their treatment at a fertility clinic, and the expenditure of considerable fees, Gez and Sarah could not have a baby. She always used to say that she was born to be a mother of a large family, and indeed we could all see her as a 'mother earth' kind of personality. She had no luck in love or fertility but she smiled through all adversity. Her relationship with Gez Jones is perhaps the subject of a book that Sarah could have written but we are left instead with this story, told by her mum and dad.

river. A four-day search ensued by river, foot, and finally helicopter. The search by local authorities continues.

At approximately 11.30 on Friday 12th May, after a thorough inspection of the rapid, it was agreed by all participants and guides that the rapid could be rafted safely.

The safety kayak ran the rapid first, followed by the cataraft and then it was deemed safe for the first two rafts to proceed. A full safety net was set up including two throw ropes, and the safety kayaker and cataraft were put in position downstream.

When the first of two rafts, carrying five passengers, including Sarah Jones and one captain, was pulled slightly off line, it dropped into a hydraulic and was stuck for several seconds before bucking violently and throwing all the passengers into the water.

The first passenger, Martin Davis, was saved by one of the throw ropes, Nick Sinfield and Peter Massey were picked up by the safety kayak and Chris Jenkins was being rescued by a throw rope from the cataraft when Sarah passed by, apparently still conscious but injured.

At this point, Juan Jose Lopez, the cataraft captain, decided to leave Chris Jenkins, who was now in relative safety, in shallow water, and pursue Sarah Jones downstream. Nick Sinfield and one of the guides, were also dispatched on foot in pursuit.

Juan Jose Lopez chased Sarah Jones down the following rapid in his cataraft but could not catch up with her. So he abandoned the cataraft and ran, cutting the corner off the next bend in the river. On seeing Sarah Jones, floating face down in the water, having passed through another rapid, he dived into the water and swam after her.

Having injured his knee in the river and seeing up ahead a particularly dangerous siphon, through which all the river passed, he feared for his own safety, and swam to the side. This point was the last recorded sighting of Sarah Jones and it is feared she has been sucked into this siphon, through which her body might not yet have passed. Juan Jose Lopez continued on foot downstream later returning to the siphon to attempt a further search.

The search immediately continued on downstream by kayak and on shore for a further 3 km, arriving at the village of Quechaulle, during which several further rapids were passed. Two groups then searched back up each shore and no signs were found.

The passengers decided to return to the village of Cotahuasi, on foot, accompanied by a Spanish-speaking passenger whilst all the guides continued to search for Ms. Jones.

This included a thorough search of the siphon area and a team continued, by raft and kayak downstream to the junction of the Rio Cotahuasi and the Rio Maran, a further three days away. No sign of the body was found and it was concluded by all the guides that there was no hope of survival for a person last seen unconscious.

The search was further continued by helicopter including several trips up and down the whole area of the actual accident and suspect siphon after which the kayak and raft crew were airlifted back to Arequipa.

Police are continuing to search the area and the lower reaches of the Rio Cotahuasi where local villagers have also been alerted and offered a reward for any information leading to the recovery of Sarah Jones.

On this day, 16th May 2000, this is a full account of the accident. It is hoped that the body may yet be recovered within the following fort-night, by local authorities and inhabitants.

Later the owner took us on a tour of Arequipa, a nice town. We had lunch and were shown various places that Sarah had visited including the famous monastery in Arequipa. Throughout the day we took turns to be strong and there were times when we were all calm and normal. Then the awful anguish would wash over us again. Grief is not constant even at the beginning. It comes in huge, tumultuous waves. We also had to meet the British Consul in Arequipa that day to collect the police report (in Spanish) and statements from people on the trip (signed before the Honorary Consul). We hoped these would help us obtain a death certificate. The Consul did his best but could not console us.

On Wednesday May 24th, we left Arequipa at 6.30 a.m. in a minibus (with exceptionally bare tyres) for a long drive through some high mountains (up to 14,000 feet) to go to Cotahuasi town. Most of the driving was on dirt roads and it would have been a nightmare if Francesca had been with us. We all cried at intervals. "How on earth are we going to manage without her?" I asked Anna who just shook her head. The scenery was stunning, wonderful snow-capped mountains, over the rocks a lovely green moss that only grows above a certain altitude and lots of llamas either grazing alone or being herded along by Andean villagers. There were few people and no tourists once we'd left Arequipa. We slept on and off, Matthew felt ill, we had all been taking our Diamox but some of us felt side-effects like bad 'pins and needles' so we all abandoned the tablets by the end of that day.

We arrived in Cotahuasi town and checked in at the hostel. Although the court-yard was pretty, it was a very basic place. The five of us had one room to share with six beds. Anna and Matthew walked into town to find a public telephone to make calls. Anna was able to telephone Francesca every day even though we were in such a remote spot.

The following day, Thursday, we went into the town first thing. There were no tourists there at all, at least no one that was not South American. Everyone stared at us and particularly at Rosie, this light-skinned little European girl. They were not hostile but curious. It was like something out of the last century. A strange, primitive town full of horses, mules and donkeys. We set off after breakfast for a one-hour drive and then a two-hour trek along the Cotahuasi river to the Sipia falls. Sarah had been on that route. She had lunched at the Sipia falls. The guides and the owner moved off while we held our little ceremony. The closest thing we had to a funeral. We took turns reading out messages and letters to Sarah and throwing each into the river with some wild lupins we had picked earlier, some photographs and little memen-toes. Sarah had given Mick three little bicycle tyre levers before she left for Peru. He threw one into the river and said, "I used to have three of these and now I have two. I used to have three children and now I have two." Rosie had made a key-ring she threw in. Cindy's photographs and letters went in along with messages from Carol, Sarah's cousin Simon and his wife Jo, and others. We ended up with our arms around each other reading together the words of Bob Dylan's "Forever Young", a song that has given all of us strength over the years. I was once chairman of an occupation committee to save a rehabilitation centre and every day when I was driving to and from the barricades I played "Forever Young" to inspire me. It was also appropriate in the circumstances, Sarah would be 'forever young' and the words described her character to a large extent. The typed song went into the river. We all felt emotionally drained when we joined the others for lunch.

After lunch we set off for the two-hour trek back to the van. Rosie, who had coped so well until then, started to wilt. She said to me at one point, "I can't go on." I poured some water over her head as it was very hot. The tour leader managed to hire a horse and a mule from a nearby farm. We put Rosie on the horse for the last stretch of about 20 minutes. Matthew was most in need of the mule but he is scared of horses and mules and refused the offer. Mick was also scared so Anna and I took turns. We loved the scenery and thought that Sarah had chosen a beautiful spot to die, but she should not have left us in such misery.

We had another night in the hostel. I got up in the middle of the night to go to the toilet across the courtyard, which had flooded. I had to inch my way around the edge, feeling very disturbed. We had another long drive on the Friday back to Arequipa.

As we left on Saturday morning, one of the staff at the hotel, a short middle-aged woman, said in broken English, "Sarah, nice, Sarah nice smile, Sarah nice hair." I broke down weeping. She held me and said, "Tranquilla, Senora, tranquilla." The local Peruvian people were always warm and kind.

We set off to the airport for an early flight to Cusco, a really beautiful city where Sarah had been planning to spend most of her six months in Peru. She had been staying in the Hotel Centenario where her luggage and her mountain bike were stored. She had found herself a flat that she was planning to move into after the rafting trip.

Max Milligan met us at the airport. He was a warm, welcoming man who hugged us all. The co-owner of the travel company was also there and a Swiss guy. We went to the hotel, the Centenario, for a wash and brush-up. I kept thinking, "This is the day Rosie and I were due to fly out to Amsterdam and tomorrow we were due to meet Sarah in Lima." We went out to look at beautiful Cusco, the Inca city. Rosie started to feel ill, apparently altitude sickness. Anna took her back to the hotel. Mick took over in the afternoon while Anna came out with Matt, the owner of the travel company and me. We loved Cusco. That evening we had a really good meal in the Inca Inn. Max was there; the co-owner and the Swiss guy came too. It was the day of the Peruvian elections so we were not supposed to drink alcohol. The owner sorted it out though – it meant we had to drink wine in tea cups! Meals were the best times for us. We felt less distressed and weepy then. The drives and the plane journeys were worst as there was too much time to think. Mornings were also bad. As soon as we woke up the thought of no more Sarah hit us with a horrible jolt. As the day wore on, things were slightly more bearable.

On Sunday morning we had to go through Sarah's belongings in the hotel. She had stored them there with her mountain bike. Her best mountain bike had been left at home in England. She had bought another one specially for her six months in Peru. We had discussed the bike earlier in the trip. We did not want to take it back to England. Matthew had suggested we give it to Juan Carlos. Sarah had spoken warmly of Juan Carlos whom she had met on her two previous trips to Peru. He was the mechanic for the mountain bike trips she had been on in Peru and Bolivia. He was also a very good mountain biker. The owner of the travel company told us he was good enough for the national Peruvian team but he had a very poor bike tied up with bits of wire and string. We all thought it was a good idea to give the bike to Juan Carlos: Sarah would have approved and we liked the idea of her bike being ridden over the Peruvian Andes. The owner managed to find Juan Carlos, who lived in Cusco. He came to the hotel, and we told him (through the owner) that we wanted him to have Sarah's bike. At first he said, "No." "You must," we said, "Sarah would have wanted it and we want to know her bike is being ridden here." He agreed and hugged us all. He was a lovely, warm, smiling man and we knew why Sarah liked him so much. His English was poor but he kept repeating, "Sarah lovely, Sarah happy." Everyone was weeping, but it helped when people spoke about Sarah with warmth and approval.

One of the very worst things was having to go through Sarah's bags. She had a considerable amount of luggage because she'd packed for six months. Her belongings from the rafting trip were also delivered to Cusco. We had to go through everything – her passport, her money, her clean clothes, her dirty clothes, her toilet bag, everything. We all wept furiously, all together. Up until then we had taken turns. We brought all the luggage into our room. Anna, Rosie and Matthew joined us. We considered delaying the sorting through until we returned to England but Matthew thought there might be coca leaves inside her bags. Coca leaves are taken in the form of tea to combat altitude sickness. We all drank it in Peru, even Rosie. For a while it was the only thing she could face eating or drinking because of her altitude sickness. The thought of explaining this to a customs official in England, however, was too much so we braved the sorting of the luggage. No coca leaves were found and we just made ourselves utterly miserable.

We went out again on Sunday to look at the Inca wall with its famous 12-sided stone. I saw a silver bracelet in a jewellers that was modelled on the Inca wall. Mick persuaded me to buy it. Most of my traveller's cheques were at the hotel so the owner of the jewellers – in fact the jeweller himself – came back with me in a taxi where we sorted out the payment. Ever since I bought it, this bracelet has been one of my favourite pieces of jewellery. We learned that the jeweller's wife had died a year or so earlier and he was still very sad. As always, we felt a bond with anyone who had suffered grief. Mick wanted to buy jewellery for Anna, Rosie and Matthew. We bought necklaces for the females and a silver chain for Matt.

On Sunday evening we went out with the owner of the travel company for dinner. Again he found a good restaurant. We joined up with some friends of his. People were talking about their favourite places in the world. Places in South America were mentioned, Mick talked about Australia, I mentioned Siena and then Rosie, sitting on my right, leaned over to me and said, "I like Bury St Edmunds." I laughed and said, "I like Bury St Edmunds too." I knew she hated Peru. She was still feeling so sick, every so often I'd take her outside and she heaved but did not vomit. She just felt so miserable. She said she never wanted to go to Peru again. Then she added, "Until I'm grown up." She had coped well apart from the two days in Cusco. We had been told in the Cotahuasi valley that less than one hundred 'gringos' had been to that valley and the youngest foreigner ever to go there was our Rosie who was 12 at the time. I'm proud to say that even when she felt ill she never whinged.

The next morning we had to leave Cusco early to go to Lima. The owner had arranged for us to have a city tour of the capital to kill time. We were not in the mood, we all felt so wretched. The young woman who met us at Lima airport, our tour guide, had not been told of the circumstances. Her English was good and she was a pleasant and competent enough young woman who probably wondered why we were all so miserable. Eventually Mick explained. She took us to the Gold Museum and then to various cathedrals and churches. We were feeling desperate and did not want to be tourists, we wanted to go home. We asked the guide to take us to a good restaurant for lunch. She did and we asked her to leave us there for three hours. As usual, we felt better sitting in a restaurant. The food and service were excellent. For my first course I had the local speciality, ceviche (marinated fish) that I'd had before and love. Rosie had perked up. As soon as we got to Lima and its lower altitude she felt better and was able to eat for the first time in days. We sat there drinking wine and feeling so grateful not to be looking at churches and museums. Our guide took us to the airport. We were distressed at check in because we knew we had too much luggage (all Sarah's luggage came back with us). I had to explain to various airport staff and we were allowed to check in everything at no extra cost.

Somehow we got through the tedious journey. We arrived home Tuesday evening. Carol, Peter and Francesca were at the airport to meet us. It was good to see Francesca again looking so healthy and normal, but we were so emotionally and physically drained we could hardly move. Carol cooked for us that evening and washed up. We were still sobbing for much of the time. Monday was the day Rosie, Sarah and I were due to go to Arequipa and Tuesday we were supposed to be travelling to the Colca Canyon. All the time I kept thinking, "We should be there now with Sarah." I doubt that more than a minute or two went by at that time without me thinking of her. My treasured, lovely, beautiful, wonderful girl. I kept wishing our story was not true.

∽

CHAPTER THREE

You were not fragile until you were fearless

2003

Our intention in this book is to provide the reader with two perspectives on grief by switching to and from Barbara's year 2000 journal and our joint analysis and description of life three years after the bereavement of our daughter. Our objective is to offer the reader a kind of map of the chronology of grief. We hope the reader will notice a change, a development in our mood and attitude towards daily life. We hope we are not becoming more resigned to our fate as time passes, and indeed we consciously fight against such a thing happening. Belonging to The Compassionate Friends is proving to be most beneficial to us. The TCF gives us a platform, not only for debate but also for reflection; its annual gathering gives us a vehicle for a special pilgrimage to Sarah, it gives us space and time to spend completely in the presence as it were of our lost daughter; and as time goes on it gives us a sense of responsibility as we meet more parents, new to the loss of a child, who need our help, sympathy and sometimes advice. Thus TCF offers bereaved parents many things: it is both supportive of us and at the same time demands support from us. No club can do more.

In her year 2000 journal Barbara refers to the different approaches to life exhibited by us in the first year of bereavement. These differences continue. While we are both lucky to be leading fulfilling professional lives that keep us busily occupied in mental processes, we do not share the same interest in physical health. Barbara, who was never involved in sport throughout the first thirty years of our marriage is now more than ever keen to pursue top physical fitness, while Mick, who was always involved in sport, even to the extent of playing regular football until he was 53 years old, is, in his 68th year, much less interested in pursuing physical fitness although he still goes swimming two or three times a week.

We both continue to think a lot about Sarah and doubt whether a day ever passes when we do not speak of her, and in both our cases, we sometimes speak to her as it were. In Mick's case this 'talking to Sarah' has at times taken the form of poetry. Judged by the number of poems submitted to the TCF journal, Mick is not exceptional in turning to poetry as a medium for his thoughts and reflections. It is one of Mick's ambitions to set up a poetry workshop at one of the conferences so that parents can share their thoughts about writing poetry, can read meaningful poems about loss that can be found in the literature of the UK, and practise ways of improving written communication in verse. One of the themes Mick is particularly interested in looking at closely is the development of verse writing as the years of bereavement pass on. Is there a different approach to verse written say ten years after loss from five years after or one year? Do parent writers change their outlook, can these changes be recognised? As we noted above, Mick's poetry currently takes the form of a conversation with Sarah, and this is usually prompted by an observation at home that reminds him of her. Below is one example:

> Fragile things have lasted years
> Since you died:
> Glasses, dishes, plastic spoons, whatever.
> I can't understand their durability in the face of your loss.

> Nor can I comprehend
> The daffodils coming to life again,
> Or my pond fish still here
> When you are gone.

> You were not fragile until you were fearless.
> When the waters, rocks and stones
> Showed how easy it was
> To break you.

> Had you been more discerning,
> Less careless, more caring of yourself,
> You could still be here, washing these things —
> Breaking them, not yourself.

> Or looking out of this window
> At the returning flowers of Spring.
> Perhaps feeding the fish
> That now rise to the surface again.

> I think a lot about the moment
> Your resolve would have broken
> That instant when you said to yourself
> "That's it, that's enough!" Or words to that effect.

> That's how you would have gone,
> I like to think:
> No time to make a decisive break from
> The world or consciousness or us?

The rest of May 2000

A number of e-mails, letters and cards had arrived while we were away, including messages from colleagues in Turkey, Hong Kong and Denmark. There was also a letter from Susan Routledge who had been on the trip with Sarah. She was on the second raft. Like all bereaved people, we constantly went through a whole host of 'if onlys'. "If only Sarah had been on the second raft." "If only Sarah had broken her leg while snowboarding in Andorra two weeks before going to Peru." "If only Mick had been taken ill and Sarah had been called home to see him." And so on, and so on. That still happens today, more than a year later.

Here is Susan's letter.

Dear Mr and Mrs Wilson,

I hope you don't mind me writing to you but I was on the rafting trip with Sarah and wanted to get in touch with you.

Sarah and I were the only two girls on the trip and so we inevitably spent quite a lot of time together, sharing hotel rooms, sleeping space at the campsites etc.

Although I had only known Sarah for a few days I felt (and I hope she did) that we had become friends. This sort of trip always brings people close together very quickly and you talk about things that you probably wouldn't discuss on more conventional holidays.

One thing that sticks in my mind is Sarah saying how close she was to her family. She obviously loved you all very much as I'm sure you knew. She was really looking forward to her mum and Rosie coming out and was full of plans for the visit. She was wondering whether she could stand being away from you all for so many months.

Everyone on the trip got on extremely well and there was lots of laughing and chatting. Sarah and I were made 'honorary boys' and Sarah introduced us to a game of deciding who would play each of us if there were a film of the trip, which kept us occupied for hours.

On the last night before the rafting, Sarah and I were the last two to go to bed as we sat up talking and complaining about the 'boys'' lack of stamina.

I wasn't on Sarah's raft and I know that Martin and Max and the guides have told you what happened. I just wanted to let you know that we had all got to like Sarah very much and I just can't imagine your grief. She was having a good time before the rafting and if you would like copies of any photographs I have of her when I get them developed then please let me know. I realise that this may not be something you want to deal with at the moment and please don't feel you have to reply to this letter.

If you do want to contact me, however, then please write to me at the above address or e-mail me, or ring me.

I don't really know how to end this letter, just I'm so very sorry.

Love,

Susan Routledge

I e-mailed Julia to tell her we had returned safely.

Dear Julia,

We are all safely back. Still feeling desperately unhappy. We are not sleeping well and I have developed a cold. The trip was emotionally and physically exhausting. The 12-hour road trip took us to a really remote and beautiful area. We stayed in a very basic hostel and the next day had a one-hour drive and a two-hour trek to the river where we held our sad little ceremony – reading out messages to Sarah and throwing in some photos, letters, flowers and mementoes. Apparently there are less than one hundred foreigners who have been down that valley (Rosie was almost certainly the youngest). Rosie coped very well although she did suffer from altitude sickness in Cusco. It was a good thing we didn't take Francesca as we wouldn't have been able to do much at all. We were shown and taken to lots of places associated with Sarah. People in the hotels remembered her and tried to sympathise in their broken English so we spent a lot of time crying. We found the right man to give her bike to and he rode to the Cusco airport on the bike to say goodbye. One of the worst moments was having to go through her belongings in Cusco. We all broke down in the hotel room. I doubt we'll ever be the same again. I find it all so unbearable.

About work, Julia, I will try to come in on Monday the 5th but I hope Tom will still go to the UMG for me. You can organise a morning business meeting if there are enough people around. I will answer any questions about Sarah and then we'd better stop talking about her at work as far as possible. Can you tell the person in Washington that I won't be able to go to the meeting in October after all. Please tell Kate Bernhardt the news as well. She is a good friend of mine who met Sarah a few years ago.

It looks as if we will have to change the date of the memorial service as we can't get the place we want on the right day. I'll keep you posted. We have to try to see the solicitor today to sort out the certificate of presumed death. We have various documents from the British Consulate in

Arequipa. There is always something. The nightmare doesn't end. You can phone me if you want.

Barbara

Later that day we went to see our solicitor. We took the statements from Peru. He checked with a friend of his who was Chief Coroner for Suffolk about the 'Order of presumed death'. The Coroner had never heard of this, neither had other people with whom he checked. At the time of writing we are still trying to obtain a death certificate.

We also received a piece about Sarah that had been put out on the internet by a mountain biking friend, Brant. I did not think it captured the Sarah I knew, but Mick liked it, and said that it was indeed a side of Sarah that perhaps she hid from us to some extent.

WE MISS YOU SARAH

by Brant

Sarah Jones, known to many of us as a bike journalist and mtb enthusiast has been killed in a rafting accident in Peru.

Just over a week ago, I got an email from a friend, telling me that Sarah had been lost overboard on a rafting trip, just a few days into her six-month stay in South America. It came as the blow you'd expect, as many of the bike community had seen her last at BIKE2000, looking so excited about her trip abroad. We chatted, I half-heartedly promised to get together when she got back, and said goodbye.

On the 12th May, she fell overboard on a rafting trip, was knocked unconscious and was swept down river.

I'll miss her for lots of reasons. I remember the first time I met Sarah. Riding a Salsa round a crap cross-country course somewhere in the Midlands, she gave me a copy of "Bad News" the fanzine that she'd written. It was full of bikes, sex and weird stuff. Slowly she forged a path for herself in the weird industry that is UK mountainbiking. Able to drink most of us under the table, I've had the worse hangovers of my life following an evening in Sarah's company.

The picture we have of her (cheers Chipps) sums her up well. My only disappointment is that I know Sarah will be annoyed, as she's only got a half, not a full pint!

We miss you Sarah.

June 2000

On Thursday June 1st, Matt returned to the States. He felt he needed to go back but once there he felt he had gone back too soon. His friends had sent a stretch limousine to meet him and had taken him out for a posh meal. Rosie, Sarah and I should have been returning to Arequipa from the Colca Canyon on June 1st. I went back to the gym that day, 'seeing' Sarah on various pieces of the equipment. On Thursday evening, Mick and I took Anna, Francesca, Anna's friend and her two children, Simon and Jo and their two children, Cameron and Molly, out for a meal (Rosie was in Brighton with her dad). It was still easier, somehow, in restaurants even though we still cried there and, of course, talked about Sarah non-stop.

I wrote some letters thanking people or apologising for cancelling talks and workshops and then returned to work on June 5th with absolute dread. Mick had gone in every day feeling the need for work as a distraction. Anna, also a clinical psychologist, returned the same day as me. I spend part of the week in Cambridge at a research unit and part of the week in Ely at a rehabilitation centre. On Monday 5th I was in Cambridge. I arrived at 7.20 a.m., left my bags and went swimming at the hospital pool. I managed to get away without speaking to anyone. Back to my office feeling very apprehensive. Julia was there and said, "You've lost so much weight, you look tiny." I had lost some weight, not a huge amount but I did look shrunken. Rosie had said to me recently, "Grandma, your face has got smaller." "I'm shrinking, Rosie," I said, "into a little old lady." That day I stayed until 5 p.m. (something I rarely did after that for months). I went through the post and started replying. I had a meeting with Agnes and another with Hazel. I went to, and chaired, the weekly Monday business meeting, crying for most of the way through. I also managed to draft a book review and revise a chapter I was writing for the *Encyclopaedia of Cognitive Science*. That was the day Sarah, Rosie and I should be leaving Machu Picchu to return to Cusco.

On Tuesday June 6th, I went to the gym first and then to the Oliver Zangwill Centre for Neuropsychological Rehabilitation in Ely. I felt much worse there; the academic work in Cambridge was easier to cope with than seeing patients. Although I did relatively little clinical work at the centre, being director of research, I saw patients walking around. I kept thinking that if Sarah had sustained a head injury like many of our patients, I would have known how to get help and how to arrange for rehabilitation. Similarly, if she had sustained brain damage due to shortage of oxygen – which she could have done if she'd been saved from near-drowning – then I would have known what to do. I thought of the families of our brain-injured clients and how those families were luckier than me. I thought however brain-damaged Sarah might be, I could do something for her. I could do nothing with her dead. In fact it was to be five months before I could see a patient again.

Later in the morning I went into the kitchen to make a coffee. I tried to do it when no one was around. I didn't want to speak to anyone, but one of the patients was in the kitchen. He was very amnesic; his memory was extremely impaired. Nevertheless he knew I was in trouble (the staff and patients had been told the week before what had happened). This young man had written in his book, "be nice to Barbara she's had a terrible tragedy". He came up to me in the kitchen and said, "I'm really sorry, Barbara, I want you to know we're all with you." "Except my daughter," I said. "Why, what's happened to her?" came the response. It was so funny in one way, a typical amnesic person's answer. He was so appropriate yet could not remember why he had to be nice to me.

I spent most of the morning in my room crying. My colleague, Jonathan Evans, talked to me and handled my grief very well but most of the others did not inter- rupt, did not come in and did not talk to me. I am sure they felt they were doing the right thing. They did not want to intrude, they wanted to give me space, but they should have come in and given me the opportunity to talk and cry. Letting bereaved people talk and cry is one of the best things others can do. If you don't know what to say to a bereaved person, *don't* say, "I don't know what to say." You could try saying, "Tell me about Sarah (or whoever it is), what was she like?" Or if it is someone you know well, say, "I remember the last time I met her / when we went to such and such a place together / how good she was at parties," or something like that.

The other thing I could not bear were the people who said, "I couldn't live with it." That made me want to scream. "I can't live with it," I'd think, "but I have no choice, I can't give up. Anna, Mick and Matthew could not go through this again, and what about those little girls, who've had enough to cope with." It is OK to say something like, "This is the hardest thing to bear, losing a child," or, "My brother died and I remember how hard my parents found that to cope with." I gave up at 12.30. I felt I'd had enough, I thought that no one could get angry with me, I'd been through the worst and if I wanted to go home then go home I would.

At home I collected Francesca from her nursery school, talked to one of the teachers about Sarah, crying all the while.

I e-mailed my friend Kate in America and she e-mailed back:

Dear Kate,

Thank you for your lovely letter which arrived yesterday. It is still so terribly hard to bear. We all loved her so much and feel in total despair. We went to Peru – a beautiful country – to collect some documents and see the river where she died and where we held a little ceremony. It was so sad though. She should have been having a wonderful six months there and Rosie and I were due to meet her in Peru on May 28th for a 10- day holiday. We can't stop crying and thinking about her. She was so beautiful and lovely and kind. The thought of life without her is intoler- able at present. Yet we know we have to keep going because of the others. Sarah was my greatest joy in life. When people talk of a broken heart, this is what they must mean. My heart is broken.

We are going to have the memorial service on Sunday October 1ˢᵗ from 2 to 4 pm in Bury St Edmunds. Let us know if you can come. We have room for 200 people but I know there are many more than that who would like to attend.

Keep in touch,

With love from Barbara and Mick

Dear Barbara,

I know that Sarah was your greatest joy – it showed in your face every time you spoke of her. We are heartbroken over here, too, and can barely believe it's really true.

I will talk with Ralph and see if we – or at least I – can come to the memorial service. Although I barely knew Sarah, it seems very important to be present as people honor her life.

We love both of you very much.

Kate

The following day I was back in Cambridge. I swam first. One of the regulars said "How are you?", as I was getting ready after my swim. That was it – I broke down again and had to tell her what happened. She was willing to talk but I wanted to escape. I went back to my room and started reading and marking a PhD thesis from New Zealand. I had agreed months ago to be the external examiner and now felt it was too much effort to send it back with an explanation. In fact, this was just the kind of work I was able to do. I was alone in my room, able to cry in peace and work at my own pace. I realised that my cognitive functioning had slowed down considerably. I do not think I would have believed how much grief can slow down one's thinking until I experienced it. Later I went over to the brain imaging centre to meet Narinder, a colleague from Southampton, who was in Cambridge with a patient. The patient stayed in the imaging centre and Narinder came back to my room. He talked about river searches, he had checked with the British rescue services to obtain their advice, he let me talk and he let me cry.

Narinder is a Hindu, he is very straightforward, he does not eat meat and is in many ways a reserved man yet he dealt with my grief well, much better than most British men. He told me at one point that his mother had been the only survivor of 12 children. "How awful," I thought before thinking, "You have known death, that's why you cope so well with a person's grief." I took Narinder over to see another colleague in the main hospital and on the way back passed the main reception. Above the desk, on the wall, was a plaque that read "Whatever it is, it will pass". I was furious, thinking, "How dare they put up something so banal? There will be bereaved people in here, there will be people whose relatives are in terrible pain or who may be dying.

They should not put up such a trivial statement. Why not a line from Shakespeare, or a poem or something uplifting – but not that trite rubbish." Ever since I have tried to avoid going past that entrance. Instead I use a side entrance or, if I have to go past, I avert my eyes from the offensive plaque.

That day I left at 1.00 p.m. feeling desolate. I arranged to see a bereavement counsellor on Friday afternoon. I had been reading a little about grief. Anna gave me a copy of Colin Murray Parkes' book *Studies of Grief in Adult Life* and I found myself going back to it again and again, although it was more to do with the grief of widows rather than bereaved parents. As the weeks went on, though, I found more and more books that spoke directly to me and these I devoured with passion. I could not get enough of them.

I took Rosie to the orthodontist late that afternoon for the appointment she should have had on May 15th – the day we heard. I sat in the waiting room fighting back tears and hoping no one would speak to me. Apart from practical things, that I coped with, nobody said anything, so once more, in public, we looked like normal people. There was no news from the solicitor nor from Peru. Life felt like a nightmare still. That evening there was an e-mail from Peru telling us about other procedures that were to be put in place.

We had received several bouquets of flowers. The house was full of flowers for weeks. On Tuesday 7th, a beautiful display arrived from Tom, Sophie and Andy, three colleagues from work. Andy had got to know Sarah quite well the year before when we were all at a neuropsychology conference together in South Africa. Tom worked in the same rehabilitation research group as me in Cambridge. I e-mailed Tom to thank him, Sophie and Andy for the flowers. Inadvertently I signed off, "With love from Sarah." I did not spot this until the following day when I was re-reading all the e-mails that had been received and been sent. I also sent an e-mail to Sarah that day. I said, "Sarah, please come back to me, I miss you so much." The e-mail went, it did not bounce back, but of course there was no reply.

None of our family has any religious beliefs. We are convinced atheists. I cannot see a mechanism by which one could 'go to heaven' or 'be resurrected', or how a soul could be liberated from a body. I do not believe in an afterlife, nor do I believe that Sarah's spirit has survived somehow. Death is final, she has gone for ever, we will never see her again and will not be reunited with her after our own deaths. Religion makes me uncomfortable, people are too sure of what they believe without any evidence. Of course, if I did believe, Sarah's death might be easier to bear, but I cannot make myself believe just because it would be comforting. Several people told us they were praying for us. I did not get angry with them – they were all trying to help in their own way – but I certainly did not think it did any good. I suppose that, on the whole, religious people were able to cope with our grief. Jewish friends usually found something helpful to say.

A colleague from the Baha'i faith wrote a comforting letter and a Christian friend from America kept in frequent touch. Some others with no religion though were equally comforting. Women tended to cope better than men, with exceptions, and

American men tended to cope better than British men, again with exceptions. Among the British men, younger ones tended to be better than older ones. To some extent this depended on whether or not they had experienced grief. One of Sarah's young friends, Jason, who ran a bike shop in Bury St Edmunds, was very good, exceptionally understanding. I learned that he had lost his mother when he was 14 years old.

On the morning of Thursday June 8th, I felt a little calmer. I went to the gym before going to Ely. I worked on the PhD thesis, e-mails and letters. People called me – some knew and some did not. In every case I cried throughout. One colleague called who did not know. I told her and began crying. She was then crying and told me she had had a still-born baby. I could not bear anyone to be unhappy. I hated hearing any bad news. I wanted the world to be perfect with no more pain and horror for anyone. I managed to stay until 3.35 that day. Went home to more letters, cards and e-mails. Many tears that evening. Mick, Anna and Matthew were still so distressed. Matt telephoned every day from America and each time he cried.

Another weepy morning on Friday June 9th – it was four weeks since Sarah had died. For 22 weeks every Friday I thought "(so many) weeks since Sarah died" and every Monday I thought "(so many) weeks since we heard the news". I managed at work until 11.35. An e-mail arrived from Roy Sugarman (a South African neuro-psychologist) who had met Sarah the summer before at a meeting in South Africa).

Dear Barbara and Mick,

I read your letter several times before I could comprehend what it said. My heart breaks for you, and the unspeakable horror of such a thing. I can only imagine what you are both going through, every parent's night-mare, and made worse, if that's possible, by the horrific details of the loss.

Ros and I are devastated by the news, and wish we could make a dent in the sadness or lighten the loss in some way, but with regret we know we can't, and probably nothing can.

All we can do is send you our fondest love, our prayers for you all, we think of you daily, and pray for a lightening of your grief, and in the Jewish tradition, a long life for you all.

Barbara, we are just so, so sorry.

Please keep us posted with details on how you are doing.

Love, Roy and Ros Sugarman

Other Jewish friends wished us a long life but some did not. Later I asked Yehuda Ben-Yishay, an American–Israeli colleague about this. He said the 'story' concerning the 'a long life' wish is a well-intentioned, naive, uninformed idea. To the contrary, all you say to the bereaved is: "May God comfort you along with all the mourners of Zion and Jerusalem!" This is the ritual formula of observant Jews. You are forbidden to greet the bereaved; you must refrain from offering any (psychobabble) types of platitudes; you are admonished to listen to the words of the bereaved and to, quietly, let them cry and recite the events leading up to and following the death of their loved one. Moreover, the bereaved themselves are forbidden to greet people during the first seven days after the burial; they are forbidden during the first 30 days to attend other people's funerals (they have their own sorrow to deal with) and so on.

That afternoon I went to see a bereavement counsellor. She was fine, a nice woman. I talked a lot and cried a lot and accepted some written materials. I did not really see how she could help. I had many people to talk to and we did talk about Sarah very frequently. Mick, Anna, Matthew and I talked. Carol talked to us and listened to us, people at work talked. I did not need someone to open my heart to, so although the counsellor did nothing wrong, I thought I probably would not see her again and I didn't.

I stopped in town on the way back from the counsellor to try to change our GP to Anna's GP, who had gone to so much trouble over Francesca's proposed trip to Peru. The receptionist at the new doctor's was very cool and unfriendly and said the doctor was not taking any new patients. I told her about Sarah but she was not interested. I asked her to check with the doctor and tell her I was Anna Vizor's mother. Later that afternoon she phoned back to say the doctor would accept us and I should go to collect the forms. I was pleased we could change doctors but had been upset at the receptionist's manner. We were so fragile and vulnerable and hated anything that went wrong. We wanted to sink down into oblivion to escape from any trouble.

Two letters arrived about that time. One from an old friend who had been present when I went into labour with Sarah at a Russian evening class 37 years earlier. The second arrived from a colleague in Australia. Both were letters that gave considerable comfort as well as considerable pain.

Dear Barbara and Mick,

I'm writing straight after Mick's devastating phone call. There's nothing of comfort I can say — it is too dreadful to bear. I just want you to know that I'm thinking about you and feeling for you. I can't begin to imagine how you are — my youngest sister hung herself in September and I couldn't bear that — but how do you cope with the sudden and shocking loss of a child?

I said to Mick that, from Christmas letters, I've followed some of Sarah's adventures and my first thought was that she has died as she has lived — on the edge and always experiencing life to the full. I remember her as a remarkable little girl — loving stories and full of imagination — a beautiful girl too — it is too sad — so unfair. Mick mentioned a memorial service in October. If you wouldn't mind — we'd very much like to come to that.

My sister died in Australia and I flew out to her memorial service — which was a very moving tribute to her life — full of happy and funny memories of Pat. It was deeply sad — but a very positive experience — too soon to be a healing one — but nevertheless a good day.

We've had so much sadness this last year — Jim's sister has lost a second son (brain tumour), my brother's son is dying of Aids. I'm very sorry that you've now got an unbearable sadness in your lives. I wish you strength and send you my love.

With love, Ann

Dearest Barbara and Mick,

I have been thinking of you so much in the past four weeks. The pain and grief you are enduring must be intolerable and unrelenting. It is so hard to know what to say, and whether messages from others are at all helpful, but I just want you to know that I am thinking of you and have been very deeply saddened by Sarah's death.

I know that Sarah meant so much to you, and that you meant a great deal to her. Not many daughters choose to spend their work and leisure time with their parents. You have obviously created the kind of relationship where this would happen. She really enjoyed your company. You have been the most wonderful parents to all your children — parents and friends. This is why this is just so, so unfair. Sarah was lovely and kind and generous and adventurous — just like you.

I guess the hardest thing is that you have to keep going for the others, to whom you are equally good parents and grandparents. But I really hope you can get some time and space to grieve in whatever way you want.

You have been such dear friends to me, and if there is anything I can do from this great distance, to help you, please let me know.

Take care of yourselves.

With much love

from Jennie

Mornings continued to be tough. It was so horrible waking up with that black, leaden weight striking one's heart. Every single thing I did, I thought of Sarah and what a terrible tragedy it was that she died and how we were never, ever, ever going to see her again or laugh with her or take her to a restaurant or travel with her. It was so very, very hard to bear.

As June 11th was Sarah's 37th birthday, Carol had decided to hold a birthday party for her. Carol was always organising family gatherings and Sarah had loved them as we all did, so it seemed appropriate (as well as kind) for Carol to do this. Cindy, Sarah's oldest friend, arrived and we all set off for the 25-minute drive to Carol's house. Although I cried a great deal, it was lovely there. All the children played nicely together. Cameron, Carol's grandson, gave me a necklace he had bought at a car boot sale. He was very endearing and I sobbed even more. His little sister Molly was a darling. She had been born in February, three months before Sarah went to Peru. Sarah loved Molly, she thought Molly looked like her. There was certainly a strong family resemblance. The very last piece of video we have of Sarah is of her with Molly, then aged about one month. Simon was using the video camera and Sarah was saying to Molly, "Who's that, is that your daddy?" Beautiful, lovely Sarah I want you back, you would enjoy this afternoon.

At about this time a book arrived from a colleague in America called *When Bad Things Happen to Good People*, by Harold Kushner. Kushner was a rabbi whose son Aaron had died of progeria (rapid ageing). I read the book, but it was not particularly relevant to me as it was written from a religious viewpoint. The main message of the book was that it is not God who causes bad things to happen but people. I did feel for the man because he had lost his son whom he probably treasured as much as I treasured my special daughter.

Apart from the Murray Parkes book, the first I read after Sarah died, I had also read one loaned by the counsellor. This was called *The Courage to Grieve*, by Judy Tatelbaum. I read this with some interest and had highlighted the following passage as being worth remembering.

> All the hardships that you face in life, all the tests and tribulations, all the nightmares, and all the losses, most people still view as curses, as punishments by God, as something negative. If you would only know that nothing that comes to you is negative. I mean nothing. All the trials and tribulations, and the biggest losses that you ever experience, things that make you say, "If I had known about this, I would never have been able to make it through," are gifts to you. It's like somebody had to – what do you call that when you make the hot iron into a tool? – you have to temper the iron. It is an opportunity that you are given to grow. That is the sole purpose of existence on this planet Earth. You will not grow if you sit in a beautiful garden, and somebody brings you gorgeous food on a silver platter. But you will grow if you are sick, if you are in pain, if you experience losses, and if you do not put your head in the sand, but take the pain and learn to accept it, not as a curse or a punishment, but as a gift to you with a very, very specific purpose.

This passage was taken from Elisabeth Kübler-Ross, *On Death and Dying*.

I struggled through work, some days slightly easier than others. Tears every day and I was still sleeping badly. Matthew seemed in such distress in New York that Mick and I decided to go and spend a week with him. I started to organise the tickets and flights. I gave my first talk since the accident, but it did not really count as it was just to two colleagues working with Mick. I knew them both and it was not like giving a public lecture. Nevertheless, I realised I had to start gently. I spoke on 'neuropsychological assessment' and managed to get through without crying.

I also attended a multi-disciplinary research meeting on recovery from coma. I did not do so well there and cried copiously. Most of the people knew me and knew what had happened but there was one young neurologist who had not been to these meetings before. He must have found it very strange to see this woman weeping so overtly. I asked the Professor of Neurosurgery, John Pickard, to explain why I was crying. I was still leaving work early and in fact that lasted for almost a year. Previously I had been known for my energy. Some people called me a workaholic. Although this was not true, I did work hard, I rarely wasted time and I had bags of energy. Not any more though. I had energy for the gym and felt as if I could not tire myself out there however hard I worked out, but I had no energy for other things. It took about a year to get my energy levels back so that I could do a full day's work but I still feel slowed down inside. I sometimes could not face going into work at all and sat at home dealing with e-mails, reading theses and writing reports. I was still slow, however, and cognitively challenged.

Mick went swimming sometimes and never missed work, although he, too, came home earlier. One morning at the pool a man said to him in the changing room, "Am I right in thinking you've had a tragedy in the family?" He went on to tell Mick that he had lost his 28-year-old son eight years ago in a car accident. The son had been a brilliant scientist. This man knew all the feelings we were going through. He said, "You don't get over it, but it does get easier to bear." We were beginning to realise that we were not so unusual in losing a son or daughter. We had known hardly any bereaved parents before Sarah's death but now we kept meeting them or hearing about them.

Anna was my main support, although Mick was also good. Anna seemed more depressed than overtly weepy. She said that most of the time she felt Sarah was going to come back and it was not true. We all thought this and felt the terrible pity of it all.

Every now and again a letter would arrive for Sarah. Some were bills so we telephoned the organisation or person who had written the letter to explain what had happened. Usually someone on the other end of the telephone said, "We will need to see the death certificate." At first I said, "There isn't a death certificate, we are still trying to get one." After a number of calls like this, I pre-empted the statement by saying angrily, "And you can't see the death certificate because there isn't one and it's going to be a long-drawn-out process to get one." Again some people were kind though, and handled us with sensitivity. I remember Mick and I going into Sarah's bank and explaining. A woman there took us into a side room, said how sorry she was, and seemed comfortable with our crying. It did not stop later letters from the bank arriving for Sarah even though our kind person said she would inform the right people.

Francesca continued to draw pictures of 'a lady stepping in the river'. One morning she woke up and said to Anna, "I had a dream. A lady stepped into the river and it was very cold." She seemed fine and had always talked freely about Sarah, death and dying but I worried about her being constantly surrounded by crying adults. If I caught my breath or started to cry, her little head would dart round to check whether I was crying. She was on the computer one day when Anna and I were watching her. She said something funny and we both laughed (it is possible to laugh in the midst of grief). Francesca looked up at us and said, "Have I cheered you up?" We told her she had.

On Friday June 16th, five weeks to the day that Sarah died, I noted in my diary that I wept a great deal after seeing some correspondence from the owner of the travel company and some more sympathetic e-mails from colleagues. One important thing happened though. A colleague, Ian Robertson, telephoned to tell me to contact a solicitor called Graeme Peart who was the secretary of an organisation for bereaved parents called 'The Compassionate Friends' which helped people who had lost children including adult children. I tried to get hold of Graeme Peart on Friday afternoon. He was out, but his secretary said he would telephone me on Monday. This was the first time I had ever heard of The Compassionate Friends – a group that we came to admire considerably.

That evening Mick had an e-mail from the owner of the travel company in Peru. We both thought that he was not keeping in touch sufficiently. We wanted news every day even if it was to say, "There is no news." We felt he was annoyed with us for expecting greater contact. In the e-mail he said that he had just received Mick's e-mail, that his computer had been hit by a virus that appeared to be attacking outgoing e-mails so he was writing from someone else's computer, and that he had a message for us that he had been trying to send for the past two days but that wouldn't go for some reason. He said that he would like us to appreciate that we would be the first to know if there was any news and that, if he had a daily bit of news worth sending, he would tell us – but he didn't have this. He told us that they were doing everything possible at their end, in accordance with the plan we had agreed to, and asked us to be patient.

He went on to say that the previous evening he had spoken with one of their guides who had just returned from the Cotahuasi canyon. His party had conducted a search five days downriver from Puerte Pullao and had found nothing. They were of the opinion that the body was most probably stuck under the rock that had been previously indicated – too dangerous a place from which to attempt any sort of recovery. The river appeared to be lower than it had been when we were there. The guide had also talked to the locals of Velinga and Quechualla, who were still on the look-out, but they had found nothing.

The e-mail concluded with the news that another group of kayakers who were going down the Rio Cotahuasi had been asked to search, and that Pepe Lopez, in coordination with the police and with locals, was to lead a group into the canyon on foot, taking up to 10 days to search both banks of the river down as far as Toccec. If there was any information received from these groups, we were again assured, we would be the first to know.

The following day Carol, Mick and I set off for Stratford-upon-Avon to see a performance of *Henry IV, Part I*. We had booked this before Sarah's death. We arrived early and went to Anne Hathaway's cottage. We all loved the garden, full of traditional English flowers. The day was beautiful but my heart was heavy and I still cried frequently. Intellectually I knew it was a good performance but my heart was not in it. I thought of Sarah all the way through. I thought of her all the time, in the car, in the gym, in the swimming pool, when I was cooking, when I was washing up, it was non-stop and totally exhausting. I was so tired, I fell asleep during the play and again before dinner in the hotel room. I changed at this time from being unable to sleep to sleeping all the time. I even began to sleep at work for a few minutes at a time. I would put my head on my desk and doze off.

On Monday I cried a lot at work in the morning. This was partly because Graeme Peart phoned. He listened while I told my very tearful story. Then he told me that his daughter had also drowned. She was four years old and had drowned in a school swimming lesson. It was so sad. Everything was so very hard to bear. Graeme Peart told us that The Compassionate Friends society was having a weekend gathering in Leicestershire in July. He said there would be about 200 people there and many would have been bereaved in the past year. He said he took six months off work when his daughter died. I had only taken three weeks so did not feel so bad about leaving early and taking the odd day off. I certainly did not feel guilty. I thought, "Nobody can say anything to me when I've been through this awful tragedy." There were calm periods and by mid-June the calm periods were probably getting longer but the bad periods would suddenly re-emerge with a vengeance and then everything was as bad as it had ever been — like a kick from a horse or an iron rod thumping one in the chest.

When I arrived home on Monday there was a letter from another colleague saying all the right things. I loved these letters, I wanted them but they were so painful and brought our tears on strongly. That evening I spoke on the telephone to Celia, one of Sarah's mountain biking friends. She said that Sarah did take risks and had already had some lucky escapes. Poor Sarah, poor us. She really did not think she was in danger. Any time I said to her that her life or exploits sounded risky, she always said, "I'll be all right."

I took another day's leave the next day to get ready for America. Matt was at the airport in New York to meet us. It was good to see him. We pottered about that afternoon and treated ourselves to a good meal that evening. On Thursday I went for a swim and later we set off for the Metropolitan Museum of Art. I remembered my first trip to New York in 1981 when I attended a workshop. Every evening one of the museums was open late, so after the workshop I would go to whichever museum was open late that day. On Thursday, it was the Metropolitan Museum of Art. On the way there I had felt hungry and decided to buy a hamburger from one of the little stalls to be seen all over New York. Fortunately, there was a hamburger stall right at the bottom of the steps to the Met. I marched straight up to the man and said, "Could I have a hamburger please?" He looked at me strangely and said, "Ma'am, this ain't a hamburger stall, this is a commercial." In confusion I looked around and saw cameras and a model in a fur coat. At first I felt foolish but then saw the funny side of the incident and I often tell that story when I am lecturing in America.

On Friday we hired a car and drove upstate to Lake Mohonk and the Catskills. We stayed at a strange baroque-style hotel I had discovered in *The Historic Hotels of America* book. We all had a good weekend there − three swims in the cold lake, good food, good service and beautiful scenery. We all cried less than we had on other days. We returned to Manhattan on Sunday and went out with a group of Matt's friends on Sunday evening. They were a zany, cosmopolitan group from a variety of ethnic backgrounds. We all ended up in a circle hugging each other and crying. Made a tearful goodbye to Matt on Monday 26th and flew home. We arrived at our home after midnight. There were loads of e-mails, cards and letters that had arrived while we were away. I read them all, naturally crying throughout. Two letters I particularly appreciated at this time were from American colleagues. One was from Jim Becker, a psychologist from Pittsburgh who knew Sarah.

Dear Barbara, Mick, Anna and Rosie,

I don't know where to begin or what to say. I cannot imagine what you are going through. To lose a daughter, sister, friend so far before her time is simply appalling. Sarah was so full of life and energy, I find it inconceivable that she is lost to us.

I have taken the very great liberty of having a book sent to you all from amazon.com − it has been some comfort to others, and I thought that you might find it so, as well.

I know that you all have many friends who are concerned for you. As I have been speaking to colleagues and friends around the world, they have all said how difficult this has been, and that all of us will help in any way that we can.

It is ironic that I actually visited Arequipa as a youth (well, 13-year-old). I remember little about the city, except that, even for Peru, it was pretty much off the beaten track. It wasn't on the top 10 spots for tourists, and I can well imagine that having to travel that far outside of the city put you well into the South American version of the outback. That somehow seems quite the sort of place that Sarah would have wanted to travel through − and the fact that she was to live in Cuzco I think is also in keeping with her personality. I remember Cuzco as a pretty, but backwater town (lo, those many years ago) but I understand that it, too, had developed its share of risk. Clearly, this was a young woman who had clear ideas about how to live life. She grabbed it by the collar and held on for a wild ride – but it was a ride that only she could have endured.

I realise that all of this probably sounds terribly trite, but it is well meant. I know that there is nothing of substance that I can say that will be of any consequence, and nature abhors a vacuum (so I ramble ever onward).

Please realise that all of your friends are thinking of you, and will do whatever it takes to help you pull through this terrible time. It seems bad now, it will seem worse, but eventually it will get better (not over, not forgotten, just better).

Please do let me know if there is *anything* I can do.

I am thinking of you often.

Jim

Here is my reply:

Dear Jim,

Mick and I returned home from New York last night to receive your letter. Thank you very much. It was a good letter and, although I cried when I read it, it was kind of you to say the things you did. It was also good to hear from someone who knows Peru. We thought it was a beautiful country, particularly the Cotahuasi Valley where Sarah died. Apparently, less than 100 foreigners have visited the valley and the youngest was our granddaughter Rosie who is 12. We didn't take Francesca, the four-year-old, as the doctor was worried about the altitude. As it was, Rosie suffered from altitude sickness and was unwell for three days. Cusco was charming and we only wish we had been to Peru under better circumstances. It was Sarah's third time there and she loved it. We were in the States to see Matthew (Sarah's younger brother) who has taken this very badly. We all have and it doesn't seem to get much easier.

I had a helpful letter from Audrey Holland who obviously knows this horrible anguish we are going through. We are in touch with a group for bereaved parents and will probably go to a weekend of workshops the group is organising. It must get easier with time although I can't believe I will ever get used to the thought of never seeing Sarah again – her lovely smile and her beautiful face and her boundless goodness.

Mick and I will be at the INS in Brussels (our first conference since the accident – so I hope we can cope). Will you be there? Thanks for writing and we hope to see you soon.

Barbara & Mick

The second letter was from Audrey Holland, a speech and language pathologist whose son, Ben, had been murdered in Tucson about two years earlier. I remember hearing about it at the time and thinking, "How awful!" but I did not really appreciate how Audrey must have felt. Now, of course, I could imagine her grief more clearly. I wanted to hear from her — bereaved parents had more to say to me than anyone.

Dear Barbara,

Judy suggested that I just write you at the company — I have been searching for a better address for weeks.

You are continuously on my mind — I reach out to you from a shared devastation of losing a child. I have few words of wisdom, only a firm conviction that you live through this by doing what *you* have to do, not necessarily what others tell you. Work was my salvation; others say totally absenting oneself from life is best. But it will be what you have to do. It shouldn't happen to us, this loss, but it did. And Barbara, we go on — not particularly because we want to, but because we have to, planting memories of our beautiful lost children, making sure they are remembered by remembering them, continuing to love them, and, I think, honouring them by getting on each day — one at a time.

I cannot comprehend why Sarah's time to die was now, as Ben's time to die was almost two years ago. But I do know now, I am learning, that death is part of life, and fitting it in, accepting it, making it part of ourselves is not a shallow and meaningless endeavor.

I enclose a meditation that is for me particularly helpful — perhaps it will make sense to you too in this senseless time.

You are in my daily meditations, and I send you strength to get through each day. If you want to talk and email, or if I can help in any way, please please let me know.

With love, respect and faith in you,

Audrey Holland

And my reply:

Dear Audrey,

Thank you for writing. I know you understand the anguish we are going through having been there yourself. When I heard about your son's death two years ago I was appalled but I did not have much idea of how you really felt. I do now and my heart goes out to you too. It really is too big a loss to bear. I know we have to go on because of the others around us but it is too hard. Mick and I have two other children and two grandchildren but Sarah was our firstborn and the one we were closest to. We have become closer to the others now but will always regret the loss of our shining treasure.

I have always been passionate about my work but now it all seems so meaningless. I go in each day but spend most of the time crying. I can't face seeing patients or going to meetings. The most I can do is the post, reading the odd report or thesis and a bit of writing. I am so slow and inefficient though that I feel I shouldn't be paid. Mick is coping a bit better but he is also in a bad way. Sarah's sister Anna and brother Matthew are also suffering. Matthew is living in the USA at present but phones home every day in tears. We have just returned from the States where we went to try to cheer him up. It worked for a while but we were very tearful at the airport yesterday when we said goodbye and I think Matthew will be home soon. He and Sarah had many friends in common and shared similar tastes in music. He always felt able to talk to her and rely on her to help sort out his problems. Anna is very depressed, Sarah was her best friend, her main babysitter and close confidante. All three were born within three years of each other and were very close. In fact we almost always saw each other every day and if we couldn't meet we were on the telephone all the time.

We have been in touch with a group called Compassionate Friends (for bereaved parents). You probably know about them? There is a weekend coming up soon organised by this group. I think Mick and I will go.

Thank you again for writing, Audrey. It helps to know people get through this somehow. Are you still able to feel that life is good? Do you ever get through a day without thinking of Ben? (Our Matthew was nearly a Ben but a friend had a Ben a few days before and we didn't want to be copycats.)

I hope we can keep in touch and meet again one of these days.

With love from

Barbara

I went into work late the next day, to the Oliver Zangwill Centre. I was dealing with replies to cards, e-mails and letters so cried all morning. I had cancelled almost everything, or Julia had on my behalf. Sue came in to talk to me, I felt the staff there were trying, they did not know whether to leave me in peace or talk to me and set me off crying again. Talking is better. As I said to several people, "The best way you can help is to let me talk and let me cry." I cried so much I could not go to the canteen for lunch because of my swollen eyes.

I booked two places for Mick and me at The Compassionate Friends weekend in Leicestershire for the coming weekend. I was not at all sure that it was the right thing to do. I felt I was 'clutching at straws' and prepared to do anything that might ease our immense pain. Although I had felt a little better in New York, since coming home the grief, regret and yearning were all as bad as ever.

Another bad day the following day. I went to the gym first and then into Addenbrooke's. Because I was late I had a job to find a parking space. It took me 25 minutes from driving into the hospital to reaching my room. I felt so depressed. When I walked in Julia said Mick had phoned. I called home and Mick was in a terrible state and wracked with sobs. He had been drafting the wording for the invitation to the memorial service and he wanted to check this with me. First he said, "I can see her out there now. I can see her smile. I can see her washing her car." We were both sobbing and that was me set for the day. He wanted to use a poem of William Wordsworth's on the invitation – one I also felt was very appropriate for the invitation.

We had postcards made for the invitations with a photograph of Sarah on one side and the wording on the other side (see pages 57 and 58).

Later I met with Agnes and talked mostly about Sarah and our attempts to get a death certificate. I was crying for most of the morning and felt useless. Perhaps I should not have gone back to work so quickly. I seriously considered resigning from work but I had read or heard somewhere that one should not make major decisions like leaving work or moving house for at least a year after bereavement. I certainly did not want to move house. I love our house and Sarah spent her last five months here before going to Peru, so Sarah's presence was all around. Her dressing gown still hung on the back of her bedroom door (and still does to this day). If Mick or I buried our faces in it, we could smell her. Matt once put on Sarah's dressing gown one morning and Mick became very upset, so it now hangs permanently on the door and nobody is allowed to move it. I decided to postpone any decisions about work.

Early in the afternoon I received an e-mail from a young Chilean psychiatrist working at Addenbrooke's with German Berrios. His name was Alvaro Barrera. He had been recruited to give Sarah Spanish lessons several months before she left for Peru. Their lessons were held once a week, in my office. I e-mailed him and sent a copy of the letter we had been e-mailing friends and colleagues. I also asked if he would be willing to translate the Peruvian Police report for the Foreign Office. He agreed and also said he would come to the memorial service on October 1st.

We had heard from the British Embassy a day or so earlier with a recommendation that we use an American lawyer based in Lima, to try to get the death certificate issued over there. The Foreign Office was unwilling to issue the certificate, explaining that the Peruvians would have to issue it because she died there.

A slumber did my spirit seal;
I had no human fears;
She seemed a thing that could not feel
The touch of earthly years

No motion has she now, no force;
She neither hears nor sees;
Rolled round in earth's diurnal course,
With rocks, and stones, and trees.

(William Wordsworth)

You are invited to attend a service in celebration of Sarah's life.
This will take place at the Athenaeum Building, Angel Square,
Bury St Edmunds, Suffolk on Sunday, 1 October 2000,
between the hours of 1.00 and 4.00 p.m.

Programme:

1.00 p.m. assemble in the lounge for a drink and snack:
there will be a photographic exhibition and guests will be
invited to sign a book of remembrance.

2.00 p.m. assemble in the ballroom for the service, which will
consist of short speeches by friends and family and the
playing of some of Sarah's favourite songs.

4.00 p.m. assemble in lounge for a farewell

Please come if you can: Sarah would love you to be there

Barbara and Mick Wilson

This is how I told an American friend, Stephanie:

Dear Stephanie,

Don't worry about getting to England for the Memorial Service. I didn't expect you to come as California is so far away. Mick and I had a few days in New York with Matthew and that was OK although we were all tearful at the airport. When we got home things were just as bad as ever what with lots more cards and letters. Then we heard from the lawyer yesterday that the British Embassy in Lima suggest to get a death certificate we need to go to a Peruvian judge and it will take at least two years for him to even hear the case. They recommend getting an American lawyer, which we will have to pay for. The Foreign Office in London seems unwilling to do anything and say the Peruvians must issue the death certificate. We have already spent a small fortune with no results and we are finding this extremely stressful. The searches have now ended with nothing to show for it but expenses.

We are now in touch with a group called The Compassionate Friends, which is a support group for bereaved parents. They are having a weekend of workshops, discussions, etc. from July 7th to 9th and Mick and I have booked places.

Enjoy China.

With love from

Barbara

I telephoned Graeme Peart, a solicitor as well as secretary of The Compassionate Friends. He said he thought we should go along with the suggestion to hire a lawyer in Lima. We also talked about the coming weekend in Leicestershire. He said we would be identified as a newly bereaved family and would be looked after. I thought about the lawyer in Lima, and the company Sarah travelled with and the searches. It seemed as if South Americans were making money out of my daughter's death. I did a few more work things and felt worn out with crying. I left at 3.25. Once I arrived home I had several more calls. One was from Matthew who was still tearful; one was from Carol, we both sobbed throughout; one was from my cousin June, another tearful session. It felt so unbearable, much too big a loss for anyone to cope with. Graeme Peart had told me earlier on the phone that it will get worse before it gets better.

I felt a little calmer the next day despite two emotion-provoking e-mails from Audrey Holland and German Berrios.

Here is Audrey's e-mail:

Dear Barbara – I am so honored that you wrote – I know what effort it all takes. I am pleased to hear that you are making an effort just to do the smallest things at work – I think it really turns into a godsend in the long run to have such distractions. And I urge you, urge you, to try Compassionate Friends as well – I had a grief counselor, a close friend whose son had committed suicide, and who was and is a significant factor in keeping me together – it can really, really help.

You ask, does a day go by when I don't think of Ben? No it doesn't, but in all truth, I don't think such a day ever went by me without a thought for Ben and Katie (his sister) before his death. It is just more obvious now. But what has also happened is that substantially more of these thoughts are about the positives of his life, rather than the negatives of his death – such things just happen as part of a healing process – but they cannot be pushed.

Oh Barbara, I just wish I could sit and cry with you – you are in my daily meditations, without fail – Love, Audrey.

. . . and German's

Dearest Barbara & Mike,

Thank you for telling us about your harrowing trip to Peru. We feel heartbroken and in full sympathy. Thank you also for describing for us the beautiful farewell ceremony in which you told Sarah that you will never forget her. For ever, she is now part of a strange and wonderful world, that of the harsh and unforgiving geography of Peru, with which she had fallen so much in love. May she rest in peace and live for ever in the hearts of all those who loved her.

Doris and I are distressed at the fact that we shall miss her memorial service as we shall be in Peru at the time. In fact we return from Lima on the 7 October. I have asked already Alvaro Barrera to represent me officially. We stand by for whatever we can do to help you all to bear your pain.

Love from

Doris & German

I showed Julie and Agnes some photographs from Peru that had recently been developed. Alvaro Barrera came to collect the document he had agreed to translate. The Foreign Office had asked us to do this, although I could not understand why they did not translate it themselves as they have a South American department. Alvaro told me that he and Sarah were friends and how terrible it was. I cried all the time he was there. Soon after he left I went over to the hospital with four colleagues to hear a talk by Dr Keith Andrews, the head of the Royal Hospital for Neurodisability in Putney, London. I know Keith reasonably well. He came over to speak to me about Sarah and my eyes filled up again. Nevertheless, I managed to sit through his talk without crying. I felt it was a good talk for me to listen to as I knew the topic and found Keith easy to listen to. I met one woman who used to work in our unit. She did not find it easy to say the right things but she came up to me and patted my hand. I felt comforted by that — she did her best in a situation that was awkward for her.

I went back to work on a chapter I was writing, some other paper work and some calls. Left at 3.10. When I arrived home that evening, the book from Jim Becker had arrived. This was *A Broken Heart Still Beats*, edited by Anne McCracken and Mary Semel, both of whom had lost sons. This was to become my favourite anthology of writings about grief. I include three of my favourite pieces from the book. The first by one of the book editors (Mary Semel); the second by Ann Finkbeiner who lost a son in a train crash; and the third by David Morrell whose son died of cancer at the age of 15. Prose meant more to me than poetry and, with the odd exception, like Wordsworth's 'A slumber did my spirit seal', it still does. These three pieces all said things I knew to be true of my family.

WHAT KIND OF UNIVERSE IS THIS ANYWAY?

by Mary Semel

When Alexander was killed, my feeling that there was any sense or order in the universe was destroyed. Not only did I have searing, agonizing pain inside of me, but the plug was pulled on the force of gravity. I was free-falling into chaos.

I had no faith in divine benevolence to begin with: there is just too much wanton suffering for me to believe everything works out for the good. But I trusted in laws of nature or chance to keep me and my children safe: healthy children grow up, good parents are rewarded, and normal people have normal lives. Children bury parents, not the reverse. You don't question whether you believe in gravity; you just assume that your feet will hit the floor when you get up in the morning and your coffee cup will stay on the table. And you also assume that if you follow the rules, your healthy, exuberant sixteen-year-old son will be home for dinner.

I ranted and raved at a God I didn't believe in. How could He allow the most wonderful boy in the world, who was full of life yesterday, to be dead today? I loved Alexander so much and tried so hard to be a good mother. How could He let this happen to me? What was the point of me investing my heart and soul — not to mention time, energy, and money — into nursing, diapering, bathing, educating, and molding this child if he was to die at sixteen? What kind of monster could play such a cruel joke?

There are old, sick people waiting to die, there are unhappy people for whom life is a burden, there are parents who abuse and neglect children, there are children who cause their parents nothing but grief. Why do they live while my happy, handsome son, who had the world at his beckoning, lies in his grave and I am destroyed?

My outraged soul screamed for answers to these questions even as I knew they would never come. The same is true for all the other bereaved parents I have ever met or read about, from Job on. Some eventually find peace in the faith that there is purpose beyond human understanding; others, like Anne and me, make do with random chance, a roll of the dice — an explanation that is less satisfying, but more compatible with reality as we know it.

Years have passed and the questioning does not consume me as it used to, but the questions remain. Still, when I pick up the morning paper and read about a tragedy that has befallen an innocent child and its suffering parents, I am haunted by the question, "What kind of universe is this anyway?"

(Reproduced from McCracken & Semel, *A Broken Heart Still Beats*)

STUNNING PAIN

by Ann K. Finkbeiner

A science journalist, Finkbeiner took her eighteen-year-old son, T.C. Colley, to the Baltimore train station, kissed him goodbye, and told him she was proud of him. He was eager to get back to his girlfriend and his school, the Rhode Island School of Design, after Christmas vacation. Twenty minutes later, a freight train hit T.C.'s train, killing him and fifteen other passengers, many of them also college students.

With reality comes pain, and the pain, when it comes, is stunning. The pain is actually physical, mostly in your stomach and chest. Your chest feels crushed and you can't seem to catch your breath. I remember feeling pinned like a butterfly, or somehow eviscerated. One woman drew an arc that started at her head and ended at her knees and said, "His death was cut out of here." The pain comes in waves — moves in, backs off, then in again. People try describing it with superlatives or metaphors, then give up the attempt. And no one wants to try too hard anyway; they'd much rather talk about how, with time, the waves of pain gradually became less

frequent. "Now when I think of him," one woman said, "I don't get that wrenching, I don't know the word to use, that wrenching feeling."
(Reproduced from Finkbeiner, *After the Death of a Child*)

EXTRACT FROM *FIREFLIES*

by David Morrell

Morrell is best known for creating the character of Rambo, the hero of books and movies. He also wrote "Fireflies", a blend of fact and fantasy about the death of his fifteen-year-old son Matthew from cancer.

> When you lose a child (and you truly loved that child and weren't just an indifferent caretaker or that scum of existence, a brutalizer), you search for some meaning, some justification, anything to ease your agony. You think about God and whether He exists and what kind of God would allow something so heinous as Matthew's death. You think about ultimates, about the point of existence and whether there's an afterlife and what it would be like. Would Matthew be waiting when his father, mother and sister died? Would he be the same?
>
> You question everything. You grasp at anything. To make sense of what seems to have no sense. To find meaning in what you despair might be the ultimate meaning: nothingness. You seek in all places, all cultures. You search in all philosophies and faiths.
>
> Reincarnation? Plato believed in it. For that matter, a full half of the world's present population believes in it. In the East. As the theory goes, we struggle through various stages of existence, not always human, sometimes animal or even plant, rising until we've perfected our spirit sufficiently to abandon material existence and join forever in bliss with God.
>
> A complicated but comforting belief. Because there's a point to life, a pay-off. Certainly it's easier to accept than the notion that God tortures us here on earth to punish us for our sins so we'll be happy with Him in Heaven. In that case, how do we explain the death of an infant, who couldn't possibly have sinned? Or the death of a fifteen-year-old boy, who by all accounts was remarkable and never harmed anyone?
> (Reproduced from McCracken & Semel, *A Broken Heart Still Beats*)

I took another day off the following day as Rosie was off school because the teachers had a training day. I kept reminding myself of all the weekends and evenings I had worked over the past years. "I am in credit with work," I thought. Once I would have felt so terribly guilty about missing work but now all my priorities had changed.

I arranged to go to lunch with Carol and Rosie. We met Mick in town and all went to Café Rouge. Although we had a pleasant meal, it was so sad to think I would never see my lovely, happy girl again. She used to tease me, saying, "Mum, you think you're perfect," and I would reply, "But Sarah, I am. Everything I do is right." We never argued, she made me laugh, she cheered me up. She also defended people. If I complained about a difficult colleague Sarah would say something like "He's probably had a row with his wife," or "Well you caught her at a bad moment." She had a naive belief that people were good. She loved her food, she had a zest for everything. She was beautiful, charismatic, my firstborn and my treasure.

We all went to look at the rooms we had booked for the memorial service at the Athenaeum. Mick had made all the arrangements there. We were pleased with the beautiful ballroom and the extra rooms for the photographic display we wanted to have. Matthew was to be in charge of the music. He and Sarah had similar tastes in music and he certainly knew what she liked. We often played her music at home in the evenings. The music never failed to provoke our tears. Even the songs I did not like would lead to weeping. Matt once played us a song he said was Sarah's all-time favourite. The song was called "Another Girl, Another Planet" by The Only Ones and would never get on to my top ten, but one of the reasons we found this song so powerful was the first line, "I always flirt with death". How ironic. How predictive. How awful. (Almost a year later, when Mick and I got to the place in the river where they think Sarah is trapped, we played Sarah's songs in a little ceremony we had prepared, and for Mick this song meant most, with its harsh punk rhythms fitting in with the noise and fierce movement of the rapids.)

July 2000

In my diary I noted that on July 1st I went to the gym and then had a lazy day watching television. Although this may seem a normal day to some people, it was not at all normal for me. I never used to be lazy, I never wasted time, I was always so energetic. Now the only energy I had was for the gym. The lassitude surprised me. I would not have believed the drain in energy that follows bereavement and accompanies grief.

We had a beautiful letter from Jean Ferrandis on July 1st. Jean is a well-known French flautist who had known us since he was a young boy. His mother had met Mick before either of them was married, working for the International Voluntary Service. They remained friends and when our children were younger, we visited them in Nice. They came to stay with us in England and once we all went camping together in Corsica. Jean's letter was like a poem and can be seen later, included in the programme for the memorial service.

Matthew telephoned almost every day, always in tears. He could not decide whether to stay in the States or come home to England. During his Saturday call he said that he had dreamed about me, Mick, Anna, Rosie and himself. Sarah was not in his dream and that made him sad. Anna had also had two dreams about Sarah recently. One was sad, in which she was incredulous at seeing Sarah and saying, "Sarah, you are really alive!" and one happy dream where the two of them were sitting on the floor chatting. In the first few months I only ever dreamt about Sarah twice. My first dream was on the night of May 16th, the second night after we heard the news. She came in rather stunned but essentially fine. I called out to everyone that Sarah was OK and it had all been a terrible mistake. The second dream was two nights later. Sarah walked into the house and I said, "You're real Sarah. It can't be a dream because I can see in colour (she had a green sweater on) and you don't dream in colour." Well, obviously one does dream in colour. Oh dear, oh dear, oh dear, how painful it all was. We were all surprised at how infrequently we dreamed about her. I wanted to have pleasant, happy, comforting dreams but even today, I have had only a few further dreams about Sarah – at least that I can remember. Matt also told me about a dream when Sarah came home to find he had moved into her room and she became cross with him saying he had to go as it was her room. Anna had a similar dream where she took some of Sarah's clothes and Sarah got angry, demanding them back.

The crying continued. Mick had a horrible cold at the beginning of July. He was very unwell and I feared he would succumb to pneumonia. He did not, and I remained well throughout this harrowing time. Apart from a slight, trivial cold when we returned from Peru, nothing had been wrong with me. I expected to be susceptible to any virus or illness going but I seemed resistant to everything. Perhaps it was all the exercise I engaged in? I thought if anything happens to anyone now, I could not bear it. I made Mick promise that he would live until he was 84. I thought by then I might be strong enough to cope. Why choose 84? Well, he once completed a questionnaire in a Sunday colour supplement that with his good blood pressure and parental history, he should live until he was 84. I also worried about Anna. She had so much driving to do to get to and from work in Norwich that I felt she was in danger. If anything happened to her how would her daughters cope and how would I cope? I worried less about Matthew and I am not sure why. I needed to speak to him every day and he needed to speak to us. Everyone felt so vulnerable. Even as I said to people, "The worst has happened," part of me knew that it could be worse. I could lose another child, I could lose my grandchildren and two deaths would be worse than one.

On Monday July 3rd, there was an afternoon meeting with five colleagues including William, the director of the Unit. I was quiet and withdrawn. William came to my room afterwards to ask how I was coping. He wanted to be supportive, he was supportive, but I was exhausted with crying. He said to me, "Just do what you can." I thought this was a helpful comment, he was giving permission for me to take things slowly. I realised I was lucky at work. My colleagues were supportive and let me take things at my own pace. Anna, too, had supportive colleagues but it was harder for her. She had students to deal with and more meetings to go to. She could not hide in her room as much as I could. On that same evening we were informed from Peru that one of Sarah's shoes had been found. Unbearable news! All those searches, all the efforts, all the money spent and only one shoe has come to light. It was discovered on the bank of the river just down from where they think Sarah might be. My poor Sarah, with one bare foot, where are you now?

I was still leaving work early, crying for chunks of the day. I told Julia about the one shoe being found and that set me off. I did some work, writing a chapter, but I was so very slow. At this time I was cooking most of the evening meals. Before this Mick had cooked about four days a week and I cooked at weekends. I sometimes cooked a meal during the week and sometimes we ate out. Now cooking was one of the things I felt able to do along with the gym, swimming, reading, sunbathing, watching television and lazing around. The thing I felt least able to do was see patients. I thought, "However brain-injured they are, their families have them." Furthermore, I could not be bothered with other people's problems at this stage. Other things I found hard were meetings and anything too demanding.

The following day, July 5th, was the first day the tears were less frequent. I cried every now and again rather than every half an hour or so. I went to the travel agent in the hospital to book a holiday to Egypt. Mick had said a week or two earlier that after the memorial service in October we should treat ourselves to a holiday. The first two trips I tried to book were full because we were travelling the week of half-term. The third one was OK. Matt had been to Egypt a year or so earlier and said it was the best holiday he had ever had. Neither Mick nor I had been there so we decided to go. We also wanted a holiday with lots to do and not too much time sitting around thinking about Sarah and the terrible tragedy that had happened to our family.

If I had thought the crying was soon to cease, I was mistaken and cried almost as much the next day, Thursday 6th, as I had done since May 15th. I had a call from an old colleague and one who knew Sarah. He wanted to be helpful but he said all the wrong things. He tried to stop me crying, perhaps because he felt uncomfortable. When I said I could not face seeing patients he said, "Oh come on, you've got so much to offer." I felt as if I had nothing to offer. I told him I was thinking of taking early retirement and he tried to dissuade me. I got fed up with his incompetence. Grieving people do not want to be told what they should do or how they should think. They need to be listened to. I would probably have been less hostile if he had suggested I wait a while before making any decisions. The best thing, however, would have been something like, "I can understand why you feel like that."

Friday July 7th was the day we went to the weekend meeting of The Compassionate Friends. We were both nervous. We knew it would be emotionally draining and we did not know how we would get on with the other bereaved parents. Although we were calmer, the tears hit us suddenly and unexpectedly. They also stopped quickly. It was a strange sensation, not like ordinary crying which subsides gradually. This grief-stricken crying would be fierce, sudden and then stop without a slowing-down period. Matt also seemed a little calmer during his daily calls from the States. Anna was low. She was quiet more than tearful and very supportive to me. She was always willing to listen. I was very glad to have Anna around so much but I knew I should have had two daughters not one. The family seemed so shrunken. I wished I'd had more children when I was younger. I should have had six, not three. I looked at mothers and daughters in the street and thought, "I hope their daughters grow up safely."

We arrived at the TCF weekend event just after 5.00 p.m., went to the registration desk in great trepidation and were greeted by one of the 'old hands', Dinah Perkins. She looked at us and said, "Is this your first time?" I burst into tears and said, "Yes, our daughter died eight weeks ago." "Eight weeks!" she answered, "You come with me." She arranged for someone to take our bags to our room, explained a few things to us and saw to our registration. She was good and kind and we were just so overcome with sadness and grief. The next thing we went to was a 'Newcomers' Group'. We did not like it, we felt uncomfortable, and the group leader did not seem to be particularly competent in our eyes. We then joined others to go to a dedication for a rose garden. We did not think much of that either – it was too religious for our tastes. We knew that The Compassionate Friends was not a purely religious group – it was for all religions and for those without religion. Nevertheless, the dedication was religious.

At dinner we were invited to join the table of the person who had led the Newcomers' Group. We were not very comfortable there, although we met a woman from Suffolk, Eileen, who was the only other Suffolk person there. She had lost her only son Oliver in a car accident in 1993. She had also had a stillborn son years before and she was a widow. I said to Anna, when we had first heard about Sarah, "I could have been a widow with an only child," and now I had met one. We also met an English couple, David and Janet, living in Belgium. They had lost a daughter, Eleanor, from cancer in 1988. As Mick and I were going to be in Belgium the following week for a conference, we arranged to meet up with them for dinner. We drank too much wine, did not sleep well and woke up Saturday morning feeling very low. We decided we would leave after breakfast.

Dinah Perkins came up to us at breakfast to find out how we were. We said we were thinking of leaving. She said, "Why don't you go to the keynote speech? Sit near the back in case you need to leave, but give it a try." We thought we might as well do that.

The keynote speech was the beginning of our commitment to The Compassionate Friends. The speaker was a nun – Sister Frances Dominica. She had started 'Helen House' – the first hospice for children – in Oxford in 1980. She told us about Helen – the girl Helen House was named after – who is still alive but comatose. She told us how she started to help Helen's parents and then took the very sick little girl into her own cell at the convent to give the parents time with their other child and each other. This was a woman who did things. She set up the hospice and several others have followed since then. I thought, "This is a really good person." Sister Frances Dominica was a delight to listen to. I felt so pleased to know there were good people around and privileged that I had been able to listen to her.

After coffee we went to a discussion group called 'Sudden Death'. Typically there are about 12 people or so in each group; the leader introduces himself or herself and then each person in the group says who they are, where they come from and a few words about their son or daughter. Then the discussions start and may go in several directions. We thought the Sudden Death group was good despite being full of heart-breaking stories. We heard about children dying in pain, dying after long-drawn-out illnesses, being murdered, committing suicide. We kept thinking, "At least our Sarah did not die in pain, she was happy up to the end – well almost to the end as we don't know about the last few minutes. At least she was enjoying her final hours." We learned fairly early on though that each bereaved family seems to need to find people worse off than themselves, so for us it was, "At least she didn't die over a long period in pain". Those whose children had died in such a manner said to us, "At least we have a body." People kept telling us how brave and strong we were to go to such a meeting after only eight weeks. We were not brave and strong, we were just normal people trying to cope and find something to ease our pain and take us through this passage of grief.

We found ourselves drawn to many of the people at the workshop. There was a woman whose daughter died eight years ago aged $17\frac{1}{2}$ of a pulmonary embolism. Another woman had lost her $6\frac{1}{2}$-year-old daughter of a brain haemorrhage. Then there was the woman whose 19-year-old son died in a climbing accident. She said, "If he wasn't taking risks he wasn't happy." That sounds like Sarah, I thought. The saddest story to me was of a 13-year-old who had died in agony, surviving for 26 hours with gangrene of her internal organs following chemotherapy for leukaemia. A couple from Teesside whom we had met and liked the night before were there. Their son was killed in a car accident 18 months before. They were still very raw and fairly recently bereaved. We were by far and away the most newly bereaved, however, and also the most tearful.

After lunch we joined a tour to the Bosworth Field battleground where Richard III lost his crown to Henry VII in 1485. That went well. We talked to several people about their losses and their children. There is an immediate bond between bereaved parents that crosses all walks of life and social class. Mick spent a while talking to a man whose son had committed suicide. Mick seemed very affected by this story. We felt the parents whose children had committed suicide had a harder cross to bear.

Dinner was better. We joined a table full of people we found it easy to get on with including the two leaders from the morning workshop, Sheila and Peter Clarke, and the Pringles who were the main organisers of the weekend.

After dinner we decided to go to a session called 'The Power of Music' where participants can play a piece of music that means something to them or to their dead children. We had taken Bob Dylan's "Forever Young" but it was on CD and the tape recorder could not play CDs. Most of the songs played were too sentimental for our tastes but a couple were good and moving. One father played a piece composed by his deceased daughter.

The following morning we went to a session on poetry and prose that we particularly enjoyed. Patricia and David Lloyd ran it and chose some excellent pieces, most of which they read themselves. Mick read the Wordsworth poem we had selected for the memorial invitations and a few other people read things. One piece Trish and David

Lloyd chose and read was from A. S. Byatt's *The July Ghost*. I had not known this before and was much affected by it. A. S. Byatt had lost a son herself when he was eight years old, I believe. One of the reasons why this story touched me so much was that the author becomes concerned with grammar. She hears her husband say about their son "He is dead" and she thinks "*is* dead, *is* dead", this present tense will always be the present however long her son is dead. She also chides herself for being concerned with grammar at such a time. I was intrigued as Mick and I had recently had a discussion about grammar. It made me aware that after death one is tripped up by grammar. We frequently spoke of Sarah in the present tense, "Sarah loves potatoes", or "Sarah enjoys that kind of music". We gradually changed from "Sarah loves that" to "Sarah loved that" and from "Sarah enjoys that" to "Sarah would have enjoyed that". Even today, though, we are likely to talk about Sarah in the present tense. Sometimes for a split second I forget about her death and I might think to myself, "I wonder if Sarah will phone today." Once the thought has crossed my mind, I remember immediately that she has gone and gone forever.

Another poem that struck home was "The Elephant in the Room" by Terry Kettering, written about people who avoid talking about the dead person. This is Terry Kettering's poem:

THE ELEPHANT IN THE ROOM

by Terry Kettering

There's an elephant in the room.
It is large and squatting, so it is hard to get around it.
Yet we squeeze by with, "How are you?"
And "I'm fine"...
And a thousand other forms of trivial chatter.
We talk about the weather.
We talk about work.
We talk about everything else...
Except the elephant in the room.

There's an elephant in the room.
We all know it is there.
We are thinking about the elephant as we talk together.
It is constantly on our minds,
For, you see, it is a very big elephant.
It has hurt us all.
But we do not talk about the elephant in the room.
Oh, please, say her name.
Oh, please, say "Barbara" again.

Oh, please, let's talk about the elephant in the room.
For if we talk about her death,
Perhaps we can talk about her life?
Can I say "Barbara" to you and not have you look away?
For if I cannot, then you are leaving me
Alone . . .
In a room . . .
With an elephant.

(Reproduced from *Bereavement Magazine*)

The whole programme was in four parts. These were the readings:

Introduction
Shakespeare − *King John*, Act 3, Scene 3, line 92
 − *Macbeth*, Act 4, Scene 3, line 209; Act 5, Scene 3, line 40
D. H. Lawrence − "Giorno dei Morti"
Part 1. Early days − shock and anguish
Henry Carey − "The Distressed Father"
Alan Lloyd − "Feet"
Pat Neil − "In the Course of a Day"
Walter de la Mare − "Autumn"
Patricia Lloyd − "Silent Witness"
Elizabeth Jennings − "For a Child Born Dead"
Elizabeth Chapman − From "A Little Child's Wreath"
William Wordsworth − Sonnet 27, "Surprised by Joy"
Part 2. The full reality dawns − difficulties in communicating as family members grieve in their different ways
A. S. Byatt − "The July Ghost" (an extract)
Robert Frost − "Home Burial"
Sylvia Read − "Orcival − Puy de Dome"
Part 3. Communication with the wider world − people's responses, helpful and otherwise
Pat Neil − "Prisoner"
From a SANDS remembrance service − "Men do not Cry"
Sylvia Read − "Dialogue for Jenny"
Alan Lloyd − "After a Death"
Rabindranath Tagore − "Lines"
Karen Nelson − "Masques"
Terry Kettering − "The Elephant in the Room"
Part 4. Older mellowing grief. Surviving. Hope for tomorrow
Elizabeth Morris − "Storytellers in the Circle of Weavers"
Jack Hirschman − "October 11, 1990"
Patricia Lloyd − "Remembrances"
Alan Lloyd − "Anniversary Snapshots"

Linda Zelenka – "Old Grief"
Charles Dickens – "Nothing Dies and is Forgotten"
Gerard Hughes – Extract from "Oh God, Where are You?"

Everyone we met was kind to us and all recognised how early it was for us. There was one comment we heard though, that caused us distress. This was, "The second year is worse than the first." That could not be true, nothing could be worse than our grief in those early months. I was clinging on to the hope and belief that in a year's time this awful pain and despair would have subsided, at least a little. One woman who said it so tritely had no idea what a blow this was to the newly bereaved. The couple from Teesside who were 18 months down the line and still wracked with grief, recognised our dismay and were able to say to us that the second year was not worse.

After the coffee break Mick wanted to read the paper. I wanted to go to another workshop. He checked out, then sat in the lobby reading. I went to another session called "Does grief ever end?" This was run by Iris and Joe Lawley, co-founders of The Compassionate Friends. Even though they lost their son 30 years earlier, Joe Lawley shed some tears in the workshop. I was awed by this. Thirty years after his son's death and he still cried. I thought this was another good workshop and I realised that only the Newcomer's Group on the first evening had not worked for us. It was a very sad and emotional occasion but two things were said that I clung on to and remember regularly. Iris Lawley said at one point, "Instead of an open wound, grief becomes a scar." The woman who had lost her little girl aged $6\frac{1}{2}$ also said, "My life now is full and meaningful." I needed to hear that. A woman from Northern Ireland looked after me, regularly passing tissues and being supportive.

I met up with Mick for lunch and we talked to Freda and Max Bonner who had lost a son aged 28 who died of a rare form of cancer. He was a Buddhist. We also spoke to a couple from the Netherlands, Jan and Betsy, whose daughter, Marieke, had been killed in a diving accident in Kuwait. Like us, they felt they had to go to Kuwait and be as close as they could to the place where she died. We also met a woman whose son had died in a motorcycle accident in Peru. She felt differently from us though. She had never been to Peru, did not want to go and did not like Peru. In contrast, we felt tied to the country, loved it and its people and were sure we would go back.

The closing ceremony was another occasion where we wept a great deal – particularly me. We made our goodbyes to various people and left. I was shattered and fell asleep within 10 minutes of leaving. We arrived home and went round to see Anna who was well but sad. We had not spoken to Matt for several days.

On reflection I felt the weekend was well worth going to, despite being so emotionally draining. We were all in the same club. A club none of us wanted to join and yet we needed to meet people who knew how we felt. There were four main sources from where I found succour. First was that there were so many worse deaths than Sarah's. Although the loss was as bad as anyone's, it would have been worse to know she had died in pain or awful circumstances. In the national news, this was the time the little eight-year-old girl, Sarah Payne, was missing. We all knew she must have been murdered even though her parents were hoping she would be found alive. She was later found dead. That was a much worse death. The second thing that helped was to have met so many good people. I wanted everything and everyone to be good. There should be no more pain and sorrow in the world. Our pain was huge and sufficient for the rest of time. Mick, Anna, Matthew and I all felt we had become better people, more tolerant, less worried about trivia. At the same time we had not been bad people before Sarah's death and would have preferred to stay as we were. The third thing I took away from the weekend was that people do manage their grief better over time. Nobody was as tearful and distraught as us, even though tears flowed freely from many people. I could see there was a possibility of living some kind of life not constantly wracked by pain, despair and agony. Finally, Iris Lawley's comment on the open wound becoming a scar helped me through. I wanted to be in a time when the wound would start to scar over.

I had one day back at work before setting off to a conference in Brussels. That day I told Julie about the weekend, which made the tears flow. I spent much of the morning crying but picked up a bit in the afternoon. I spoke to Matthew and thought he sounded better. I began to think the intense crying period was coming to an end. How would we get through the International Neuropsychological Society Conference in Brussels though? This was our first conference and a big occasion for us. I had organised a symposium. Mick was exhibiting neuropsychological test materials. We both knew that many acquaintances of ours would be there. Some would know the awful news but many would not. We took photocopies of the letter about Sarah with us to distribute to people. David and Janet, the people we met at The Compassionate Friends, lived in Brussels and had given us instructions on how to reach our hotel.

We left on Tuesday morning, July 11th, and drove through the Channel Tunnel on 'Le Shuttle', arriving at the Radisson. We checked in, unpacked and met up with David and Janet for dinner. They took us to a good restaurant and we enjoyed their company. Bereaved parents were so much easier to be with because we have all been through the same pain. One does not have to explain and there is never this feeling of awkwardness or embarrassment. I remember David saying over dinner, "You change your address book after bereavement." I thought, "That's true, there are people I don't want to bother with any more and there are others who have gone up in my estimation because they were so good." Another thing David and Janet said was that some people think the death of a child is contagious and avoid bereaved parents. We had all met those, although, fortunately in my case, there were few in this category.

On Wednesday morning over breakfast we met Annelise Christensen from Copenhagen. I had known her for many years and knew she had been through a troubled time following the death of her husband years earlier. She was extremely sympathetic and compassionate so the day started with great bursts of sobbing.

I had thought Mick's exhibition started Wednesday but it was Thursday, so we had a free day on Wednesday for sightseeing and a long, excellent Belgian lunch. I think the food in Brussels is superb. That evening we went out to dinner with an old friend and colleague, Mike Kopelman. We got through with only a few tears every so often.

I gave a copy of the letter to Bob Bornstein, the secretary of the International Neuropsychological Society, on Tuesday evening. He was good. Almost every Jewish person was good. They have a formula, a ritual and do not seem to feel uncomfortable when faced with grieving people. Several Jewish friends wished us a long life. Roy Sugarman said it may seem strange to do this after death but life is important.

The conference started on Thursday July 13th. Mick had a good conference and was able to keep his grief at bay while manning the stall. I was useless that day, crying in public all the time, disappearing to my room, unable to attend the talks although I did go to the Presidential Address and fell asleep for about 90 per cent of it. I was still falling asleep frequently. Most people we met were good and coped well with our anguish. A couple of men did not handle it at all well. We got through the day and went out to dinner with a gang of colleagues. Met some Italian neuropsychologists in the restaurant. They did not know, so we told them and started to weep once more. On Friday July 14th, I was a bit better and able to attend some of the talks. Met with the people in my symposium for lunch to discuss plans and timing for the following morning, when we were all speaking. The conference dinner was on Friday evening and I found that depressing. I felt trapped in a corner and having to make small talk with people I did not want to be with at that time.

Our symposium started Saturday morning. I knew I had to get through it without crying, so asked Mick not to talk about Sarah. I avoided talking to people about anything other than the symposium. I warned the others who were speaking not to mention Sarah and we survived. We had a good audience and I felt the talks went well. I was absolutely fine until we finished. Two people came up to me to say how sorry they were so there I was crying again. Later we packed up, checked out and went for a final Belgian lunch that was mouth-watering. I slept in the car on the way home and for a further eight hours that night. I felt as if I could not get enough sleep at this time.

The owner of the travel company that Sarah went with sent an e-mail that evening. There was, of course, no news but a report of the latest search, poking down into the siphons in the rocks with poles. I felt sick at the thought of this. We felt wounded. Anna was very low; Matt phoned from LA, reasonably OK. We ranged from very calm to highly emotional to being angry with Sarah for going on the trip and wounding us so deeply.

Sunday July 16th I went to the gym and the pool. I had been exercising every day. Although I needed to do this, Sarah was in my head all the time. There were videos on the television screens of cycling (Sarah's favourite sport), skateboarding (she had once represented England in the United Kingdom championships), white-water rafting (ugh! − I could not bear to watch those), surfing (she had never tried but liked the idea), and snowboarding (she had gone to Andorra snowboarding in April 2000 and found it frightening). If she had broken her leg there she would never have gone to Peru. We still went through a list of 'if onlys' every day. When I returned from the gym on Sunday morning, Mick and I had our first row since Sarah died. I did not record what we argued about but I had thought we would never argue again. Maybe this was a sign we were moving on to another stage?

Every time I thought we might be moving on, I seemed to be proved wrong. On Monday July 17th – nine weeks since we had received that phone call, I wept on and off throughout the day. All of us were very volatile, weeping one minute – one second almost – and then calm and coping again. It was not how we would have imagined grief.

Mick wanted another search to take place in the Cotahuasi valley and informed the owner of the travel company. In his reply of July 17th, he thanked Mick for his ideas for another search and thought it would be possible to organise one for the end of July or during August when the water level would be lower again. The search would concentrate on the 150-metre length of the river which had been identified by the extensive search techniques of the previous search. But much would depend upon the skill and experience of the search leader and his judgement about whether the water level was low enough to use ropes to lower people, or even hooks, into the likely areas of the river without risking the lives of the search party. It would be a highly dangerous operation, fraught with the possibility of accidents. He also informed us of the finalised costs of the previous search and the amount that remained for us to pay.

A colleague, Robyn Tate, from Australia, was at the rehabilitation centre on Tuesday 18th, giving a lunch-time talk. I introduced her, listened to the talk, asked questions, did not cry and appeared perfectly normal. Left at 2.05 p.m. though feeling I was lazy and had changed character. Although tears welled up a few times, that was the first day I did not really cry. However, I made up for it on Wednesday. I was in Cambridge when Eve popped in to send me good wishes from Ian Robertson. That was the starting point. Then Hazel and Agnes sorted out some tests they needed for a workshop they were giving the next day. I saw Sarah's handwriting on some of the boxes, so that was a tear trigger. The colleague who tried but said the wrong thing phoned later, still telling me what I should do, e.g. see patients, keep working and so on. I wept again. Left at 4.05. Mick was at a meeting in Keele. I phoned him. He said he was very low and had cried during the conference and cried at dinner. It was, I said in my diary, a bad business and just too sad that we would never see Sarah again, my lovely treasure who brought nothing but joy.

I worked at home the next day, after a fashion, dealt with e-mails and started preparing some talks I was giving in August. I had a call from someone I had not seen for a while. She kept saying, "I want you to know we are thinking of you," as if I should feel grateful. She said it in such a chirpy voice I became irritated. I was still reading the book Jim Becker had sent, I thought it was excellent but almost everything I read in it made me cry. That day I had a letter from two Mormon colleagues at Brigham Young University in Utah. They expressed their sorrow at Sarah's death and told me they had donated one of my books to their library with a memorial statement to Sarah. I felt quite touched.

Another first came on Friday 21st (10 weeks since Sarah's death). I was on an interview panel. We were interviewing for a new clinical psychologist at the Oliver Zangwill Centre. Candidates and panel members met for lunch and I had to leave. It was too banal and trivial for my frame of mind. There were two candidates, one was very good and we decided to offer him the post. I dealt with that appropriately.

Earlier in the day one of our head-injured clients walked past my open door with his mother. They were there for a follow-up visit. The mother said to me, "How are you?" Such an innocent remark and one people ask all the time. Yet, to this day, I cannot say, "Fine, how are you?" These days I usually say, "Not bad," or "Coping," or "Getting through." In the early days though, I felt I had to tell people what had happened. How could anyone who knew say, "How are you?" so casually? If they did know I would say, "Not good," or "It's been a terrible time," or "Struggling through each day." Well, I told the young man and his mother. I kept my tears in check and I had to put up with their platitudes which were well-meaning but hard to bear. Although I could tell colleagues that platitudes did not help, I could not say this to patients or their families. One thing the mother said that I could accept was, "Having a head-injured relative is like a bereavement." Left at 3.00 p.m. that day.

I e-mailed Jim Becker that day too.

Dear Jim,

I am halfway through the book you sent. There are some wonderful things in it but most make me cry. The weekend for bereaved parents was painful although we met some good people — the most terrifying aspect is how long everything takes. Some people said the second year is worse than the first and we didn't want to hear that. Others said it took about four years until they felt they were as good as they were going to get — ohhh how unbearable. Judy phoned last night and said you wanted to come to the memorial service on October 1st. Of course you are very welcome. We are sending out the invitations any day now so where shall we send yours? You might want to book a hotel in Bury St Edmunds. The best hotel is The Angel (just yards from The Athenaeum where we are holding the non-religious service). The Angel is mentioned in Charles Dickens' *Pickwick Papers*. The vaults date from the 12th century but most of the hotel is 17th century. Let me know if you want us to help with the booking.

Best wishes,

Barbara

We had a family gathering at Mick's eldest sister's house on Saturday 22nd. The afternoon at Gloria's went well enough. It was always good to see the children together. I was very quiet and sad though and spent most of the time watching the children play. The next day was a hard day as we went through some of Sarah's belongings which was painful. We were going through the motions but felt our hearts were broken. Managed to do some work on some talks for Hong Kong and thought my ability to work might be improving. I still did not know, though, whether I would ever be able to see patients again.

Every phone call, e-mail, letter and visit still made me cry. On Monday 24th I had a visit from Richard Taylor, the Chief Executive of Lifespan NHS Trust, the trust that ran the Oliver Zangwill Centre. Richard Taylor had been the man responsible for seeing the Oliver Zangwill Centre opened in 1996. I had put a business case to the Trust in 1993 and Richard was the man who took it through to fruition. He was a good listener and let me talk and cry for nearly half an hour.

Mick went off to a big psychology meeting in Stockholm on July 25th but did not have a good time there. He was bored, sad and lonely. I was in the process of sending out invitations for the memorial service. We had room for 200 people.

Narinder got in touch and told me about an anthology that I might be interested in called, *All in the End is Harvest* edited by Agnes Whitaker. I replied:

Dear Narinder,

I would like to borrow your anthology. I have read several books on bereavement but not that one. Jim Becker sent a collection of prose, poems and essays on the death of a child called *A Broken Heart Still Beats*. It had some wonderful things in it. I am glad you liked the card. I took the photo about three years ago in a café in America. Mick and I always liked that photo of Sarah. The Wordsworth poem seemed so appropriate to Sarah's death given that she really is "with rocks and stones and trees" in some wild remote valley in Peru.

The INS was OK but quite painful as I had to keep telling people about Sarah. I got through the symposium without crying and all the speakers in the symposium did a good job. I guess it will be easier next time.

Hope your three little ones are all well.

All the best,

Barbara

Mick telephoned that evening. It was July 28th – our 38th wedding anniversary. We arranged to celebrate a day late on the 29th when Mick would be back from Stockholm. Spent some time trying to arrange a holiday for the New Year. As it would be our first Christmas without Sarah, we thought we should be kind to ourselves and have a holiday in the Caribbean. The previous New Year – for the millennium – we had all gone to Mauritius and had a good time. We had a need to keep doing things to try to distract ourselves I suppose.

I met Mick at Stansted early Saturday morning and we went out for dinner that evening to our favourite restaurant, Maison Bleu, with Carol, Peter and Anna. I said in my diary, "We are surviving – still sad – but crying less and forcing ourselves to keep on with life."

Before Sarah's death I had arranged to go to Hong Kong to give some talks at a conference and to give a one-day workshop with Agnes. When Julia was cancelling most of my arrangements in the first weeks after Sarah died, she asked me whether she should cancel Hong Kong. I said, "No." It seemed so far ahead that I thought I should go and would be able to cope. I had also booked a 10-day holiday in Malaysia before the Hong Kong conference. This was with 'Explore', a travel company I had been with three times before, including a wonderful holiday to Jordan with Sarah at the end of 1999. The only trip that was in South East Asia and fitted in with the Hong Kong dates was the 10-day trip to Sarawak. It would be the first trip alone I had taken since Sarah died. Although an experienced traveller with few nerves, I was not sure how I would cope with Sarawak. I thought I would manage Hong Kong as there would be colleagues who would understand. Agnes would be there for a start. In addition, I had been to Hong Kong several times, I had ex-students working there and other people I felt comfortable with. Sarawak was an unknown.

On Monday July 31st, over lunch, Agnes said, "Are you looking forward to Sarawak?" I said that I had mixed feelings about it and then I started to cry again. One never knows when this grief is going to wash over one. Managed to remain at work until 4.50 p.m. but felt very down that evening. All the yearning, regret and wishing things were otherwise came back. We had several photographs of Sarah around the house. There was one of Sarah that I had taken in the United States a couple of years earlier. We used this photograph on the invitations to the memorial service. Sarah looked so relaxed. We had a larger, framed version in the hall. At first I could not bear to look at it, now I sometimes kissed it saying "Sarah, why did you leave us? You know how much we all loved you."

August 2000

I kept working, in slow motion, I felt. I started each day either at the gym or the pool and did not feel slowed up in those places. Cried every day, sometimes a little, sometimes a great deal. Continued to leave work early. I felt useless but, nevertheless, I was achieving quite a bit on the academic front. Mick left for Washington on August 3rd for the American Psychological Association conference. On August 7th I had to phone a credit card company who were chasing up Sarah for a payment. I had already called them several times to explain she had died. The information did not get transmitted. I telephoned again in fury but also weeping non-stop. I did not hear from them again. Arranged a flight home for Matt with British Airways. I tried to get him on the United flight with Mick but could not. I arranged that they would meet in the long-term car park. They were due to land within half an hour of each other at different terminals. It did not work out that way though. At 11.20 p.m. on Monday evening, Mick phoned to say he was going to be very late as there was something wrong with the plane. I tried to phone British Airways to see if I could get a message to Matt. After being on hold for ages, I was finally told they could not get a message to Matt and I would have to telephone Heathrow Airport. I had a bad night, I kept waking up worrying. At 6.15 a.m. Tuesday morning I telephoned Heathrow and was told that Matt would be paged and asked to telephone home. He never heard the message. I also learned that Mick's United flight from Washington had been cancelled. I kept expecting Matthew to telephone and he did not. I took Django to the vet for his booster vaccinations – back to find no message from Matt. I telephoned Anna in tears. She came round. Meanwhile I had the sense to telephone the car park at Heathrow. I should have thought of that before. Eventually I got through to a security man who said he would go and find Matt and tell him to phone home. Matt had been waiting at Mick's car for three hours. I could not believe it. He came back by train and I met him later in Cambridge. I felt highly stressed about Matt and about Mick's flight being cancelled. Anna was a rock of calmness and sense.

To add to all this I had to go to Manchester that afternoon to give a talk the following morning. I did a two-hour talk on research-led practice the next morning and felt it had gone well. I never thought of Sarah while I was talking. This must have been the longest period since she died that I had not thought of her. Nobody would have guessed I was grieving if they did not know already.

I almost got through that Wednesday, August 9th, without crying. It would have been the first full day, but in the evening I told Mick that Francesca had watched a video of Sarah and said, "Why doesn't she look at me?" Mick started sobbing and I followed suit. What a rotten time we had all been through. I had Hong Kong and Malaysia coming up and felt I should not go, I should not leave the family.

At about this time I asked Matthew and Rosie to write down what they remembered of the day we learned that Sarah had died.

Matthew wrote:

MAY 15TH, 2000

It was about 9 a.m. in Philadelphia. We had got back from N.Y. at about 6 a.m. and I had fallen asleep on the couch. We had a cordless phone and it was upstairs in Dan and Jasmine's room. I remember Dan waking me up and saying, "Why do people call you from UK so early in the mornings?" I took the phone it was Dad. "I have some terrible news," he said. "It's the worst." I did the classic and dropped the phone. He told me that Sarah had been lost. He said I had to come home and to call later. He was off to get Mum.

I put the phone down. Dan was sitting on the top of the stairs. I told him my sister had been killed. I hadn't smoked for months, I asked him for a smoke and he gave me some really horrible menthol flavoured cigarette. I went into his and Jasmine's room. "What am I supposed to do?" I said. They said to do whatever I felt like. I called Anna, expecting her to have spoken to Dad. She was so pleased to have heard from me. She obviously had not spoken to Dad. I told her Sarah was missing, probably dead. "Not my Sarah," she kept saying. She said that about ten times. Then she said, "Rosie's got the dentist." "SOD the dentist," I said. She said she had to go. I told her I would be back as soon as I could get a flight. Straight after I spoke to Anna, I had this awful feeling that I had dreamt Dad calling me. I called him back. He was driving to Cambridge to get Mum. He was crying so I knew it was true. I told him I had told Anna. I thought he might be angry that I had told her. I don't know why I felt that.

It was now about 9.30 a.m. I called Helen on her cell phone. She was in IKEA in Thurrock. I said, "We have lost Sarah." She was very sweet and said she would phone me as soon as she got home.

I then went round to Nou's. She lived about six blocks away. She had been in N.Y. with us. I had keys to her apartment and my passport was there as well. I let myself in. Her and Juan were asleep in bed. They woke up when I came in. Nou looked at me and jumped straight out of bed. "What's the matter?" she said. I couldn't speak. I finally managed, "I have to go back to England." "Is it Lainey?" she said. Lainey is the name I called Helen. I managed to tell her my sister was dead. She gave me a huge hug and burst out crying. She took charge. She got my passport and Juan, Nou and I went back to my house.

When we arrived Dan and Jasmine were awake. Dan went out to the shops and bought loads of food for breakfast and also a big bottle of Heineken beer for me. I started to call my friends in UK. I called Tracy, Ben, I tried Laura but she was away in Greece. I remember calling Ross, whilst I was on the phone I was crying. I noticed this snot hanging down from my nose to the floor. Nou came and gave me another hug, she was crying as well. "Mind your clothes," I told her, I was scared she was going to get snot on her top. She really didn't mind about that. Dan cooked this huge breakfast which I couldn't eat, I drank the beer though and was smoking non-stop.

The post came through the letter box. Nou went over and picked it up. She burst out crying again and said she didn't think I should see what arrived. I got the mail off her and there was a postcard from Sarah. It was a picture of a Peruvian mummy. Posted a few days before she died. There was also a letter from Anna with one from Rosie about how excited she was to be going to Peru with Mum. There was also a picture by Francesca.

Mum called at about 12. She had got me on a flight from Philadelphia at 6 p.m. my time. She told me that my cousin Simon would pick me up from Heathrow in the morning. She said that Anna and the kids and Carol and Peter were all round the house. She was very upset but she still sorted out all the flight info for me.

At about 2.30 Nou, Jasmine, Dan, Juan and I got a taxi to the airport. I had to pick up the ticket from British Airways desk. We all then went to a bar. We spent the next two hours drinking. Nou and Dan started to buy shots of liquor and bottles of Heineken beer. We kept toasting Sarah. It was very surreal, one minute I would be laughing and the next crying. I remember saying that the film on the plane was probably going to be *Deliverance*.

When it was time to board the plane the others all came with me. In America you can go to the departure gate even if you are not flying (this was prior to September 11, 2001). When I went up to the desk to show my ticket, the air stewardess said the flight crew were aware of what had happened and would make my flight as comfortable as possible, she was very sweet. There were about 250 people all in a line for the plane. Dan, Nou, Jasmine and Juan all gave me a hug. As I stood in the line Nou, who is 5 ft 10, has wild curly hair, which was half dyed bright red, is very stunning and was wearing a mini skirt and a crop top, shouted out, "Matt Wilson!" Everyone in the line turned around. She then said, "Every time you get sad on the plane thinking about Sarah think of these." She then pulled her top up. She was not wearing a bra and has quite substantial breasts. The whole line of people including me burst out laughing and applauding.

When I got on the plane I showed my boarding card to the hostess. She said to follow her. She led me up the aisle where she placed me in a row of three seats. She told me that they were all reserved for me because of my situation. She then told me that the whole flight crew and pilot were aware and would do whatever they could to make me more comfortable. After take off the same stewardess came up to me and asked if I wanted to eat anything. I replied, "No, but I would like some more alcohol." I'm sure she was aware that I was drunk already. She came back with five mini bottles of vodka and two cans of tonic and said if I wanted more I just had to ask.

After drinking all five bottles I passed out. I awoke about three hours later and started to cry. The same stewardess who got me the booze saw me crying and ran up the aisle to me. She sat next to me and gave me some tissues. She asked me if I wanted her to sit with me. She then asked if I wanted something else to drink. I nodded and she went off to get me something. She returned with a whole bottle of champagne. "I know it's not a celebration," she said, "but champagne's always nice." I wish I had got her name, she was such a star. In fact British Airways will always be something special to me.

Rosie wrote:

THIS IS MY MEMORY OF THE DAY I WAS TOLD ABOUT SARAH'S DEATH

I was at school and the school secretary asked me to sit on the sickbay chairs. I was very confused because I knew I shouldn't catch the bus, but why should I miss the end of the day in the classroom? I sat there when my friend came and told me I had to go back to class. I explained that Mrs Jopling had told me to stay there, so she went back to class. The bell went, so I went too. When I got outside, to my gladness, both my parents were there to meet me and take me to the orthodontists or so I thought. Mum ushered me into the car. I was now really worried because she was crying. She said, "I have some terrible news"... all that went through my mind was a question, had Francesca my sister died? "Auntie Sarah has died!" she said to my surprise and horror. My eyes filled up with tears as we turned the corner from my school onto Westley Road.

We went straight home, where I asked what was happening about my orthodontists and was told that it had been arranged for another day. Then we discussed school. When I would go back and if my class should be told. We arranged for my form tutor to tell my class the next day and for me to go back the day after.

That night we all stayed at Grandma and Grandad's where there was a lot of crying and discussing over Sarah and her good life.

Two days after Sarah's death, I went back to school. My friends had all been told and managed to take it off my mind. They were all a comfort to me and understood amazingly well. I had taken my last present from Sarah, a picture of her and a handkerchief into school also, just for more comfort.

I knew it would be difficult to get used to her not ever to be around again but I also knew I had to still live my life to the full.

❧

CHAPTER FOUR

It's OK, I can talk about it

2003

We don't panic about Sarah's loss any more. At least not in the almost constant manner we did in the immediate months after her death. It's still there, though, but it returns less often and touches us only sporadically and unexpectedly sometimes. When we are in a group we rarely think of Sarah unless she is brought into the conversation. We sometimes wonder whether anybody can tell we are bereaved parents? Of course we talk about her much of the time when the two of us are together, particularly at home. There's so much here to remind us of her, and we like that: our rooms have many portraits of Sarah, many of her clothes are still here, her dressing gown still hangs on the bedroom door where she left it. We have spoken to some bereaved parents who cannot abide anything in their house to remind them of their lost child. They refuse to look at photographs and even hide them away so that they are not reminded. We find this surprising and wonder whether those parents have come to terms with their loss, or whether they might not have made themselves ill by shutting out the truth? Here is a poem Mick wrote when he was painting our living room and came across a cupboard filled with some of Sarah's clothes.

THE LIVING ROOM

Happily painting our living room
I came to a cupboard to clear.
Among your clothes that you left here,
A black suit for formal occasions
Caught my attention.

I searched through the pockets and found
A tissue now more than two years old,
Folded neatly but yellow with age.
Unfurled it was toilet paper.

I smiled, picturing you making do with this:
You must have run out of tissues on that day
And your hands had folded the sheets
In the way you had of making things
Tightly wrapped and tucked away.

Picturing your kind hands
Doing this private act
That is now public.

We dig where we can
To find memories of you,
And picture you in acts of living.

This private thing that you did
On that day as you hurried to work
Should mean nothing to us
And would be utterly unmissed
Were you not dead.

And I'm prodded back to being a young father,
Proud of you in your pram,
With your yellow macintosh
And matching hat,
Dazzling all with your smile.

All those years we cared for you
And all those books you read,
All that learning about life
And the examples that you set
All that has gone for nothing
Now that you are dead.

You would have cared for me
You would have been at my deathbed
And I would have died in your arms
Like my mother died in mine.

We know that's how it should be −
Not hanging on to yellow tissues as
Though they mean something.

It's getting easier not to think of you,
I'm losing you again.
Sometimes bitterness is a blessing.

I carry on painting the room where we live
With a cupboard of clothes you will never wear.

We think pupils at school should be taught about death and bereavement. But is there a place for it in the national curriculum? Do children in schools learn about death? Do they ever have a chance to talk about grief? Mick remembers teaching in the 1960s when at his school most English language and literature was taught round a theme that related to the pupils' lives. A theme would be chosen and pupils would be asked to relate to this topic, taking examples from their own everyday life. Books, poems, films, popular culture would all contribute to the topic and then the pupils themselves would write about their own ideas and feelings. Sometimes a book of creative writing would be compiled or a radio broadcast would be made. Mick remembers the pupils at his school writing most movingly about death in their own families. It's strange that children are shown so much death and destruction in the cartoons that appear on television during the hours after school and before bedtime but never about the real effects of such mayhem. What effect does so much vicarious violence have on them we wonder?

At TCF meetings we regularly meet newcomers to grief who are caught up in the extremes of despair just as we were three years ago, and they frequently ask desperate questions about what is going to happen in the future. Will this pain ever stop? Will I be able to do other things? Will I be able to sleep throughout a whole night? Will I be able to get on with my work? Will I be able to enjoy myself again? Three years into grief, we are able to say "Yes" to all those questions. This does not mean that the anguish has gone away, or that we are beginning to think less about Sarah. It's just that other aspects of life – the essentials – keep pressing one to act normally in order to get by. Life goes on and has to go on. There is nothing else. We still cry and yearn for Sarah to be with us, but we can now put our feelings into a compartment labelled "Sarah". Sometimes we cannot escape being locked into the compartment, it suddenly surrounds you and won't open its doors, panic can set in and the stomach churns. Other times you choose with a sense of gratitude to be in that compartment to welcome Sarah and share your thoughts with her again.

Mick does this frequently when he is in the car driving to work or coming home. At these times he can play some of Sarah's favourite songs or songs that remind him of Sarah because they were part of our earlier life. The power of music – of all kinds – to stir the emotions is remarkable. Mick is now convinced that music is the greatest of the arts although for most of his life he has been someone who loved the theatre, novels and poetry. Now, though, it is only music that can regularly and instantly take him to Sarah. Of course we still love the theatre, and there have been moments when something is said on stage that will remind us of something we have shared

Plate 1   Animated conversation at the farewell dinner prior to leaving for Peru

Plate 2   Sarah and Barbara in Jordan: they were great travelling companions

Plate 3   We want her back: Barbara and Rosie in Peru

Plate 4   Auntie Sarah and Rosie

Plate 5   Sarah and Francesca aged three

Plate 6 Matthew and Rosie

Plate 7 Sarah in happy times as a recently married woman

Plate 8 A school photo of Sarah, Anna and Matthew aged six, five and four

Plate 9 Four-year-old Sarah playing in the garden

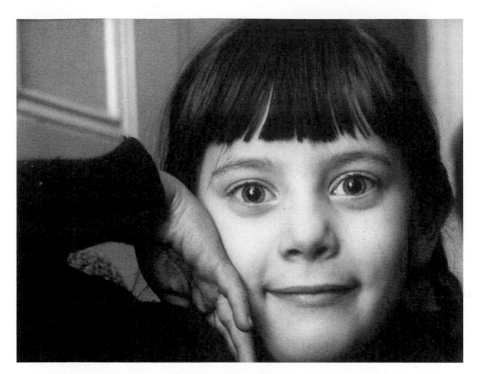

Plate 10   She was a lovely child

Plate 11   Anna, Karen (a friend) and Sarah aged about 18 or 19

Plate 12 Mountain bike racing

Plate 13 Mountain biking was Sarah's great love

Plate 14   Sarah and Juan Carlos in 1999

Plate 15   Jean Ferrandis: 'Pan himself!' *Photo: Elise Hardy – Europeart*

Plate 16 The mule pack crossing the River Cotahuasi

Plate 17 Mick and Barbara at 14,000 feet

Plate 18   Pepe Lopez: an impressive man

Plate 19   Raoul: a shy man and great cook

Plate 20   Barbara and Pepe at breakfast at the last camp

Plate 21 Pepe assisting Barbara through a small tributary stream

Plate 22 Above the river at the point where the five were thrown in

Plate 23   The last photo, two days before the fatal rafting

Plate 24   Our final river camp

Plate 25 Mick and Barbara in the cactus forest somewhere near where Sarah was last photographed

Plate 26 The final goodbye to Sarah

with Sarah and her brother and sister. These occasions are frequently a mixture of pain and joy and we sometimes cry silently together in the darkness of the theatre, hoping no one can see or hear us.

Another way in which we differ is in our thoughts about the actual death of Sarah by drowning. Mick finds it very difficult to get out of his mind the struggle that Sarah must have gone through in her final moments as the rapids swept her to her destruction. Barbara, however, can put these aside as being almost irrelevant in the context of Sarah's actual exit from life itself. In the car Mick sometimes thinks of Sarah as she is being swept down river and it's as though he wants to intervene, to shout out, "That's enough! Stop this!" He also thinks about her very last moments of life. Was she too caught up in the struggle for life and breath to consider dying? Was she resigned at the end, and therefore at peace? Did she die still thinking she would escape the rapids or be rescued? Did she, as Anna likes to think, die like those people who have been so near to death that they have for an instant died but come back from that brink, who see brightness at the end of a tunnel of darkness and reach towards the light with feelings of peace and joy? We will never know. The one solitary shoe that was found on the bank of the river is the only thing left behind and tells us nothing. We know only that she died in a raging river in a beautiful valley in the fearsome but lovely mountains of a dear and somewhat tragic country called Peru.

In the previous chapter Barbara mentioned the Spanish lessons that Sarah had been receiving before she departed for Peru. We think about the effort Sarah put into them and pity the fact that, apart from her notes on the lessons that we found amongst her possessions in Peru, all that learning is lost forever. Sarah's mind has gone just as her body has disappeared. What a strange thing to consider! When people die all their memories, opinions, learning and imaginings die with them. Yet these activities of the mind cannot rot or dissolve in themselves, they simply vanish as the brain cells stop working. Only oblivion follows, and that must be like being unconscious all the time? We wonder whether those lost products – processes – of the mind, what we would summarise as consciousness, are what people are referring to when they talk of the soul? We cannot believe that they live on, except of course as memories held in the minds of those left behind. At death these products, processes of the mind, the results of the interaction of brain cells, electricity, chemicals, simply stop flying between brain cells. There are no laws in physics that support the notion that they can live on and travel to another place after death. Yet we realise that many bereaved parents believe that this is so. We frequently hear many of them talk about their dead children as being "present" or "up there", and it is obviously of great comfort to them that they believe they will one day meet up again. In fact this might well be the prevalent view rather than our own, which is that Sarah has simply gone back to Nature, gone forever, and we will never meet her again. We must say that when it comes to grief itself there is no difference in the pain people feel: we all share similar feelings of loss of the living, conscious child.

Mick loves the fifth and final poem of William Wordsworth's 'Lucy poems' because it is both simple and powerful, conveying huge emotions in eight short lines. Indeed it is the silence between verses one and two that makes the most powerful statement. The first verse shows how confident and relaxed the poet was about Lucy while she was alive (when she was conscious). Then follows the gap between verses when nothing is said but it is obvious from the second verse that Lucy has died in this space of time as it were. So the actual awful loss of Lucy, her death (loss of consciousness) is not described. In the second verse we are told the facts of Lucy in death: she has no motion, no force, she neither hears nor sees. And then the poem ends with the extraordinary two lines when Lucy is seen as being at one with Nature now as the earth, and her body in it and indeed as part of it, rolls round its diurnal course. That is of course what is, in fact, happening to Sarah. What an image Wordsworth gives us! We can see the planet rolling and turning and know that our loved ones are still part of it. Some might regard him as a boring old man who wrote poems about daffodils but only a genius could convey so much in so few words.

August 2000

The crying continued whenever I read a letter or an e-mail or spoke to someone on the phone or face-to-face. Music made me cry, looking at photographs made me cry. I wondered if I would manage in Sarawak. Matt showed us a photograph he had taken in Peru of Juan Carlos with Sarah's bike. He also pointed out the last known photograph of Sarah, taken on her camera that we had brought back from Peru. She was in a cactus forest in the Andes in shorts and hiking boots and her rucksack on her back looking very happy. We think this was taken two or three days before she died. Mick and I sobbed together when we saw it. The pain seemed to go on and on. My lovely Sarah, my beautiful unfinished symphony.

On Saturday August 12th, 13 weeks since Sarah's death, I was getting ready for Malaysia and Hong Kong and reading another book having finished the one Jim Becker sent. The latest one was Harriet Sarnoff Schiff, *The Bereaved Parent*. I found some of it was appropriate for me. She said, for example, on page xii:

> Not long ago, a young man aged eighteen, a casual friend of our surviving son, died. Although we did not know his parents intimately, we knew them well enough to make a condolence call. They had a house full of people. Yet when they saw us they left everyone and asked us to sit with them in another room. The father put his head on my husband's shoulder and cried. My husband held the newly-bereaved man in his arms and patted him and quieted him. The mother grasped my hands.
>
> We did not possess some secret knowledge that gave us special comforting skills. What we had was something few could give them. We had experience. When they saw us, they saw a mother and father with a dead child who were able to cope.

This is why The Compassionate Friends is so important and this is why I tele-phoned German Berrios, who also knew the pain of losing a child, so soon after we had news of Sarah's death. Someone also said that one of the hardest things for bereaved parents is when the body is never found. This was cruel and hard for us, but we felt that as a family we were coping and coping better than many of the bereaved parents we read about. She also said that bereaved parents are less afraid of things. Because they have faced the ultimate tragedy, life has few fears for them. To some extent this was true for us. Certainly I was no longer afraid of what people thought, or afraid of being late and missing a flight. On the other hand, I was very afraid that something might happen to a member of the family. And, although I was not afraid of my own death, I did not want Mick, Anna, Matthew, Rosie or Francesca to have to go through grief again so soon. So I was less afraid and more afraid at the same time.

Mick took me to Stansted on Sunday August 13th. I went first to Amsterdam and then on to Hong Kong. I cried before I left home when I wondered if Sarah would telephone to wish me goodbye. Mick and I both cried as we said goodbye at Stansted.

David, an ex-student of mine, met me at the airport in Hong Kong and drove me to my hotel in Kowloon. He said in the car how sorry he was about Sarah. I cried a little then but did not break down into heaving sobs as I would have done back home. It seemed to be easier to control the tears away from home. I was staying in the Harbour Plaza for one night, leaving my work things there while I went to Sarawak and then returning to the Harbour Plaza for a further five nights. I liked the hotel. After lazing and dozing in my room for a while, I went for a swim in the roof-top pool with stunning views over Victoria Harbour. I decided to go for a walk after I'd showered and before telephoning Mick. I cried on the phone remembering that Sarah had been with me in Hong Kong about two years earlier. She enjoyed it immensely. She said she loved Hong Kong and we should bring Rosie as Rosie liked shopping so much. I thought of my lovely girl and how could it be that I would never see her again.

I decided to try to enjoy the trip to Malaysia for Sarah's sake. My travelling now would be for her. I would try to see new places through Sarah's eyes. I read a novel, *Of Marriageable Age*, by Sharon Maas. I knew Sarah would have liked it. She read a great deal. The last book she read before her death was Tony Parson's *Man and Boy*. She said in her journal that we found in Cusco she believed nobody could fail to enjoy the book. I deliberately did not take any books on bereavement with me as I knew I could not stop the tears.

On Tuesday August 15th I left the hotel by taxi at 5.30 a.m. for the train station and then the airport. The plane arrived in Kuching on time and my luggage was the second piece to come through on the carousel. Given that I had been travelling on two different airlines I had not expected to see it for a while. I changed some money and found a taxi to take me to the hotel, the Teleng Usang. I had eaten hardly anything so I went to the coffee shop downstairs and ordered some vegetable noodles and Earl Grey tea, which I consumed with relish. I decided not to phone home and to try to make this my very first day without crying. I had almost achieved this before but had not entirely succeeded.

One disappointment was the teeming rain when we landed in Kuching making me reluctant to go out. I had been on an 'Explore' trip to Madagascar two years before and it rained for the first eight days. "Please don't let Sarawak be like that," I thought. The second disappointment was that the rest of the group (flying out from London via Brunei) were late. I was told to meet the group leader at 7.00 p.m. in the hotel lobby, then received several messages each saying he would be later. The leader and the group turned up at 9.45 p.m. There were 16 people altogether including three married couples. All but three were doing the whole Borneo trip, Sarawak and Sabah. I could not do that because of the Hong Kong conference. Two other women had also opted for the 10-day Sarawak trip. Some of us went out for dinner after the briefing. One of the women said she had spent time in Peru. I kept quiet. In other circumstances I would have said, "Oh, my daughter is living there." I decided I would try not to tell anyone about Sarah as I wanted to remain calm. I managed to get through the whole day without crying.

I slept well that night. At breakfast I met up with three of the women, Patsy, Kate and Iris, to look around Kuching. The morning was free. We wandered along the waterfront and went to the Sarawak museum. Kuching means 'cat' in Malay – a pleasing thought for me. The city is attractive and I felt safe. We went back to the hotel after lunch to find a fax from Julia from someone wanting dates for a medico-legal trial next year. I tried to phone her but could not get through so it had to wait until I arrived home. It did not matter as it turned out.

At 1.30 p.m. we set off for Bako National Park. This involved a 45-minute bus ride and then a boat to the park. The setting was beautiful. We were in wooden huts set along the beach with jungle all around. I was put in a room with Iris and Jenny. Shortly after arriving we all went for a jungle walk and saw a rare proboscis monkey. The walk was a short one, only an hour. We returned to our huts and sat on the veranda sipping beer. I thought that was going to be the second consecutive day I did not cry. Was I through with the crying, I wondered? I resolved to get through the whole trip without telling anyone about Sarah. I tried to telephone Julia on the guide's handset and on Iris's mobile. Neither worked. Dinner was followed by a video on proboscis monkeys. Back on the veranda later Iris, Jenny and I were sitting chatting. Jenny was talking about her daughter and she said to me, "Do you have any children?" I had been dreading the question, "How many children do you have?" as I thought that I would not know what to say. I said, "I have three but one died three months ago." At that I started howling and stood up to run off, but Jenny caught my arm and said, "Sit down and tell us about it." It was exactly the right thing (or one of the right things) to do. I talked and sobbed and showed them photographs of Sarah and the family. I did not sleep so well that night as I kept going over and over things in my head.

On a later walk I said to Jenny, "You were very good that evening. Have you experienced grief?" She said, "No, but I am a mother."

After breakfast on Thursday we walked along the beach to get a boat to a further beach and a swim followed by a four-hour walk. However, it was too rough for the boats so we walked for $1\frac{1}{2}$ hours to yet another beach. The walk was fairly demanding but enjoyable. I was the oldest person there at 58 years old — but one of the fittest. We swam at this beach but the waves were rough. I did not do my normal half mile as I was nervous of being swept out. After a packed lunch and another 45-minute walk, we split into two groups. Nine went back the short way to the chalets and seven went for a longer walk with Ken the guide. The walk was hard but enjoyable and we saw a monitor lizard. The rain had stopped by now and the weather was good. A band of macaque monkeys came to entertain us and stole a bag of lychees from Jenny. We were nervous of them because of the possibility of rabies. We were surrounded by pretty little lizards and colourful butterflies. Dinner was followed by a night walk to see spiders and butterflies. I like spiders. I like most creatures except cockroaches and slugs. I get cross with women who scream at snakes and insects.

We left Bako National Park on Friday at 7.45 a.m. The boat took us to Bako town where the bus was waiting to take us to the Lemanek river. We stopped for an hour at Serian, a town with a lively, colourful market. We then stopped in Lachau for lunch. I had bought a phone card earlier so I could phone Mick and Julia but could not find a phone to accept the card.

We reached Lemanek river at 3.30. Our main luggage had been delivered there from Kuching. We had just taken a small bag to Bako. We had to repack at the side of the road for one night in a longhouse. Next to the longhouse was a guest house comprising little cubicles. Everything was lively and colourful. We went on a tour of the longhouse and saw skulls and tattooed men. There were lots of clever little children shinning up trees and women weaving mats. After dinner we watched some traditional dancing. Even though we knew this was put on for the tourists, we enjoyed it.

Earlier that day we had sampled fruits, including the durian that "smells like hell and tastes like heaven". I was one of the few willing to try it (like Sarah, I am more adventurous than most, I think). I rather enjoyed the durian. I also tried some rice wine that I found too sweet. It was not like Japanese sake, which I do like.

The rice wine was drunk at the traditional dancing. Before that we had a dinner cooked by our bus driver with the help of some of the local Iban people. We ate chicken, fish, rice and vegetables. The food was fairly basic and standard but I enjoyed it all. After the show it was hard to sleep. The cubicles were made of bamboo and every sound could be heard. On top of that there was a noisy group of beer-drinking Germans who kept us awake.

We were woken very early by cockerels crowing and people going to the toilet. The toilets and showers were awful. I was glad we were only there for one night. We left on boats along the brown Lemanek river. It reminded me of Brazil when Mick and I travelled by canoe down a tributary of the Amazon except there the water was green instead of brown. I thought about Sarah on the River Cotahuasi. Even though the Lemanek was safe, I would not have wanted to fall in. She fell in white, swirling water. What were her last thoughts? Did she know she was going to die? I hardly ever thought of the actual moments she was in the river. I put them out of my mind. I thought of her doing things, smiling, enjoying life. I knew Mick frequently thought of the last minutes and tortured himself with whether she was panic-stricken and in pain. Anna had told us that people who had almost died and then survived typically reported a feeling of calm in the face of the death and that is how I imagined Sarah when I did bring myself to think of those last minutes. I also thought of her saying to herself, "Sorry Mum," because she knew how much we loved her and how desperately we would miss her.

We left the boat to continue our journey by bus to Sibu, the second largest city in Sarawak. At the hotel I sorted out my clothes and gave in my laundry before meeting Iris and Jenny to go out and see the famous seven-storey pagoda. I cried very little that day. There were just a few tears when I was talking to Jenny after lunch. At this point only Iris and Jenny knew about Sarah. It was safer (in terms of putting on a normal front) to keep people in the dark. I spoke to Mick on the telephone and wished I could see him again.

We left at 7.20 a.m. for another long bus ride with a couple of stops at garages for the usual soft drinks and toilets. Trees, ferns and palms en route were interspersed with brown rivers and wooden villages of the longhouse design. There was some logging, particularly around Bintulu, but not nearly as bad as in Madagascar. Sarawak seemed a safe place. There was a good feeling there and the people were gentle although rather solemn. We reached our next stop, Niah National Park, about 2.00 p.m.

I thought about Sarah a great deal that day, particularly on the bus ride. I talked about her to Iris who was sitting next to me on the bus. I felt as if Sarah was just away somewhere, travelling. She was somewhere still full of life. It was hard to believe she was dead and I would never see her again. It just did not feel true.

The next day was Monday, 14 weeks since we had heard the news. Sarah was constantly in my thoughts but I was surprised by how well I was coping. That was probably because so few people knew and we were not constantly referring to her. I knew I was a quieter person than I had been previously. My inner sadness prevented me from being so talkative as I had once been. That may well have been a good thing. We had to get up at 5.00 a.m. and left at 5.35 to catch the high-speed water bus from Miri to Marudi. Marudi was not much of a town. The next boat was the Tutoh Express. I sat on top for a while. Although it was interesting seeing the river-bank life, it was uncomfortable. I was reading Rose Tremain's *Music and Silence* and thought it one of the best novels I had ever read. Because we had to be so strict with our luggage and were only allowed to bring a small bag with us for this leg, I thought I could get away with one book. With so much travelling though, I was reading a great deal, despite rationing myself. I was beginning to panic that I would run out of reading material. In the end someone lent me a copy of *Bridget Jones's Diary* that she had finished. I read it because I was desperate, but it wasn't my kind of book.

We reached Tutoh at 3.40 p.m. and climbed straight into another boat to go to Mulu National Park. We reached there at 5.25 p.m. so had been travelling for almost 12 hours. The park was beautiful. Mountains were all around. The river here was more green than brown. I was on my own again in a wooden chalet.

I felt low Monday evening and Tuesday morning. Went for a walk before breakfast and the day improved. We left at 9.15 and crossed the river to the elegant Royal Mulu Resort with a nice pool. I wished we were staying there. We caught the bus to the Park Headquarters and had a quick look around the exhibition there. The Royal Geographical Society had carried out a 15-month exploration in 1977/78 and had mapped the caves and the area. Twelve of us then set off for a walk. The others remained at the Park Headquarters and had a swim. I would have liked a swim too but wanted a walk more. The walk was good, through dense jungle. We saw millipedes, a frog and some hornbills flying over. On the way back we saw some magnificent butterflies. We had seen these earlier in the trip but on this day I was particularly struck by the Rajah Brooke's birdwings. They are as big as swallows and jet black with emerald green stripes on their lower wings and red heads. We had seen a few in Niah but there were crowds of them here. After lunch we set off for Lang Cave and Deer Cave. Lang was very pretty, full of stalactites and stalagmites in wonderful formations. Deer Cave, so named because deer used to congregate there to lick the salt water until they were hunted out, was very impressive. It is the tallest and widest of the Mulu caves and quite magnificent. We arrived back at Park Headquarters and the bat observatory about 4.20 and waited to see the bats. They did not appear until 6.15 p.m. I was expecting a great throng but they flew out in family groups like puffs of black smoke that elongated and spiralled.

Mulu itself was very beautiful, but our hostel was not so good. Although my room was OK, there were complaints from the others about broken windows and toilets, poor wiring, poor food, lack of wildlife, and being rushed too much. I was not one of the complainers. For a start I feel privileged to see such exotic places and I do not mind being on the move. But the main reason not to complain was that Sarah's death had put these petty irritations into perspective. We did see some exciting creatures, like a luminous millipede in one of the caves, a scorpion and some magical fireflies dancing through the trees. We had also seen several graceful stick insects and some amazing furry caterpillars. Then there was some luminous fungi in Baku so I felt content with the trip. I had talked quite a bit that day to Jenny. We were walking together at the back of the group for some of the time. I was surprised that I had not told anyone else.

I had a bad night and woke at 5.00 a.m. on the morning of Wednesday August 23rd. I forced myself to stay in bed until 5.55 then discovered there was no light, no fan and no water. I read by torchlight. The lights and water came on at 6.40. We set off just before 9.00 in longboats. I sat next to a partner of one of the three couples there. She talked and talked about her daughter, her daughter's forthcoming wedding and her daughter's forthcoming move to another country. I was low to begin with and felt worse and worse as she rattled on. I felt desperate and in the end I told her that I had recently lost a daughter. I provided the bare details. She said, "I couldn't live with that." "You have no choice," I said, and thought to myself, "I can't live with it but what do you do – put your head in the gas oven? How will the other members of the family cope with that?" It is as if those who say they couldn't live with the loss of their child are saying to me, "I love my daughter/son more than you – you can go on but I couldn't, therefore you did not love her as much as I love my child." Nobody could be loved more than my Sarah, nobody. But how will it help if I don't live with it? Should I wear my heart on my sleeve all the time? Is it fair to others to go to pieces for too long?

We stopped at a Penan village where I bought some handicrafts. The village seemed very poor. The longboat had trouble getting through the water. It was heavily laden with 19 people and heaps of luggage. We were going against the current and kept getting stuck on the shale in the shallow water. The engine was not good. The scenery, however, was lovely. Later I had a swim. I had my goggles with me so could see loads of fish. The clear, fresh water was good to swim in.

We had a picnic lunch and I moved away from the others as I wanted to be on my own. I read in the sunshine by the river bank. The group had been split into three for three separate flights on small planes to Miri. The flight was wonderful. We flew over the Pinnacles, the jungle and the river.

A group of us met up to go shopping. I tried to find a football shirt for Matt as he has a collection from all over the world. I was unlucky. I telephoned home later and spoke to Matt and to Mick. We wanted to be together again. I had felt low all day. After dinner I walked back to the hotel with Mary and David, one of the married couples. Mary said something that reminded me of Sarah and I started to weep. I had to tell them. We went to the hotel bar for a drink. I talked and talked and talked. Both were good listeners and insisted on paying for my drinks. It was not a good day emotionally although the trip as a whole was good. Mulu was particularly beautiful. I decided I liked Malaysia. The people I met were honest, there was no obvious crime, English was widely spoken and that helped. I thought I might come back.

Thursday was another early morning. I was awake at 5.30. I could get off to sleep without trouble but could not stay asleep until a reasonable time. I went down to breakfast and sat next to the one American woman on the trip. I was tearful so told her about Sarah too and wept throughout breakfast. It was as if I'd held it back for so long, the dam had burst and the grief came gushing out again.

This was the end of my 10-day tour and I left to return to Hong Kong, where David met me once more. I had left a sunny Malaysia for a very cloudy and wet Hong Kong. David said there had been a typhoon in Taiwan that had killed 11 people. It was now moving away but the tail end of it was in Hong Kong. David left me at the Harbour Plaza. I had been hoping for a swim in the rooftop pool but it was too dark and wet for that. I missed Sarah, my special girl, my travelling companion. I yearned to see her again.

That night, Thursday 24th, I had my first dream of Sarah since those first two right at the beginning. She was with us in England and I decided to tell her about her rafting death, the call from Max Milligan and our terrible grief so that she would cancel her trip. It was as if we had a warning of what would happen if she did go and we had a chance to persuade her otherwise. She actually said to me, "That's not written yet," (meaning her own death); and she said she was waiting to hear something in order to decide whether or not to pull out of the trip.

I worked on my talks on Saturday morning and read until 11.30 when someone from the conference came to collect me and two other invited speakers to take us to the Polytechnic University. Agnes had arrived and I met up with her in the afternoon. I was relieved to see her as we were doing a workshop together on Monday. I spent Saturday morning at the conference. I gave one of the keynote speeches and also gave one of the research talks. In the afternoon we went on a bus tour. The weather was appalling. It had been ever since I arrived. We went to the usual tourist places, winding up at Stanley Market. Stanley Market was hard for me not only because the last time but one I was there I was with Sarah, but also because I promised to buy her another pair of silk pyjamas decorated with suns and moons. Sarah had bought herself a pair in Stanley Market two years earlier and liked them very much. I had told her, "Next time I'm in Stanley Market, I'll buy you another pair." I saw the pyjamas but there was no point in buying them. I bought several presents for Anna, Mick, Matthew, Rosie and Francesca.

The tour ended in Aberdeen where we had a meal in the floating restaurant. Everyone had a jolly time. When I reached the hotel at 8.45 I had a call from Tatia, another ex-student of mine. She arranged for us to meet her for dinner with her husband on Monday evening after the workshop. She asked me how I was so I felt obliged to tell her about Sarah and started weeping again. In fact, Tatia knew. She had e-mailed me in Cambridge not knowing I had already left. My e-mails automatically go to Julia, so Julia had e-mailed Tatia to tell her. My heart was still aching badly.

I won the award for the best free paper and was given a cheque for one thousand Hong Kong dollars. I shared the money with the co-authors of the paper once I arrived home. I felt guilty about winning, thinking I was too senior to have been entered and a more junior person should have won. I couldn't be embarrassing at the dinner though so accepted with pleasure.

On the whole I had survived the day with few tears, apart from those I shed at lunch when I told Agnes that Julia had told Tatia about Sarah. I had moved on since the conference in Brussels the previous month.

The workshop on Monday (15 weeks since we had heard) seemed to go well. Agnes and I were talking about assessment and management of people with severe head injury. We started at 9.00 a.m. and finished at 4.30 p.m. We made our goodbyes after being photographed by some of the workshop participants. Tatia arrived. I talked and wept and talked again about Sarah. Tatia had met Sarah. So many of my colleagues knew her as she travelled with me so much. Tatia's husband joined us and we went out for a Korean barbecue. I had eaten a different style of food every evening.

Back at the hotel I packed for the journey home the following day. I thought over the day's workshop and remembered that one of the participants showed me an abstract of mine that she had found on the internet and asked for more details. It was the abstract of the workshop I had presented in Belgium on May 12th, the day Sarah died. This 'coincidence' made me feel depressed. Nevertheless I was aware that I was coping better.

As I left Hong Kong on Tuesday morning the sun was shining. This was the first time I had seen the sun since leaving Sarawak. I checked in and was upgraded once more. Some might say I was lucky to be upgraded both on the way out and on the way home. Yet I had the worst of bad luck in May. In Amsterdam while waiting for my flight to Stansted I phoned Mick. He said they had done a final search in Peru but nothing had been found. I knew it would be a waste of money asking for yet another search, but I also knew that Mick felt he had to do it. Both in Hong Kong and at Schipol Airport I 'saw' Sarah everywhere. I saw her in my mind as I had been to these places with her. There were brief moments though when I would feel a sense of peace and even joy. These feelings were momentary and did not happen often but I had one such moment on the flight about an hour after leaving Hong Kong. If I believed in such things, I would say it was Sarah telling me to be OK or that she was OK. I felt that the trip had been good for me as I had broken the pattern of crying so frequently. I still thought of Sarah all the time. I doubt two minutes ever went by when she was not in my head but the crying had certainly eased.

Mick met me at Stansted. At home, a letter and a book were waiting for me. The letter was from Ralph Lombreglia, the husband of my American friend Kate. This is what Ralph said in his letter.

Dear Barbara and Mick,

I know that Kate wrote to you months ago, but I wanted to let you know personally, though belatedly, how terribly sorry I was to hear about Sarah. I only met Sarah once (that time years ago for lunch on the hotel/restaurant patio in Harvard Square), but I was devastated and wept when I saw the e-mail from your assistant that day. I'm so terribly sorry to this minute, and I simply wanted to send you my deepest sympathy and love.

As far as we can tell now, Kate plans to attend the memorial service in October. I'm not as certain at this point that I can be there myself, though it's not out of the realm of possibility. I hope I can.

Barbara, a long time ago, on a very happy evening with you here in the living room where I'm sitting right now, while listening to a lot of great old Bob Dylan records, you told us a funny anecdote about a person who had a bat fly into the windshield of his car. Your story was complicated and full of wonderful ironies, but I used a much simplified version of it as the basis for a scene in the novel I'm writing. And then, when an editor asked me to donate something for an anthology to benefit the homeless, I took that scene and turned it into a self-sufficient story, more or less, and I'm enclosing a copy of the book for you, with heartfelt thanks.

Much love to you both,

Ralph

There was also a report of the latest search Mick had requested.

SATURDAY 19.08.00 (Arequipa − Cotahuasi village)
7:30 We start driving from Arequipa.
Everything goes on well, according to our plan and we arrived in Cotahuasi village at 19.00. After dinner we meet the man who has orga-nised the mules for tomorrow. It seems that he has prepared everything.
SUNDAY 20.08.00 (Cotahuasi village − Velinge)
8:00 We leave Cotahuasi village and driving down to the bridge where we are supposed to meet the mules (from the bridge we have to walk until the put-in, in Velinge). When we arrive at the bridge the mules have not arrived yet.
10:00 The mules are arriving and we pack them as fast as possible. At 11:00 we leave the bridge with three mules, three donkeys and a 'cowboy' who has to look after them.
19:00 In the dark we arrive at the 'old' put-in by Velinge (where the expe-dition in Mai started).
MONDAY 21.08.00 (searching the accident-spot)
8:30 We are starting from the put-in. Our plan is that we will go down the river. The others (driver and the cowboy) take down the equipment with the mules to the accident-spot. There we meet them and we will start searching from the shore.
9:30 We get to the 'accident-rapid'. We stop and have a look at the rapid. I explain what's exactly happened at the 12.05.00. Then we raft down to the spot where Pepe Lopez has seen the victim for the last time. We stop there and decide to have a look from the shore. As we know are in the following section some of the 'critical spots' located. 'Critical spots' means some locations in which we think the body of the victim might be.
    Some of the main reasons which indicates us that the body could be in this section are:
1. The body must be below the spot where Pepe Lopez has seen the victim for the last time P1. But above the flat section after the 'critical spots'.

2. In this section we find the two 'critical spots' with undercuts and siphons.
3. Below this two spots, Pepe Lopez found in the expedition of June (19.06–23.06.00) the neoprene-shoe.
4. The section after is getting flat until the next big rapid by the village of Quechualla (about 5 km further down) and there are many, as we saw undercuts and siphons.

We are starting searching in location P2 and P3.

The location P2 with the undercuts by the cliff is searched quite fast. We find nothing. The search in location P3 is more difficult. There are two big rocks in the middle of the river. This rocks must have been fell down from the cliff on the right hand side of the river. They consist of a relative soft material which the water has deeply washed out. By the search we have problems to get to some of the siphons. We work from the shore, from above the rocks and a few times from the raft. But in most of the spots it is too danger to use the raft.

The time passes by and more and more we realise that we got a very small chance to find something. At the time it gets dark we go back to the camp.

After dinner we have a briefing and discuss the situation. It is difficult for us to find a way to handle this. We got left three more days, if we like to run the river until Iquipi and search the canyon further down we have to leave tomorrow. If we leave tomorrow we got no more time left to search location P3.

But as we saw today the chance to be successful in P3 is very small. The body still might be under the rock but in that case it must be unreachable for us. And additional we got 80 km of river with a reasonable chance to find at least some of a indications about the victim.

We decide to leave tomorrow and go down to Iquipi.

TUESDAY 22.08.00 (Accident spot – 'Canyon del metro')

9:00 We start rafting down the river. Our driver and the 'cowboy' go back to the bridge with the animals. He is going to pick us up at the take-out in Iquipi.

Until Quichualla, the last village in the canyon, the river is quite easy and we got time to warm up.

Then we got to the first big rapid by Quechualla, after that the river is getting steep and faster. We continue the journey and a guide is always in front of us checking out eddies and big rocks if there might be something.

15:00 We meet some farmers who are walking down to the canyon several times a year to look after their vineyards. We talk to them, they have heard about the accident in Mai. But they have not seen or found something which could give us some more information about the victim.

17:30 We pass the 'Canyon del metro' and camp.

WEDNESDAY 23.08.00 (Canyon del centimetro – Rio Maran)

10:00 We leave our camp. The river is not anymore that steep but we have to pass several narrow gorges with strong rapids. Today we meet gold diggers, we talk to them but get no important information.

15:00 We pass the end of the Cotahuasi Canyon and soon we get to the Rio Maran. The canyon of the Rio Maran is wider and there are leaving people. So it is quite possible that we meet somebody.

17:00 We stop and camp on a beach.

THURSDAY 24.08.00 (Rio Maran – Iquipi – Arequipa)

9:00 We leave the campsite and start paddling down the river. In this section the Rio Maran is large and powerful. There are people living on fishing. We meet very few people and they had no news about the victim for us.

15:00 We arrive the take-out and meet our driver.

23:00 Arriving in Arequipa last briefing in the team.

COMMENT BY THE EXPEDITION LEADER:

Objective looking at this search I knew we had only a very small chance to find the body of the victim. It was more than three months ago when the accident happened and we had to search an enormous stretch of 90 km where the body somewhere might be.

The only indication we got was the neoprene shoe of the victim which Pepe Lopez found in June. But this was in June and if the body was under this rock, as we thought, it could have been washed out until the end of August.

After having searched this two rocks I really can not say in conclusion if there is anything down there. The only way to know this will be to stop the river and move the rocks.

On the other hand the body also might be some where down in the gorge. There are thousand of spots where it could be. And it is impossible to search all of them.

If the river will give free the body and I think this is the only chance we got, some of the gold diggers, farmers or fishermen's will find it. And most people know about the accident in Mai so it is quite sure they will contact the police.

COMMENT BY ANOTHER MEMBER OF THE EXPEDITION:

I think this type of sport always will have a big risk of danger more than others. We have to cover all of this risks in a professional way and in any situation on the river.

What I know and have seen [the name of the travel company] had the necessary guides and equipment to cover this risk.

The Cotahuasi river is characteristic for it's high gradient and the profundity of the rapids. Therefore the rescue after the accident must have been very difficult. And I think this is an accident of unlucky circumstances.

We have not seen any of the body of the victim during this expedition.

Later we had an e-mail from the owner of the travel company in which he said he had heard from the expedition leader who reported finding nothing during his search of the Cotahuasi. We would be sent the full report when it had been prepared but, from his phone conversation, he could tell us that the search concentrated on the rock under which they believed the body to be trapped. A hook had been used to search the whole area and they had eliminated the other places mentioned in the previous search as possibilities. Around the actual rock the water was incredibly deep and fast-flowing, which meant that a body could be trapped forever. The search had been continued down the river to Iquipi, but with no success. None of the locals they had talked to had anything to report. He said that he was sorry to be the bearer of this news.

That night I went off to sleep with no trouble but woke at 1.50 a.m. I forced myself to stay in bed until 4.30 a.m., hoping to go back to sleep. I didn't, so went downstairs and checked the 108 e-mails waiting for me on my computer. I went into work early. Swam and then spent the day on paperwork. I had a call from the secretary of a psychologist in the north of England. She said, "I was hoping to get Julia and not you as I didn't want to upset you." I told her, "It's OK, I can talk about it." She then told me that she had lost her own daughter three years ago from anorexia. Oh dear. She went on to say, "At least I was with her at the end." Yet another 'at least'. 'At least' our Sarah is in a beautiful country that she loved. Another thing the secretary said was that, when she heard, she wanted to write to me but the psychologist (who knows me fairly well) said she should not write. "Well, he was wrong," I replied. It is always better to write, and to hear from another bereaved parent is particularly important.

Anna and the girls came round that evening. Anna was tearful as she had been reading the newsletter from The Compassionate Friends and the SIBBS (Support in Bereavement for Brothers and Sisters) newsletter.

The last day of August saw me at the gym first, then into the Oliver Zangwill Centre where I spent the day reading papers, revising drafts of papers and other paperwork, including an e-mail to Audrey Holland.

Dear Audrey,

Well we are coping and crying less. We went to the weekend meeting of The Compassionate Friends (the group for bereaved parents) and although it was emotionally draining we were relieved that our circumstances were not as bad as some. There were parents there, for example, who had to watch their children die in agonising pain after complications during an illness. We also realised that people do survive and have meaningful lives and "the terrible wound becomes a scar". Since then, I have given my first talk, been to my first conference, presented a workshop, written a paper, marked a PhD thesis and so on. I haven't seen a patient yet. That first is due to happen on September 11th. So we are moving on, as Sarah would have wanted, and as a family I think we are doing perhaps better than expected at this stage.

I still don't go more than a few minutes without thinking about her. We did so many things together. I have just returned from a meeting in Hong Kong and I was there with Sarah two years ago. She loved HK. Every time I am in a restaurant or an airport or the gym or in the car, I think of when Sarah and I did those things together.

Despite all this, things are not as bad as they were a few weeks ago. We are now getting ready for the memorial service. We want to make it a very special day for our treasured daughter. She will remain forever now in a wild Peruvian river in a beautiful valley. The very last search has just finished and nothing was found. Sarah would have found this a romantic way to go and if she *had* to choose a death, she would probably have chosen this one.

Thank you for your continuing support.

With love from

Barbara

I left at 4.15, pleased with myself even though I still couldn't manage a whole day. Back home I found a letter from John and Alison, two of Sarah's good friends. We decided we would have a book of quotes from people who knew Sarah at the memorial service. This is John and Alison's letter in its entirety.

Dear Barbara and Mick,

We are so sorry to hear of your very sad news and apologise for not replying to your invitation to celebrate Sarah's life sooner. We would, of course, love to be there on October 1st for both you and her.

When we first heard about Sarah's accident in Peru, we tried several times to put together some words of condolence to you but we found it extremely difficult because we were so shocked and distraught by the tragedy and were always hoping for good news. We only feel able now, after receiving your invitation, to respond. We hope you understand why we have not contacted you sooner. We have taken a long time to come to terms with the loss of a good friend and can only begin to imagine how difficult this summer must have been for you and your family.

Sarah was a very good friend, we had become especially close in recent years and we have many happy memories of times spent with her. Probably the most numerous of these are to do with mountain biking; racing at the NEMBA's, the Malverns and Thetford, reading her reports, writing articles for her fanzines, her MTB/BMX parties, team time trials, night rides in Thetford in the rain! And quieter rides and evenings in Hitchin. Sarah was full of life and excellent at organising all manner of social gatherings and activities.

Yet it is strange how when you lose someone close that it is not always the big things that truly spark the memory and become really significant, but it is the everyday, seemingly ordinary things. Memories of Sarah keep cropping up unexpectedly now that she is gone. But what is reassuring and comforting is that part of her remains with us always. We have a lovely Christmas card that she sent us the year Ben was born, it's on our dining room wall. We loved the picture so much that it has been there, amongst our family photos ever since. It is a photograph of a young boy cruising down the road on his BMX bike, his head thrown back and his mouth wide with laughter and glee. Inside the card it just says, "Joy to the world", so appropriate. It reminds us of Sarah daily. We are going to put the photo you sent beside it, along with the beautiful and poignant words of Wordsworth.

Another peculiar memory we now have which will always remind us of Sarah is when we cook sausages and mash. It was one of Sarah's favourite meals that we had when she came to visit. I also remember her recommending this to John once as one of the best meals on the menu when we were out in Bury one evening with Ben, Anna, Rosie and Francesca.

It is also comforting that I have two books Sarah gave me for my birthday last year because she had particularly enjoyed them. I have just finished reading them and although it saddens me that we cannot share our thoughts on them now, owning them now means so much more because we have them forever. Our birthdays were very close, mine being 8th June, so we used to try to do something together on or around that time if we could. It was great for me to have a fellow Gemini as a friend with similar personality traits. I still feel the need for my other 'twin' sometimes and know that Sarah filled that place for me for a while. She is a great loss and we will miss her enormously. We will be glad to come to the memorial service to celebrate her life next month.

Wishing both of you, Anna, Matt and all the family our deepest sympathy during this very difficult time.

Best wishes,

Alison and John

September 2000

Much of this month was spent getting ready for the memorial service. Matthew and Mick were searching through our large collection of photographs, deciding which to use, then scanning them into the computer, enlarging them, printing them and laminating them. Matt was also in charge of the music. Mick dealt with the people at The Athenaeum, the caterers and the audio-visual man. We talked about the programme, which speakers and the order of events. I drafted a provisional programme that we stuck to with a few amendments. Anna was the first to draft her speech and had an argument with her father about which anecdotes to include.

Work continued in much the same way. I worked solidly but slowly at the academic and administrative things. I was now able to go to the post room via the gloomy and soulless underpasses of Addenbrooke's Hospital to collect the post. Such a simple thing yet I could not face it until the end of August. I started to think about my next trip with Explore. I wanted to go to Mali in North West Africa to trek among the Dogon villages and go to Timbuktu. It was a trip that Sarah would have liked, we could have done it together and I wanted to go before I was 60. The only time I could go when Explore were offering a trip was March 2001, so I decided to book for then. I bought a book on West Africa that said Mali was the 'jewel in the crown' of this region. This confirmed my decision.

On Sunday September 3rd I started to draft a piece about Sarah for The Compassionate Friends newsletter. I cried as I wrote. I read it to Mick who cried. I went to Anna's and read it to her and she cried. Mick was gathering together the quotes for the memorial service from all the cards, letters and e-mails we had received. Consequently, we were in a very tearful state over that weekend. I raged at her stupidity in doing such a trip, and for the awful, awful loss we had to bear. That Sunday I thought, "OK, we've suffered enough. Let's put it right now. Let's have her back and we'll know how awful grief is. We have learned our lesson." Our family had been so fortunate prior to this, no real hardships, healthy children, a successful marriage for Mick and me, enough money not to have to worry. But our luck ran out. We were being taught a lesson, I sometimes thought, for not knowing suffering enough.

I had been reading Agnes Whitaker's *All in the End is Harvest* and there was one piece I read over and over again. It was from a book by Christopher Leach called *Letter to a Younger Son*. His older son had died and he wrote this book to the surviving son. This was my mainstay in bereavement literature. He captured the agony and the blackness of grief but was also positive about life. Furthermore, I felt this man was like us in that he did not expect to see his son again. For him, as for us, death is final. There is no after-life − how can there be − in which we are going to meet up again. The piece that I almost learned by heart will appear later in the section on speeches from the memorial service.

I worked on the morning of Monday 4th, then took a day and a half's leave. Mick and I had booked tickets to see *Henry IV, Part II* in Stratford-upon-Avon. The evening performance was excellent. I was able to concentrate better now than I had for *Henry*

IV, Part I in July. Both of us wept in the first minute though. Northumberland learned of the death of his son Hotspur and his grief was overpowering. The actor playing Northumberland was brilliant, capturing a parent's grief with such heart-rending accuracy. Oddly, though, within the space of a few minutes we were laughing along-side the rest of the audience at the antics of Falstaff. How weird grief is in the way it can strike momentarily and disappear equally abruptly from one's consciousness. Later we thought of Shakespeare, who had lost more than one of his children, and wondered if these losses had contributed to his understanding of the deepest emotional levels in tragedy.

We returned home next morning. I had leave so went to the gym, finished reading a PhD by my ex-colleague and PhD student Linda Clare. I thought it was one of the best PhDs I had ever read. It was clinically important, of great potential importance, it linked theory and practice, it was innovative and beautifully written. I hoped the examiners would see it the same way. In fact Linda sailed through her viva the following March with no corrections to her thesis, and that is almost unheard of. I cooked for seven of us that evening and wanted Sarah to be there.

We received a letter from Janet and David in Brussels saying we remained very much in their thoughts and they would be thinking of us especially on October 1st at the memorial service. They sent us strength and courage. I also received an invitation to speak at a conference in Australia in May 2001, just after the first anniversary of Sarah's death. Mick and I both love Australia so I had no hesitation in accepting. There was a slight problem though, we were thinking that we should return to Peru and trek to the site where Sarah died. We thought we should be there on the anniversary of her death so the conditions were likely to be similar. If we went to Australia we would not be able to be in Peru for the first anniversary. We discussed this and decided to go to Australia first and from there to Peru. We would only be two weeks later than the anniversary and we believed that the conditions would not have changed a great deal in those two weeks.

I worked on my article for the newsletter. There was a 500-word limit. I cut it down to size and Mick felt I had lost the feeling from the writing. I had spent ages on it and sent it off. I cried three times at work that day, Wednesday 6th. Once when I was telling Jon about Northumberland's grief in *Henry IV, Part II*, once when I replied to an e-mail from a colleague who had known Sarah as a child and again when I was working on the piece for the newsletter. More crying over e-mails the following day. I had to tell people about Sarah every day. However many people we informed, we could not tell everyone. On Thursday 7th I was so worn out with grief and fatigue that I shut the door and lay on the floor for a few minutes. I had never done that before. I dreamt about Sarah again that night. This was the usual theme. She was really alive and not dead at all. "Who rescued you then?" I asked her. "Oh, some bloke," she said nonchalantly.

On Friday 8th, Matt came over to Cambridge and we went to look at poster boards at the MRC Centre. I had arranged to borrow a number of boards for the photo-graphic display at the memorial service. Mick wanted a big display so quite a few boards were required. We took measurements for Mick. It was 17 weeks to the day since she had died. At times it was still as hard as ever. The regret, the yearning to have her back, the anguish of our loss would sweep over us all regularly.

On Monday September 11th, I noted that I had a good day. We had been checking readings for the memorial service on Sunday. We wanted this to be a very special day to celebrate her life. Her death at this moment seemed inevitable as did the manner of her death. I thought I would probably have bad days again but Monday 11th was emotionally my best day since Sarah's death. I also saw my first patient that day. It was a man I had known for several years. I went with Fergus, my clinical psychology trainee, who was experienced and would be fully qualified in a month so I thought he would attend to the patient and I would observe. That is essentially what happened. I read Anna's speech that evening and thought it was excellent. I also read Matt's introduction to the pieces of music; that was very moving.

Anna's 36th birthday was on Wednesday September 13th. She was now the same age as Sarah was when she died. Next year Anna, 15 months younger than Sarah, would be older than Sarah. She said that would be a hard birthday for her to deal with. We went out for a birthday dinner that evening. It was not the joyous occasion it should have been. Mick was depressed and we wanted Sarah to be with us.

The memorial planning took up most of Saturday 16th and we went out with Carol and her gang on Sunday. I had always worked at the weekends and still did some now, but not nearly as much as I had before Sarah died. Work was far less important to me now. Monday 18th was another day with bouts of weeping. It was 18 weeks since we had heard the news. The loss was so huge and hard to bear, it seemed such a waste of a life. I cried more in the evening because a woman cyclist won Britain's first ever female cycling medal at the Olympic Games. We had already won a men's silver and a gold. I cried because Sarah would have been so pleased and now she would never know.

I worked on my speech and the introduction to the reading I had selected. Not surprisingly I chose the piece by Christopher Leach. A colleague of Graeme Peart's, Tom Cook, came to give a talk at the rehabilitation centre on September 19th. He came into my room afterwards. I made him some coffee. He obviously knew about Sarah and said to me "So you're back at work. How are you coping?" I talked and talked about Sarah for half an hour or more. He was a good listener and I felt he had done the right thing in asking the question. I worked on a chapter I was completing after he left and then wrote to Jane Plimsoll. She and I did our clinical training at the same time at the Institute of Psychiatry from 1975 to 1977. I had not seen her since then but I had heard from a mutual acquaintance that Jane's middle son had died unexpectedly of an undetected heart condition in the New Year. He was 19 years old. I felt I should write as one bereaved mother to another and we exchanged a few letters over the next three weeks or so.

I was still leaving work at around 4.15. This was better than when I first returned to work in June but still not good enough. One reason I left early is that I was doing most of the cooking. This was a job I found relatively easy whereas Mick, who had done most of the weekday cooking before Sarah died, seemed to find it too demanding. We had been drinking most nights, sharing a bottle of wine between us but by September felt we needed it less. In the early days we drank a lot more in the hope of getting off to sleep. Now we did not need it so much. Despite everything I was able to write papers and chapters and caught up with most of my backlog.

The next day I went into Cambridge at lunchtime to buy an outfit for the memorial service. Fortunately, I found something quickly and was back at the hospital within an hour. During the evening Mick and I checked the draft programme that Andrew Boag, Mick's designer friend, had sent to us. We thought it was lovely. I also spent a long time on the telephone to Anna discussing flowers and speeches. We felt the memorial service was going to be special but it was dominating our lives during the latter half of September.

On Friday 22nd I went to my first committee meeting since the event. I knew the other committee members well and I felt comfortable with the people. Nevertheless, I was nervous about this new 'first'. I was one of the last to arrive at the British Psychological Society's offices in London. Several people said how pleased they were to see me back. The morning passed normally. Over lunch I told them the story. They listened, apparently mesmerised. One woman told me she had lost a baby at birth. So many people have been through this experience. One is just so unaware until the event occurs. We finished at 3.20, and before I left each of the four women on the committee came to give me a hug. The men did not hug me although I would have appreciated this, but they were certainly not hostile. I felt that it had been a supportive day.

I collected the poster boards and continued with work but October 1st was looming. We could not think about much else. It was too much in our minds. We felt fragile and on an emotional tightrope. During this week the programme for the memorial service was completed. It contained the following quotes from Sarah's family and friends (some of them have appeared earlier in the book).

SOME QUOTES FROM PEOPLE WHO KNEW SARAH

We have a lovely Christmas card that Sarah sent us the year Ben was born, it's on our dining room wall. We loved the picture so much that it has been there, amongst our family photos ever since. It's a photograph of a young boy cruising down the road on his BMX bike, his head thrown back and his mouth wide with laughter and glee. Inside the card it just says, "Joy to the world", so appropriate. It reminds us of Sarah daily.

Alison & John

I simply want to tell you, that you are my English family. You all represent the best part of my childhood. I had a wonderful time fishing, playing cricket and I have to confess that my talking with Sarah was simply a great pleasure. I used to listen to her like a 'privilege'.

She was very patient with my poor English; her eyes, her state of mind was a kind of secret at that time, it was amazing and mostly different. As a child I was just fascinated.

I keep Sarah and all of you in mind forever. There are no words to express what I'm feeling. There are no words to express your suffering.

I love you.

Jean Ferrandis

I was always a little envious of the way Sarah did everything with so much enthusiasm and energy. I think it was because, no matter what, you always gave her support and understanding.

Karen Pitman

Sarah was the best person in the family and was dearly loved and treasured by all those lucky enough to have known her. We have had many communications from friends and relatives of Sarah's from around the world expressing their grief and fond memories. People who knew her when she was a childhood friend, a punk teenager, a skateboarder (for the England team), a sailor, a mountain biker, a mountain bike journalist, the office administrator for a publishing company, and just a wonderful companion, have written to say how much she will be missed.

At home we are experiencing much pain: Sarah was the heart of the family from which all of us drew our strength. We don't have to tell those who knew her well how the light of her presence lit up every social event in which she was participating.

Anna, Matthew and Rosie are accompanying us to Peru . . . Although we won't be able to manage the two-day trek in the mountains to the place where Sarah was last seen, we shall be able to get to the river to say our goodbyes. If Sarah is not found it will simply add to her legend as a very special person who has returned to nature. She was always a risk taker. She died as she lived. She was a complete person in a way that most of us are not. Although her life was short, it was full, exciting and, because of her remarkably good and forgiving nature, a life in which she was at peace with herself. Living for us now, without Sarah's love, is very hard indeed.

Mick

This was a young woman who had clear ideas about how to live life. She grabbed it by the collar and held on for a wild ride.

James T. Becker

I hope you don't mind me writing to you but I was on the rafting trip with Sarah and wanted to get in touch with you.

Sarah and I were the only two girls on the trip and so we inevitably spent quite a lot of time together, sharing hotel rooms, sleeping space at the campsites etc.

Although I had only known Sarah for a few days I felt we had become friends. This sort of trip always brings people close together very quickly and you talk about things that you probably wouldn't discuss on more conventional holidays.

One thing that sticks in my mind is Sarah saying how close she was to her family. She obviously loved you all very much as I'm sure you knew. She was really looking forward to her mum and Rosie coming out and was full of plans for the visit. She was wondering whether she could stand being away from you all for so many months.

Everyone on the trip got on very well and there was lots of laughing and chatting. Sarah and I were made 'honorary boys' and Sarah introduced us to a game of deciding who would play each of us if there were a film of the trip, which kept us occupied for hours.

On the last night before the rafting Sarah and I were the last two to go to bed as we sat up talking and complaining about the 'boys' lack of stamina.

I wasn't on Sarah's raft and I know that Martin and Max and the guides have told you what happened. I just wanted to let you know that we had all got to like Sarah very much and I just can't imagine your grief. She was having a good time before the rafting . . .

Susan Routledge

I am afraid I have some terrible news about our beloved and beautiful daughter, Sarah. Just over three weeks ago on May 12th she drowned in a rafting accident in Peru. We heard about it on May 15th. She had decided to spend six months in Peru to write for sports and travel journals and reconsider her life. She moved there on May 3rd. She went on this rafting trip before moving into a flat in Cusco. Rosie and I were due to meet her there for a 10-day holiday on May 28th. Apparently, the trip was in a remote area and on a dangerous river (grade 5, i.e. the most dangerous). Sarah kept very quiet about the trip and we had no idea she was engaged in anything so dangerous. Five people were on Sarah's raft when it overturned and four were saved. It appears that Sarah lost consciousness quite quickly and although attempts were made to rescue her, she disappeared and her body has not been found . . . We don't expect her body to be recovered now, although one of her shoes was found several weeks later, washed up on a bank.

Mick, Anna, Matthew, Rosie and I went to Peru for 10 days to meet people from the British Embassy in Lima, the British Consulate in Arequipa (the nearest town to where the accident took place), the owner of the travel company, and other people involved. We went to the River Cotahuasi where the accident took place although we couldn't get to the actual site as it was two days further on and a difficult trek. As it was, we had a 12-hour drive on dirt roads from Arequipa, then overnight in a primitive hostel, another one-hour drive and a two-hour trek to get to the nearest spot. We held a little ceremony there – reading out messages and letters to Sarah and throwing them into the river with some photographs, flowers, and a few little gifts. We have the police report and statements from people on the trip (signed before the honorary consul) and are now trying to get an order of 'presumed death' from a British coroner. Obviously we can't get a death certificate without a body. It might have to go to court which will take a while.

It is the worst thing that has ever happened to us and we are in total despair. I loved her, her father loved her, so did her brother and sister, her nieces, her aunts and uncles, her cousins and her friends. She was the best person in the family, always good and kind, fair and just – but a risk taker.

Barbara

As a traveller I am aware of the many risks that are present as one travels round different countries. However I am also aware that travelling is a passion, it makes people who they are. They have a love of life, a need to experience new cultures, meet new people and see new sights. It sounds as if Sarah was very happy, doing what she wanted to do. I know whilst I was travelling I was conscious that I had my parents to thank for giving me the confidence and freedom to fulfil my dreams. I have spent several years on the road, I don't think a day passed without a thought for my parents. Whenever I experienced something beautiful, exciting and different I would memorise it and think how happy my parents would be to see me so happy.

I have always said to my friends and family that I don't want to be a caged bird and have taken many risks whilst in the pursuit of fulfilling my dreams. I also had an accident whilst white-water rafting and it made me conscious of how much I have managed to do in my life . . . I tell my parents that should anything ever happen to me I want them to be happy in the knowledge that I achieved more in my lifetime than I ever could have hoped for.

I hope you don't mind me writing this, not only am I not particularly articulate but I am also conscious that I haven't known you for very long.

I am just hoping that you can take some comfort from my words, as a traveller and daughter, and what I would want my parents to know and feel in such tragic circumstances.

Tina Emery

I have been thinking of South Africa and our trip to Robben Island. I am so glad that I had that recent time with Sarah. She was such a wonderful, strong young woman, and I will treasure those memories. She died as she lived, courageous and adventurous and loving nature.

Know that around the world people will be holding you close and wishing you strength and courage as you begin coping with this most difficult of all losses.

Jill Winegardner

Sarah was a special person — such a pure spirit in many ways. She was a credit to you and Mick. I hope you can take some small comfort in her specialness, and in the zest she showed for the rich life she had.

Ian Robertson

Having known Sarah since she was 10 I know what a rare and special person she was. She always lived life 100 per cent and I guess that was what she was doing right up to the end. She certainly packed more into her life than some of us who are twice as old. And you were wonderful parents to her; you helped her become the person she was. Even through her most difficult times you loved her and stuck with her and believed in her. She was wise and sweet and adventurous and strong and everyone who knew her will miss her very much.

Jo Tasker

I met her briefly the week before she left. She was coming in for her Spanish lesson as I was leaving. She was really happy and excited and said how much she was looking forward to her trip. I'm sure she was having a wonderful time and was doing exactly what she wanted to do. So many people never achieve that — Sarah didn't spend her time wishing that things were different — she did something to change things. Not many people are that courageous.

Agnes Shiel

You don't know me but I felt I wanted to write to you. I went on the trip to Peru in May. I am so sorry about what happened to Sarah. I only knew

Sarah for six days but she was a lovely girl. She seems to enjoy every second of the day. She loved the outside world and was particularly excited about her trekking and mountain biking that she was about to embark on after the trip.

It was a great shock to us all on the trip – what happened on that day. I was in the boat with Sarah and I was particularly upset about what happened. It was a very distressing time in my life and I feel great sympathy for you both in your loss...

Chris Jenkins

I met her, she was beautiful and lovely and I am saddened by the news.

Irini

She was so warm, friendly and caring, with a delightful sense of humour and an infectious enthusiasm for life... Fiona often talks about the lovely weekend she had at Center Parcs when Sarah looked after her and Rosie while we wrote the grey book. She thought Sarah was great – as did we all.

And Sarah was such a wonderful person to work with too. She was always calm, patient, reliable and full of common sense. I particularly admired her ability to go straight to the crux of the matter, to make decisions speedily and confidently, and follow through to make sure things happened.

Hazel Emslie

Sarah was one of the most special people I ever met. She was always so very kind to me and I always looked forward to seeing her. She was so smart and beautiful inside and out. I'm glad she was my cousin and I'm going to miss her.

Noel

She was the loveliest sunshine to everyone who crossed her path.

Mark & Celia

I have very distinct memories of Sarah. I remember her as a very dark, striking girl who was very fond of poems. We must have shared a bedroom at one of our respective homes because I seem to recall her reciting poetry in a deep, dramatic voice before we went to sleep. I remember feeling very impressed by her and a little mystified...

Katie Woodford

On Wednesday 27th, Thursday 28th and Friday 29th of September, I was in Antwerp for a memory conference where I was giving a keynote speech and another talk. I had seriously considered cancelling this, but thought I could cope and I did. One of the organisers was very sympathetic. I met a British colleague who listened to my rambling and crying one evening when I had drunk too much, but I gave my lectures without trouble. I had never cried during a lecture or presentation so I stopped worrying about that.

I returned home on Friday evening for the final preparations and anxieties. I had selected a reading for Mick from *The July Ghost* but he did not want to read it so I agreed to do this and wrote a short introduction. Carol and Peter came for the evening and we went out to dinner with them and other friends. It was a good evening but I had a terrible night going over and over talks and arrangements for the service. The day finally arrived.

CHAPTER FIVE

I always flirt with death

2003

The memorial service for Sarah is described in the journal in this chapter. We are satisfied that the reader will get a very clear impression of Sarah from the contributions made at the ceremony and from the written comments collected together to form part of the Memorial Service Programme. In particular, we think Anna's description of her sister comes closest to revealing Sarah's character and the effect she had on others. As to these effects we refer the reader back to the written comments of Jean Ferrandis on pages 104–105 because there is a three-year follow-up to this statement that makes an interesting and we think beautiful story in itself.

The time Jean is talking about was back in the 1970s when our family used to meet up with the Ferrandis family, either in their French home in Nice or at our home in Reading. All our three children and the three Ferrandis kids had great times together on the beaches of Nice and Corsica or in the Berkshire and sometimes Suffolk countryside. It was a very happy time for all of us. Even though Barbara and Mick could speak little French and Jean's parents, Georges and Thérèse, could speak little English we still got on and laughed our way through some great times. Jean had never been to England since those days, although now in his capacity as a classical musician with an international career he travels the world extensively. Jean is one of France's leading flautists and among other honours he was awarded First Prize at the Prague Spring International Flute Competition in 1986. The late Leonard Bernstein expressed his admiration for the young flautist when, on hearing Jean play the Mozart K314 concerto for flute, exclaimed, "It's Pan himself!" Later the great conductor was inspired to compose a cadenza especially for Jean.

In March 2003 Jean paid his first visit to England since his childhood. He was to play a concert for solo flute and accompanying piano. The venue was the Wigmore Hall in London and we were all invited. It was a wonderful occasion at a most prestigious venue and the two musicians (Graham Scott played piano) were excellent and indeed inspiring. At the end of the concert the musicians were warmly applauded and came back to play two encores. Even this was not enough for the audience so Jean and Graham Scott came back for a third time. Jean stressed that the staff wanted ". . . to go 'ome" and said he would play just one more piece. To our amazement he spoke calmly to the audience, telling them that he had an English family, the Wilsons, and he was thinking of us and in particular Sarah. He went on to say that he was playing the final piece in memory of Sarah. It was a song by Bartok and was called "Star". He played this slow and beautiful song with great tenderness and Mick was reminded of the magical night he and Barbara slept out under the stars at 14,000 feet in the Cotahuasi valley where Sarah now rests. He thought particularly of the beautiful Southern Cross constellation that looks down on the valley and his heart was filled with sorrow for his lost child and joy for the beauty of the world, its music, and for people like Jean Ferrandis. A month or two later Jean faxed us details of the song:

> In Hungarian it is called Csillagok, it is a popular children's song . . . This song is just wonderful, nostalgic but not sad. In fact the last piano chord is in Major, full of hope and light. I think it is written for Sarah.
>
> Love Jean

October 2000

THE DAY OF THE MEMORIAL SERVICE

During the morning Mick, Matthew and Paul (Anna's ex-husband) were setting up the display. We had photographs of Sarah from birth until two or three days before she died. Mick arranged these in themes: Infancy, Childhood, Young Woman, a Wonderful Auntie and Sarah and Barbara. We also had some of Sarah's bikes there and her rocking horse, Pegasus, that we bought for her on hire purchase when she was seven years old. She loved the horse and one of her early poems was about Pegasus. I remember it now:

> Pegasus, Pegasus
> My white horse
> I ride you to London
> To Ipswich, everywhere

Among the photographic display were quotes from books we had been reading.

> A month ago, at this very hour, I was a different woman. I have a photo-graph from that day. I am at a party launching the publication in Spain of my most recent novel. I am wearing a silver necklace and bracelets and an aubergine-coloured dress. My nails are manicured and my smile confi-dent. I am a century younger than I am today. I don't know that woman; in four weeks, sorrow has transformed me.
>
> (Reproduced from *Paula* by Isabel Allende.)

Undo it, take it back, make every day the previous one until I am returned to the day before the one that made you gone. Or set me on an aeroplane travelling west, crossing the date line again and again, losing this day, then that, until the day of loss still lies ahead, and you are here instead of sorrow.

(Reproduced from Rapoport, *A Woman's Book of Grieving*)

THE EXISTENCE OF LOVE

I had thought that your death
Was a waste and a destruction,
A pain of grief hardly to be endured.
I am only beginning to learn
That your life was a gift and a growing
And a loving left with me.
That desperation of death
Destroyed the existence of love,
But the fact of death
Cannot destroy what has been given.
I am learning to look at your life again
Instead of your death and your departing.

(Reproduced from Pizer, *Selected Poems 1963–1983*)

As long as you mention my name, I live!
African proverb

We had plenty of help in getting things ready. We asked people to gather at 1.00 p.m. for lunch and the display. As I arrived at the Athenaeum, just before 1.00, I could see that many people had already arrived. I stood just inside the entrance to greet people and invite them to go upstairs for the display and lunch. Rosie was with me for most of the time. Simon took over towards the end. I hardly saw the display but I know it was stunning. The photographs took up three sides of a fair-sized room.

I hugged most people whether I knew them or not. I did not know all of Sarah's biking friends or Cindy's friends from Berkshire that Sarah knew well. Some people were crying. I hardly cried that day. I wanted to be strong for the visitors. Also I remember going to a memorial service for a friend of Anna's, who died in a car accident about 18 years ago. He, too, was a special person, full of character and his 'own man'. His service was emotional and memorable but his mother was strong. She comforted everyone else. I never forgot her behaviour that day and wanted to be like her. About 200 people came (the maximum we could seat in the hall). A few people went to the hall early. Mick had arranged a video loop to show a video of

Sarah and other members of the family over the years. My mother who died in 1992 was also on the video.

We ushered everyone in just before 2.00. They all picked up a programme. I wanted family and close friends in the first two rows. Once each person was seated, we began. Mick welcomed everyone and I gave the first talk "Our Daughter". I then took over as chairperson to introduce the others. Anna followed me with "My sister" and then Rosie and Francesca talked about "Our Auntie". Anna had to lift Francesca to the microphone and she just said two sentences. Matt then introduced the first song, "Don't Think Twice, It's Alright". We regarded it as epitomising Bob Dylan's sensitivity and sense of irony. Cindy went next with "Growing up Together" and two more recent friends from Bury St Edmunds, Nick and Linda, talked about "Our Friend". Nick gave the speech. The second song was "Another Girl, Another Planet". Hazel then spoke about "A Colleague" and Celia talked about Sarah as "A mountain biker". Matt introduced the third song, "Just like Fred Astaire". I then read from *The July Ghost* by A. S. Byatt before Susan Routledge spoke about "Sarah in Peru". We showed part of the video of the Cotahuasi Valley that we had filmed in Peru in May. Song number four was The Waterboys' "Fisherman's Blues". Then came the second reading from *Letter to a Younger Son*. Mick concluded the talks with a piece entitled "She who kisses the joy as it flies" (a quotation from one of William Blake's poems). He also read out an e-mail from Max Milligan and then a card from The Finnish Neuropsychological Society. The last song had to be Dylan's "Forever Young". I then thanked everyone and asked them to go back upstairs for a glass of wine.

These are the talks:

SARAH: OUR DAUGHTER

From the moment I married Mick in July 1962, I wanted a baby and I particularly wanted a girl. Sarah was born just over ten months later. Immediately after her birth the midwife said, "She is the most beautiful baby we've seen in a long time." Anna, our second child, arrived 15 months later and Matthew, our last, was born 18 months after Anna. So we had 'three under three' and we loved it. We were 1960s hippies and travelled around the country visiting friends and taking our lovely children, our cats and our stick insects with us. We didn't own a car then so travelled on public transport attracting a few stares and comments.

Sarah was always a joy. An imaginative and clever child, she taught herself to read at three years old and taught herself the times tables with her pieces of Lego. I would hear her say to herself, "Four of the eights make 32." She was a dreamer, planning events and making up stories. For a long time she had an invisible bear to protect her. I once mentioned this to a school doctor and wondered whether I should be worried. The sensible doctor said, "Well bears are cuddly, we'll start worrying when she gets an invisible tiger." Years later I told this to Sarah and she said, "But I *did* have an invisible tiger, I just never told you about it."

I once made Sarah cross. She came into our bedroom crying and said, "I dreamt you turned into a packet of biscuits and somebody ate you all up." I started to laugh and she was most annoyed saying, "It's not funny, I was very upset."

My most enduring memory of Sarah as a child is with a book propped up behind the taps in the bathroom while she cleaned her teeth. She was always a great reader and couldn't bear to put her book away while she did the mundane things.

On leaving school Sarah became a punk with weird hairstyles and strange clothes. We did not like it but felt we had no choice but to live with it. Although Sarah was living in a series of squats then, she turned up regularly to do some washing, get something to eat and scrounge some money. Our friend, Jo Tasker, was one of the few people to pay Sarah a compliment at that time. She once looked at her bright blue hair and said, "Sarah, you look like an exotic bird."

After four years, Sarah wrote two plays about her punk lifestyle, put it all behind her and went off to university where she became secretary of the sailing club. She taught herself navigation and undertook some risky trips crossing the Channel. She phoned me once from the Channel Islands and said "I've been out in a gale force 8 wind and had to be strapped to the boat and every time a wave came it lifted me right in the air. Oh, and a Frenchman in the next boat drowned yesterday." "Oh Sarah, come home," I wailed. "But I love it," she replied. I realise now, she probably had more than a few lucky escapes in her time.

Sarah took up mountain biking when she met the man she was to marry and they became keen bikers. They started their infamous fanzine "Bad News" and also wrote for *Mountain Bike UK*.

As Sarah was by now working for her Dad in the publishing company, she and I frequently travelled to international conferences together. Sarah ran the exhibition and display and I presented papers and talks. We went to the USA, Hong Kong, Japan, South America, South Africa and other places. We also holidayed together, including a fantastic trip to Jordan for New Year 1998. During all of these trips, I can't remember a single row with her. She was an enthusiast about travel, food, people, sport and life in general. She made me laugh if I was too serious, introduced me to the gym so I could get fit for a trip to Madagascar, made me see the good in people and was my closest friend as well as my treasured daughter.

Sarah went on a mountain biking adventure holiday to Peru in 1998 and cycled in the Andes and in the Amazon basin. She fell in love with the country and returned the following year for more biking in Peru and rafting in Bolivia. Here she fell in love with rafting, unfortunately. She came back from that trip saying it was the best thing she'd ever done and she wanted to live in Peru for 6 months in the first instance to see if she wanted to stay. She also wanted to concentrate on her writing and reconsider her life.

Although Mick and I felt desolate at the thought of her being so far away (after all we were used to seeing her nearly every day), we also felt proud of her for doing something courageous and different.

Sarah gave up her job, her flat and her cats and last Christmas moved back home to save money for Peru. For the Millennium, Mick, Sarah, Anna, Matthew, Rosie, Francesca and I went to Mauritius and had our best New Year ever. At the end of April we had Sarah's farewell dinner at Ravenswood Hall with her aunt and uncle, Carol and Peter, her cousin Simon and cousin-in-law, Jo. We had a smashing time and at the end Sarah beamed at Carol, Peter, Simon and Jo and said, "See you all in November."

She left for Peru on May 3rd. Mick took her to the airport and they had to leave at 5 a.m. The night before, Sarah said to me, "I won't wake you up." "Oh yes," I said, "come and say goodbye," which she did. Rosie and I were due to meet her in Peru at the end of May for a 10-day holiday. It was to be my birthday present for Sarah who would have been 37 on June 11th.

On May 7th Sarah left for a 12-day trek with white-water rafting included. We knew she was going to do this but we did not know she was rafting on a grade 5 (i.e. the most dangerous) river, advertised (we discovered later) as "Extreme world class rafting". She drowned on May 12th and was last seen floating face down, unconscious. Her body has not been found. We did not know about her death until Monday May 15th. The day before we heard we were travelling back from the memorial service of a colleague in Brighton. We had seen his elderly mother there and I said, "How terrible to outlive your children." On the way home from Brighton I said to Mick, "Life is good at the moment, work is going well, the kids are sorted and we don't have to worry about money." We didn't know then that Sarah was already dead.

We know we have to carry on living, there is really no choice about it but life without our precious, beloved, treasured daughter is hard indeed.

Goodbye, darling girl.

Anna's speech

SARAH – MY SISTER

Sarah once said to me that the number 4 was special to her. This was because she had been 4 years old when she first realised that she was

Sarah, herself, and that nobody else was her, and nobody else would live her life. She told me this with such passion in her voice that I suddenly realised that this was still an amazing revelation to her. It was not something she had ever taken for granted. Sarah lived her life as if every day was Christmas Day, and she'd just been given two fantastic presents, herself and the world around her. She always made the most of what she was given, whether it was the toys we had as children from which she created fantastic imaginary games, or the chance to go on a trip that most of us would have been too cautious to take. Whilst I'd sometimes thought as a child that I was tougher and more worldly-wise than Sarah, it was Sarah who threw herself into things she wanted to do, Sarah who threw herself out of things she didn't want to do, and Sarah who genuinely appreciated what life had to offer her. Sarah was my brave, wise, big sister.

Sarah had a message to give to the world. Those of you who knew her well will recall how she wanted to scream from the rooftops that life was special, that the world had much to offer, and that each individual person within it was unique. I was and still am more ordinary. I, like most people, have spent too much time complaining about little things like lack of money, a minor injustice, my job, when what really matters is that being alive is a great gift that we can take so much from. Sarah should have lived a thousand years so others could have experienced her greater wisdom.

When we were children I was more frightened of the world than Sarah. Sarah, being older, more confident and optimistic than I, helped me to see that life could be fun and that we had a choice about what we took from it. I would watch in awe at how she was able to create day-long adventures out of a stretch of sand and her own mind. As an adult she still remembered the times we spent on holiday as if they had happened yesterday – her ability to remain positive was unsurpassable. She also showed me that neither as individuals, nor as a family were we in any way ordinary. Whilst I would worry if our parents had a row, she would laugh and soothe me, saying, "Oh Anna, our parents are so happy." Sarah often said to me that she had always known our parents were almost unique in their love for each other and for their children. We enjoyed a free childhood with hippy parents who taught us to love ourselves and other people, to speak our own minds and to remain true to ourselves. Sarah always appreciated our luck at having been born into this family.

Sarah's desire to make the most of her life was clear from an early age. She had an insatiable appetite for enjoyment and a determination to end things that were not for her. As teenagers our parents would occasionally go out for the evening or even overnight and let us have parties in their house! Sarah would invite everybody she knew and tell them to invite everybody they knew. On one occasion there were at least 300 people in our house, some of them having travelled from London. I hated every minute of them – worrying about the spilt cider and fag-burns. Sarah spent every one of those evenings, every single minute of them, partying. Sarah equally threw herself out of things with similar drama. As a Brownie she thought the Brown Owl stupid and so told her to "sod off". I followed her out and that was the end of Brownies for both of us. When she was 15 she wanted to give up O-level Art but was told she had to take it. When it was clarified that if you failed your Mock you couldn't sit the exam, Sarah sat through a whole 3-hour Mock exam in which she was supposed to draw a fish until 5 minutes before the end when she scribbled a cartoon drawing in one tiny corner of the page. I, being in the year below, was shown this drawing in my Art lesson as an example of a fail. We, however, all knew that this was no ordinary failure of ability, but a statement. Most people were not so daring, however much they wanted to concentrate on life's pleasures.

During her late teens, Sarah became a punk and believe me she didn't do that by halves either: she was the queen of Reading Punks. Whilst this was a time of embarrassment and anguish for my parents, I feel I must acknowledge it for Sarah. Sarah was hugely proud of that time in her life and would not want it to be passed over. Punk culture was and still is strongly associated with hedonism, hence the difficulty for society at that time. In a sense Sarah was hedonistic then, no surprise, given her age. But that was not why Sarah was proud of being a punk. She was proud because it was new and it was creative. Punk rockers were politically crea-tive – they made people think. And they were visually creative – they made people look. Sarah wanted people to look at her – she wanted people to notice and she wanted people to think about what she had to say – "Look at me, I'm alive, I can do things, I'm unique, life is special, to be lived." How better could she have said these things at that time at her age than to become a punk?

Sarah's desire to make the most of her experiences meant that, when the punk lifestyle started to get the better of her, rather than the other way round, she gave it all up and joined me in Brighton at university. She quickly developed into an adult incapable of being negative about anyone or anything. Whilst I would fight against people, she would fight to embrace them. She would meet new people and immediately determine to reward them with attention and fun. She arranged parties, trips out, games, even a new sport for her friends. She was the life and soul of any group event. People loved her. I remember when we first moved into a shared house in Brighton and within hours a man there who'd been most reluctant for us two 'student-types' to move in, pointing at Sarah and saying, "That one, she's a diamond."

There were only ever two things that really made Sarah unhappy – the ending of her marriage and her inability to have children. When her marriage ended she was incapable of resenting her situation and continued to see only the good in her husband. She continued to love him because of this, and the loss of one she loved was felt keenly until the end. She, however, still managed to make the most of her situation. Whilst many people spend years grieving and bitter, she only got low for minutes at a time and would then focus on her next opportunity. Some people would say that she should have come to terms with it, talked about it more. But this worked for Sarah. She didn't want to change her view of life and deliberate over things like people aren't always great or that love is fallible. She wanted to remain positive forever, and if this involved seeing her husband in a way different from how most see their ex's, then so be it. Similarly her lack of children did not become a huge source of bitterness, merely a sadness that served as a reminder to her of how important children are. She threw her maternal energies into looking after my children in particular, but also the children of her friends. She was present at Rosie's birth and for the first six months of Rosie's life in our shared house. I had desperately wanted a girl but thought I was carrying a boy. When the midwife said it was a girl I remember Sarah's face, lit up, saying, "Oh Anna, it's a girl, it's a girl!" She often said to me that that was one of the most special days in her life and particularly remembered travelling back to the house on that special Christmas Day, the Christmas lights glowing over Brighton, and discussing with the taxi-driver this amazing experience and the aptness of Rosie's name which they concluded was neither too posh nor too common. Sarah shared a special bond with Rosie. They shared many adventures together, Sarah acting as friend, big sister and second mother to Rosie. Whilst this bond was particularly close, Sarah also became close to Francesca, working out that things like cooking cakes would engage this rather independent and less affectionate child. Indeed, Sarah was always able to see each individual child as just that – she had a great gift for finding out what each child wanted from her and then providing it. During the last year of her life I lived with a friend and her two children. Sarah quickly found that the little girl wanted to put Sarah's earrings in and out and the boy, a little baby then, was fascinated with her watch. She dutifully provided them with these enjoyments whenever she was round.

This was Sarah: someone who could make something good for others out of her own sadness; someone who refused to allow a sadness to rule her or in any way change her view of the world to a less positive colour; someone who always appreciated what life gave her and someone who wanted to share that with others. She was a huge influence upon me and many others but now I must carry on through life without my sister in her proper place. There were so many things I expected to happen over the years. I thought she'd be there to bring me out of myself, to show me the good things in life, to help me laugh when life is difficult. I thought we might live together as two slightly dotty spinsters as we'd planned. That she would hold my hand, share my children's happiness, be a second grandmother to their kids, keep me mobile, outward and alive.

"But enough," Sarah would say. Whilst I am sure that if she knew what had happened to her and to us she would be hugely saddened, I also know that she would see something in it. She would stand here and say to us all, "But I had a good happy life and look, what a way to go. I couldn't have chosen a better way to go; it was so dramatic and so romantic. I'm at one with nature, remember me and have a great time living."

SARAH JONES – MY AUNTIE

Sarah was my auntie and she meant a lot to me. If I needed something from in or around town, Sarah would either get it for me, or take me into town with her after school. For Christmas, Sarah would take me into town to do Christmas shopping for all my family and friends. She would also go into town with me to buy my Christmas or birthday present, usually in January, to catch the January sales.

Eight weeks before Sarah went to Peru she took me in to Amanda Jones Beauty and Nail Salon to get our ears pierced. Sarah was getting her ears done for the second time and I was getting mine done for the first time. Sarah said, "I bagsy getting my ears pierced first," but I said "Oh, I wanted my ears pierced first," so Sarah, being her usual kind self, said "OK, I'll be last in getting my ears pierced, just for you."

In September 1999 Sarah took me on a cycling weekend in Reading with Trailbreak. We went on a few cycling trips and races, one of which was a family trip. Celia, Sarah and I went off, we had about four hours to get around the trail and get back before the time was up. We were on our way back when we realised that we only had 10 minutes left. We were climbing a slight hill which I found difficult. We could not stop or else we wouldn't get back in time. I climbed the hill with great difficulty but I didn't stop. We got back within the time, with 2 minutes to spare and Sarah said to me "We wouldn't have made the time if you had stopped. Well done Rosie!"

I love my Auntie Sarah. She is my only close Auntie. She cared about me and I could talk to her about everything and anything.

Sarah and I were similar in the way we dressed, both liked and enjoyed shopping and also our hair (as you can probably see!). This may be because for the first year of being on this planet, I lived with Sarah in a flat in Brighton.

Sarah was an important part of my life and I was very upset when I heard that she had passed away.

Francesca's speech

Me and Sarah made some cakes and she brought me a La La suit.

Matt's introduction to song number one

There is an ancient Tibetan saying which goes "It is better to live one year as a tiger than 100 years as a sheep." Well Sarah roared and burned bright for nearly 37 years . . . It wasn't enough.

On May the 15th this year, I was in Philadelphia. It was 9.00 a.m. where I was, five hours behind UK time. Dan, one of my flatmates, woke me up and told me there was a call from England. I took the phone, it was Dad telling me that we had lost Sarah.

This was definitely the worst day of my life. It was made worse because of the fact that I was so far away from home. Mum managed to get me on a flight that afternoon. I landed at Heathrow where my cousin Simon was waiting to take me home. I will always remember coming through customs and seeing all these people being reunited with their friends and family and all looking so happy. Simon and I were just crying.

Well it's down to me to introduce some of Sarah's favourite songs. Not an easy task as she had such a wide and varied taste in music. Over the last two months or so I have gone over Sarah's record collection, playing various tracks to Mum, Dad and Anna, trying to choose the ones she would have wanted played. I hope we got it right, Sarah.

When Sarah, Anna and I were children, our parents were hippies. We grew up listening to The Beatles, Joni Mitchell and Bob Dylan. I think Bob Dylan had the biggest influence on us. I know that Sarah listened to Dylan regularly. This first track was Sarah's favourite Dylan track. Many years ago she told me that she once wrote it as a Dear John letter to some bloke she had been seeing. I'm sure that if Sarah could see us all here today she would say something like, "Don't think twice, it's alright."

GROWING UP TOGETHER – Cindy

I first met Sarah in January 1971 – we were eight years old. It was Sarah's first day at Long Lane Primary School in Reading. The teacher asked me to show Sarah where her coat peg was. I remember looking across and seeing this girl, dressed in 'hippie' clothes, pale face, big eyes, long dark brown plaits and *serious* looking. In fact it turned out that she had a great sense of fun, adventurous, creative, intelligent, passionate, loyal and loving person and she became my best friend for the next 30 years.

I don't have one story to tell you about these early years of our childhood – just hundreds of memories playing over the woods – forming the Red Fox Gang – Sarah producing the Red Fox Gang Magazine; we loved animals – thought we'd be vets when we grew up, played make believe – got bored – got the giggles – moaned about school – talked and talked, fell out, made up, joined guides, went camping, left guides (without any badges), loved Abba, hated the Osmonds, would only wear flares and were generally inseparable.

Sarah was unconventional, adventurous – she'd be the one to go out and give things a go – she was also someone who developed intense passion about things. At around 16 years of age – Sarah got into Punk – leather jacket, leopard skin trousers, spiky multi-coloured hair, curled lip – adventurous, she took off on her own, following Siouxsie and the Banshees around the country.

She discovered skateboarding and it became her life, travelling around the country, competition events, and it wasn't about winning for Sarah, it was about being a part of the action, exhilaration, meeting new people, making new friends, then sailing in Brighton, then mountain biking – where again she became a well-known, well-loved person.

Sarah was a party girl – up for nights out in London – dancing 'til 4 – out to the Candy Bar with Vanessa and the girls, raucous dinner parties, staying up into the early hours with red wine and chatting – it was her that introduced me to the magic of 'Resolve' for the morning after.

Sarah had a strong sense of justice and spoke her mind in defence of what she believed to be right. When we were eight, I remember her losing her jumper and, getting cold, she told the teachers who did nothing. I remember her marching into the teachers' rest room and telling them that they were not doing their job, she was only eight, she was cold and she demanded that they help her find her jumper. They did.

Sarah was a good-hearted, generous person. Not 'vanillery-nice', but genuine, warm, non-judgemental. She got on well with so many different people – she was so easy to like and have fun with – friends in Reading here today remember dinner parties, fancy dress, and seeing her in 1999 with a bang and a 'duckboard'.

Sarah was a great friend. Karen told me how she will never forget Sarah's decision to throw a party for Karen after a relationship break-up, because she always believed she had to go on, get out there and make the most of life.

For me, Sarah offered unjudgemental, unconditional friendship, love and support. When my parents split up – she was there for me, when I came out she applauded and supported me, and when my relationship broke down – she was loyal to me.

Sarah loved her family. Mick, Barbara, Anna, Matt, Rosie, Francesca – she always spoke of them and they are a close and wonderful family.

Meeting Sarah and her family has been a massive influence in my life. I got to learn new things, think new thoughts, I got to see I could do more, and my life is different and richer for that. I know it sounds trite, but I would not be like I am if I had not known Sarah, and her family, and had her as part of my life for so many years.

I hold hundreds of memories of Sarah, all part of a colourful, powerful tapestry of our long friendship. I loved her, I admired her and I miss her – she'll always be with me.

OUR FRIEND – Nick (and Linda)

I first met Sarah eight years ago through mountain biking and although I am sure everyone will have different memories of her, these are a few words which help capture the spirit of my friendship with Sarah over the past eight years.

Ours was an easy, low-maintenance friendship, which had to survive periods of inactivity due to our busy schedules much like many friendships. But I always knew that it just took a phone call to carry on where we'd left off.

Sarah had a great sense of occasion, she was never happier than when she was planning the next event and wanted to get as many people involved as possible. She had a natural enthusiasm for life and for making life more exciting and loved to bring all her friends together, 'borrowing' Barbara and Mick's house to hold themed mountain bike parties, night-time bike races, beer-drinking challenges, desert island disc parties, chilli cooking contests, all carried off with her usual gusto.

One particular event sticks in my mind. Sarah organised a night-time bike race through Thetford Forest involving friends from all over the country. It was decided that half-way round the course everyone should stop and drink a beer. It transpired that each team arrived at this point at around the same time and proceeded to guzzle the beer which had been hidden there earlier in the day. Unfortunately the local constabulary happened to be passing and were attracted by the lights. Strangely they decided that 30 people covered in mud drinking beer in the middle of the night at the edge of the forest was not normal behaviour – even around Thetford.

Sarah was not always known for her diplomacy but immediately took the matter in hand and although I never knew exactly what it was she said, she managed to persuade the policemen that everything was totally in order allowing the event to continue.

Not only was she a strong and committed cyclist, she would whole-heartedly throw herself into anything that she did. Having mentioned to Sarah that my wife and I were thinking of joining a new gym being opened locally, it came as no great surprise when I finally got around to my first visit some weeks later, I discovered Sarah's name on the notice board for most improved fitness level, and while I would struggle to find excuses not to go, Sarah would be there as often as she could, soon getting to know everybody there.

Sarah was a character who wouldn't let things get in the way, although she was a late learner when it came to getting her driving licence, she had no reticence once she had achieved it. She immediately used the car as her passport to the whole country and would travel independently great distances to attend events and visit friends. She soon progressed from the motorised roller-skate that she had passed her test in to an Alfa Romeo, which she felt was far more in keeping with her lifestyle. I was always struck by her enjoyment of travel, which for a single person must often be quite daunting.

We shared a love of football and Sarah played it more often and with more ferocity than me or most men I know. We would often get together to watch crucial England matches on TV over a beer or two, which would normally end in dismal defeat! She inherited her support of Ipswich Town from her father and with me being a keen Norwich City fan – Ipswich's sworn enemy – as you might imagine it led to some lively debates. I am sure Sarah would be giving me a lot of stick over the positions of our teams now.

Living in Bury St Edmunds we are lucky enough to have our own fine local brewery – Greene King. Sarah did her best to sample their wares whenever possible and enjoyed introducing her unwary friends from the United States to some potent local brews that are quite unlike the Budweiser they are used to. Coincidentally, this would often be the night before an arduous bike ride. It was as if she was single-handedly trying to create a demand for Greene King Abbot Ale in California.

One such night was an invitational Abbot Ale drinking competition which one of our more robust local friends won easily but then did not resurface for several days.

I spoke this week to another good friend of ours who wasn't able to be here today, an American by the name of Greg Fuquay. Greg returned to his home in Alabama 18 months ago but asked for his unusually concise memory of Sarah to be passed on, I can't replicate Greg's accent, a mixture of Ipswich and Alabama twang but I do agree with his words: "Sarah was cool."

Matt's introduction to song number two

Most people have a favourite song or piece of music. I know I have. I sometimes have conversations with my closest friends about what are our favourite songs and what we would like played at our funerals. I had this conversation with Sarah. So I know for sure that this next song was her all-time favourite, and also the one she wanted played at her funeral. I know it's not quite a funeral but I guess it's close enough.

There is some irony in this tune. The opening line is "I always flirt with death." Something Sarah did on a regular basis. Also in the last verse there is the line "Long journeys wear me out, but I know I can't live without it". Again, this relates to Sarah. Here is Sarah's favourite song, "Another Girl, Another Planet".

SARAH – A COLLEAGUE, by Hazel Emslie

Although I had been in fairly regular contact with TVTC for a number of years because of the tests I had helped Alan Baddeley develop, I didn't really get to work with Sarah until I was asked to join Barbara and Jon Evans in devising a one-day training course on Selecting and Administering Cognitive Tests. The idea was that Sarah would do all the organising and Barbara, Jon and I would do the teaching.

Barbara suggested that we should all go away for a long weekend to write a book to accompany the workshop and told me to bring my eight-year-old daughter because Sarah was bringing Rosie. Sarah would look after Fiona for me during the day while we were writing the book.

So off we went to Center Parcs and Sarah would collect Fiona after breakfast and return her in the evening when we finished work. And she organised a wonderful programme of activities for the girls, cycling, nature walks, indoor sports, swimming – Fiona had a great time and thought Sarah was wonderful – and Jon, Barbara and I finished the book.

Then the workshops started and this is when I began to learn that Sarah wasn't just a very nice person, she was also a wonderful colleague.

We must have done between 20 and 25 workshops in the last five or six years. Sarah, of course, did all the hard work — she did the publicity, answered hundreds of phone calls, sent out all the letters plus the Center Parcs book, and on the day of the workshop, no matter how early I got there, Sarah was already there. She brought the score sheets we would need, always ensured we had the correct number of tests and manuals, she brought the tea, coffee, hot water, milk, biscuits and cups and was there to welcome the participants and put them at their ease. This was all done in such a calm, efficient manner with the minimum of fuss. All we had to do was concentrate on the teaching. Then during the day she appeared at break times with the tea and coffee and at lunch time she was there again to hand out what she always referred to as "your dinner money" before she took the participants across to the hospital concourse where they could buy their lunch. We really enjoyed all our workshops days — Sarah was fun to work with and was utterly reliable.

Between workshops there were often queries about what we had taught and the tests we had covered. Sarah always knew when to answer the questions herself and when to pass them on to the authors. When asked for a decision she would make one there and then, clearly and confidently. She was a very good communicator, had lots of patience, had a delightful sense of humour and an infectious enthusiasm for life.

It was a pleasure to work with Sarah. She was warm and friendly, elegant and reliable with a quiet confidence I always admired. I have nothing but very happy memories of the times we worked together and feel honoured to be asked to speak today about Sarah as a colleague.

A MOUNTAIN BIKER — Celia

Sarah, friend and partner in crime.

I was fortunate to know Sarah for the last year of her life. It was one of those friendships where we met and it felt as if we'd known each other all our lives.

During the time I knew Sarah, she spent most of her weekends away with the Trailbreak crowd. Wherever Sarah was, there was always laughter, fun and excitement, a dare and a joke and lots of adventure. She was a very well-known mountain biker and always had time to give someone a hand and help out.

She also introduced Mountain Bike Football to the Trailbreak week-ends, a sport which she and Gez invented. I got dragged into helping her and in memory of Sarah we will keep the tradition an ongoing event.

Sarah and I spent many an hour on the phone and our trips travelling to weekends away together were always special times where we shared a lot of laughs but sometimes also a tear or two.

She had the most incredible zest for life and wherever she went people always liked her very much.

Knowing Sarah as such a close friend I also knew her sad side – deep down in this brave little person. I think Sarah planned to go and make her peace at the river in Peru and knowing Sarah the way I did, I think she did it, which is why I think she was happy when she was taken away from us.

I'd like to finish by reading a quote from Kahlil Gibran's book, *The Prophet*:

And a youth said, Speak to us of Friendship
And he answered, saying:
Your friend is your needs answered.
He is your field which you sow with love and
Reap with thanksgiving.
And he is your board and your fireside.
For you come to him with your hunger, and you seek him for peace.

When your friend speaks his mind you fear not
The "nay" in your own mind, nor do you withhold the "ay."
And when he is silent your heart ceases not to
Listen to his heart;
For without words, in friendship, all thoughts, all
Desires, all expectations are born and shared, with
Joy that is unacclaimed.
When you part from your friend, you grieve not;
For that which you love most in him may be
Clearer in his absence, as the mountain to the climber
Is clearer from the plain.
                    (Reproduced from Gibran (1923) *The Prophet*)

Sarah was the loveliest sunshine to everyone that crossed her path. There are no words for our loss. But Sarah will remain, forever, that magnificent spark in my memory.

Matt's introduction to song number three

I used to work with Sarah, in fact she was my boss for a couple of years for Dad's company. When Dad wasn't around we had the radio on. We rarely agreed on what songs we liked. There was one tune, however, that we did both like. It is by a band called JAMES and the track is 'Feel like Fred Astaire'. Sarah always said this song made her feel very happy.

Barbara's introduction to a reading from *The July Ghost*

About three months ago I had a call at work from Mick. He was drafting the invitations to the memorial service and wanted my advice about the wording. He said, "I want to say, 'Do come, Sarah would love you to be there', but that sounds as if she were alive. If I say, 'Do come, Sarah would have loved you to be there', that sounds inelegant. What shall I say?" I replied, "Say, 'Do come, Sarah would love you to be there', that sounds right to me." "Yes," said Mick, "Death overcomes grammar."

Soon after that we went to a meeting of The Compassionate Friends and attended a session of poetry and prose readings. One of the readings was from A. S. Byatt's *The July Ghost*. A. S. Byatt lost her own son. In the story she describes a woman who takes in a lodger in July. On several occasions the lodger sees a boy in the garden – it is the ghost of the woman's son who was killed. One of the things that struck me was the woman describing her reaction when she heard the boy was dead: "is dead, that will go on and on and on – to the end of time". The continuous present tense bothered her and then she felt how ridiculous to be concerned with grammar at this time.

It was so similar to our concern with grammar that I wanted to read part of the story to you. Noel is the woman's husband.

"When it happened, they got Noel, and Noel came in and shouted my name, like he did the other day, that's why I screamed, because it – seemed the same – and then they said, he is dead, and I thought coolly, is dead, that will go on and on and on till the end of time, it's a continuous present tense, one thinks the most ridiculous things, there I was thinking about grammar, the verb to be, when it ends to be dead . . . And then I came out into the garden, and I half saw, in my mind's eye, a kind of ghost of his face, just the eyes and hair, coming towards me – like every day waiting for him to come home, the way you think of your son, with such pleasure, when he's – not there – and I – I thought – no, I won't see him, because he is dead, and I won't dream about him because he is dead, I'll be rational and practical and continue to live because one must, and there was Noel . . .

"I got it wrong, you see. I was so sensible, and then I was so shocked because I couldn't get to want anything – I couldn't talk to Noel – I – I – made Noel take away, destroy, all the photos, I – didn't dream, you can will not to dream. I didn't . . . visit a grave, flowers, there isn't any

point. I was so sensible. Only my body wouldn't stop waiting and all it
wants is to — to see that boy. That boy. That boy you — saw."

SARAH IN PERU — Susan

There were 10 of us plus the guides on the trip to Peru. As the only two
girls on the trip Sarah and I inevitably spent quite a bit of time together.

The trip started in Arequipa where we had our last night in a decent
hotel with proper beds and hot showers. This was where I first met
Sarah and we got on well from the start.

We had been warned that our luggage was severely restricted but Sarah
decided that the one essential she could not manage without was her
hair-removing wax. A girl after my own heart, I thought!

We then had a 10-hour bus journey to the town of Cotahuasi. As we
had to go via the airport to pick up some missing luggage, Sarah had the
opportunity to buy a bottle of Johnnie Walker just to keep us warm at
night.

Definitely a girl after my own heart.

On the bus trip we passed through spectacular scenery and we all got
to know each other well, 10 hours is a very long time to spend on a bus!

Sarah was excited and apprehensive about having "packed it all in" for
six months and worried about being homesick but determined to make
the most of it.

In Cotahuasi town we stayed in a hostel. Sarah and I shared a room
which was pretty basic — we were warned it might be better to sleep in
our bags rather than the beds! And to avoid the shower at all costs.

We then had a three-day trek to the river. This was when Sarah introduced us to the game of "If they made a film of this trip who would play
you?" For some reason I gather the boys cast French and Saunders as
Sarah and I . . . not sure why.

The trek was spectacular if a bit vertigo-inducing. I gather Sarah didn't
have the greatest head for heights. She did spot some brilliant downhill
mountain bike tracks though and she had clearly had a great time when
she had been in Peru before on the mountain bike run.

We walked through cactus forests and swam at the edge of a fantastic
waterfall and camped out under the stars.

When we reached the river we set up camp. The girls' dormitory was
two patches of sand which were just long enough for Sarah and I to sleep
on. We then spent what seemed like hours digging rocks out of our 'beds'.
Luckily, we both found it very funny (I'm not too sure why) and we were
very proud of our efforts, despite having so little room we couldn't even
turn over at night.

One day we went to a hot sulphur pool. When we got out, having floated around for a bit, Sarah produced razor and gel and shaved her legs. I was very impressed that she wasn't prepared to let standards slip.

Because we were getting up at dawn, everyone tended to go to bed fairly early particularly as the canyon was so deep that the sun disappeared from view at about 4 o'clock. Despite being younger and probably fitter than Sarah and I, the boys generally were in bed long before us. Our big challenge each night was to stay up until 9 o'clock and most nights we made it, helped by the odd nip of the previously mentioned Johnnie Walker cooled in the river.

On trips like this you tend to talk about personal things quite freely and what was clear from Sarah was how much she loved her family and friends.

My strongest memory of Sarah is one day lying by the river sunbathing, under a brilliant blue sky, looking at the most amazing country.

Sarah said that it made her realise how lucky we were to be able to do this sort of trip and experience these things and we both agreed that life was for living and not to be wasted.

We didn't know Sarah as well as the rest of you but she certainly lived life. We're all glad we met her.

Matt's introduction to song number four

When we went to Peru the week after Sarah's death, one of the hardest days for us all was the day we had to go through Sarah's belongings in a hotel in Cusco. Dad said we should just ship everything back, however, I thought it was likely that Sarah would have some coca leaves in her bag. Although these leaves are legal in Peru, they are highly illegal in the UK. We did not find any. However, we did find her CD Walkman. Anna and I had bought this for Sarah the previous Christmas. She seemed delighted with this gift though said that she would only have room to take about five CDs with her. I'm sure she struggled with what to take. When we found the Walkman, the CD that was in it was by a band called The Waterboys. I knew that the first track on the album was a favourite of Sarah's. So here is "Fisherman's Blues".

Barbara's introduction to a reading from *Letter to a Younger Son*

In the weeks after Sarah's death I needed to read about death, grief, and bereavement, particularly about bereaved parents. This reading, together with support from family and friends helped me through those black, black days. Some of the support was fantastic, the immediate family was the most important but my sister-in-law Carol was a huge strength and help. My secretary, Julia, gave enormous practical help, my friend and colleague, Narinder, really turned up trumps and there were of course many others to whom I will always be grateful for allowing me to talk and to cry without expecting me to pick up the pieces before I was ready.

One piece of writing I returned to many times was a letter written by a father to his younger son after the older son had died. I want to read part of this to you now.

Christopher Leach's book, *Letter to a Younger Son* is about the death of a child but some of its conclusions could be applicable to anyone.

"[Death] can cast us down for more than the necessary period of mourning. It can blight our days, so that we exist forever in that chill, unexpected land. It can whisper to us that life is ultimately meaningless. If what awaits us at the end is our own obliteration, and the same grief we now feel is transferred like a disease to those who love us, what is the point in going on, of ambition, of rearing children who too will one day fail and fall? It can hang like an albatross about our necks; or enclose our heart in ice; or change us so deeply that even our closest friends turn away. At its worst, death has taken one life; and is offered another.

And yet it can enrich us. We can live for those who have gone. We can pack into our lives that extra time the dead have given us. For they have given us time: the expanded moment that comes when we realize that, for us, the blood still moves; the world is still there to be explored and made over; that, for now, this minute, this hour, this day, we are free of pain and hunger; that, though we still mourn in the deepest part of our being, death has liberated us, has made us see the transitory nature of everything; and life, being transitory, is thus infinitely more precious; commanding more attention than ever we gave it when we went on our way, still unthinking children, before death opened our minds, sharpened our eyes; and set us free. . . .

What have I discovered?

I have discovered the ache of loss, the coming of a deeper grief than I thought possible. I have witnessed the extinction of a personality, and have been made to face the continuing certainty that never again shall I see that loved individual. I have discovered the transitoriness of all things; and their consequent worth while they are with me. I have discovered the uncaring nature of the universe; and yet, as a living entity, I am sustained in an attempt to permit me wholeness. I have discovered that men make religions out of their own limited apprehensions of their world; and that, outside their own imaginings, exists a mystery which they can never name, only trust. I have discovered that tragedy need not diminish those who suffer it; that it has a positive aspect; and that, having won through to some kind of angry acceptance, brings a more realistic view of life, and a deeper resonance.

What have I learned?

I have learned what is important. That, faced with the ultimate, things move to a correct proportion. That every day free of pain is a bonus. That there exists in myself acres of my nature which are still undiscovered: one has been opened by grief – what others may be known in the future, sprung by a more disciplined art, or travel, or meetings with strangers? I have learned to be wary: the time that is left is savoured now, dwelt upon, treasured. I have learned compassion: I know what it is to mourn. I have learned, too late in one respect, that I have not cared enough. And now it is too late: for him. But not for you. [I have learned the strength of my own creativity: that, called upon, it never fails to respond, and joyfully. It rushes in to heal; and for that I am grateful.] I have learned to expect death; and although I resent its intrusion, I grant its cold necessity.

What do I believe?

I believe I share in the making of the universe, perhaps many universes. I am engaged in a stupendous working out of forces, the nature of which I have only the minutest of understanding; and yet know intuitively that I, and even the smallest atom-fizzing rock, are somehow part of an experiment which is in its first, possibly uncertain stages. I believe in life; and my belief is strengthened by death. I believe that somewhere there exists an answer, but that the wrong questions are being asked; or even that no question is needed. I believe it is not what happens to a man that matters, but his opinion of what happens. I believe to laugh at life is better, and saner, than condemning it: the experiment may be the work of a mad scientist, but to die laughing is not a bad way to go.

And I have always believed, in life, the best is yet to come. I cannot speak for the other side, the dark."

(Reproduced from Leach, Letter to a Younger Son)

Mick's speech

SARAH: SHE "WHO KISSES THE JOY AS IT FLIES"

One of the things that came across while I was looking through all the family videos to see what moments we shared with Sarah, was that whenever there was a family occasion when speeches were made, I tended to ramble on and on and on, so, those of you from the extended family who have suffered from my previous speeches in the past, will be glad to know that I'm going to keep my speech very short today. Anyway, we have heard some exceptional accounts of Sarah's life from others already, and I'd like to single out our lovely daughter Anna's remarkable tribute: I think it should be published one day so that others outside this hall can appreciate what Sarah meant to us all. Certainly, when I first heard it I realised that Anna had got down to the very roots of Sarah's life and soul, and that I had very little to add that would enhance her portrait of Sarah.

I quoted William Blake for the title of my speech because whenever I think of Sarah now, I think of these lines. The whole quotation is:

He who binds to himself a joy
Doth the winged life destroy
But he who kisses the joy as it flies
Lives in Eternity's sunrise.

What I think Blake is telling us is that those of us who are always trying to hold on to happiness in the form of possessions, money, friendship, power, success, or even love, fail to achieve real happiness because the act of possessing nullifies any joy that we might experience. Whereas, those very few bright spirits among us who do not try to possess, hold on to, or bind to themselves the things or people they love, can experience joy. Sarah, I know, kissed "the joy as it flies". She was such a good person who allowed others to live their own lives. She was never interested in binding anyone to her own will. That, I think, is why she was such an exceptional person who is missed so much by all of us. And that is why she will, for all of us, always live "in Eternity's sunrise". Another way of putting this is to recognise that Sarah was an innocent person who was genuinely good. I don't mean 'good' in the conventional sense. Indeed, I don't think Sarah can be judged by convention: she was certainly capable of great anger at times, which sometimes exploded into magnificent verbal abuse. For example, I remember a time when the family was having a meal at a local restaurant and an elderly man and his partner were critical of Francesca because she was standing on her chair. Sarah rounded on him by saying she hoped he would go to hell and be plagued by noisy children for the rest of his time there. Also, I think – although she voted Labour – I think she was inclined towards liberalism as far as her sexuality was concerned. But Sarah was innocent in the deepest sense, so much so that I believe she was capable of making me believe in a time when all mankind was innocent, a time before the fall of man – in its mythological sense, a time when we were all innocent perhaps.

I frequently said to Barbara that Sarah had a peace which passed all understanding, and indeed this biblical reference is apt for her. I also said on several occasions in recent times, that Sarah was my true heroine. And I believed this because she was so strong in adversity, she always bounced back. She had a lot to bounce back from in recent years, not least the fact that she lived on her own for two years prior to moving in with us for her last five months. For those two years she had to return to her little rural flat, with nobody but her two cats for company. Yet she smiled through this, and got on with her life of entertaining and organising biking adventures for her friends. She was a great hostess who cared deeply for her guests. She also bounced back from being childless and never resorted to feeling sorry for herself, even though her greatest ambition was to be a mother of a large family. And what a mother she would have been! We only have to look at some of the photographs of Sarah with her nieces to see how much love she gave them. And how terribly sad it is that she won't be able to continue being their supportive carer through to their own motherhoods. We want her back, we need her, there are many, many decades she should have been with us . . . But I must try not to bind her to me. I have to let go, I have to kiss the joy as it flies.

Max Milligan's e-mail

In Cuzco and the Cotahuasi Canyon I briefly got to know Sarah, a woman who you all knew extremely well.

The Sarah I met in Peru seems to have been the sum of all those memories you must have of her. She had decided what she wanted to do with her life and had reached a point where she could do it.

Therein lies the tragedy of her early death; but also the tiny solace we can gain from the fact that she ended her days doing exactly what she loved to do.

Like me, she had found herself living out the fantasy of making a career of adventure travel. Numerous articles in magazines and websites had enabled her to come to such a place of great beauty and excitement not as a tourist, but as someone who was involved, who stayed awhile longer, who got to know and love Peru and return again.

Here she was, as an Adventure Travel Writer. 'Adventure Travel', the phrase says it all. One thinks of "Out of Africa", "Indiana Jones", Mount Everest, the Amazon. It was our fantasy, suddenly come true.

She asked me if I would like to take photographs to go with her articles about Mountain Biking, Trekking and River Rafting, and I said "Yes".

I soon found out that she was tough and brave with a sharp sense of humour and actually far more adventurous than a lot of us male outdoors types like to think ourselves, something she took great pleasure in!

The night before Sarah died, we sat around the campfire on the sandy banks of the river. The moon was nearly full and the landscape surrounding us, extremely dramatic. We thanked our lucky stars that we were there, in real wilderness, beyond the noise, pollution and everyday-life problems that every traveller loves to avoid.

The conversation swung, as it often does, to the risks involved and those dear friends we had each lost, engaged in such dangerous pursuits. In remembering our lost friends, it was as if their memories encouraged us to get out there and live out our dreams, not to be timid. Sarah was clear: "Better to go out here, than under a bus."

We all agreed. Any one of us could die, yet none of us would dream of giving it up. We believed when your number was up, it would be time to go, no matter where you were, or what you were doing.

The intensity of such a life is what she lived for, and it reminds me of a line from "If", Rudyard Kipling's impossibly idealistic poem, "If you can fill the unforgiving minute, with sixty seconds worth of distance run"... Sarah filled her minutes, days and months and it was my pleasure to have run with her, if only for a short while.

I remember her with a smile. As we stood in a circle in the traditional team bonding before a big rapid, she said, "It's alright for you, you can jump out of the boat anytime, and snap away without looking like a wimp." She smiled and as the raft pulled away she shouted, "and I'm not at all sure you're the person to be trusted with the chocolate rations." Minutes later she was gone.

I think of her today from here in Peru, and of Barbara, Mick, Anna and Matthew and about the short time left to each of us before we see her again.

The Finnish Neuropsychological Society of which Barbara is an honorary lifetime member sent a card and flowers. The card said:

The brave don't live long but the cautious don't live at all. Here's to the brave.

Barbara's introduction to the final song

We are going to finish with a song whose words we read out at the River Cotahuasi in May when we held our little ceremony for Sarah. It is another Dylan song that we all love, "Forever Young", and, of course, Sarah will be Forever Young now.

We felt the day had gone well and Sarah would have loved it. Many, many people were crying. I was sitting between Mick and Matthew who sobbed at every piece of music. I had my arms around the two of them. There was a mirror in front of us. I had not realised that people behind could see us in this mirror. Robert, Julia's husband, said that seeing the three of us like that had upset him the most. Alison (Jon's wife) said she found Francesca's few words really moved her. Jon and Alison have a daughter Hannah slightly older than Francesca.

People now had a clearer picture of Sarah. Even those of us who knew her so well learned about new aspects of her personality. My cousin Ann who had not seen Sarah since she was two or three years old, said, "I feel I know her now."

In addition to Susan, there were two young men who had been on Sarah's raft, Chris and Martin. I was talking to the three of them afterwards and heard once more that Sarah appeared to have been in distress early on. "How do you know?" I asked, "Was she screaming, was she bleeding?" "No, no," came the reply. "Well what makes everyone say she appeared to be in distress?" I asked. The three looked at each other as if deciding whether we should be told. Finally Martin said that when she was seen in the water, her head was at a strange angle. They thought she had broken her neck or dislocated her shoulder. Martin told me that everyone believed she had lost consciousness very quickly and that she may have died from these injuries and not from drowning. I thought a dislocated shoulder would not kill her in a few seconds but maybe a broken neck did. I felt so anguished for my poor daughter – poor, poor Sarah. They were right to tell me, but it was so hard. Chris, the youngest of the three and the last to be rescued, was clearly distressed. I asked them what they thought of the video. Chris said, "I couldn't look at it." I felt very close to these three young people, the last ones to see Sarah alive.

People left and we went home feeling pleased, exhausted and emotionally drained. As I feared, I slept badly that night and went over all the talks, the songs, the videos, what people had said, how good the Athenaeum staff had been and a million other things. The next two days were bad. I had been strong on Sunday but no longer. It felt like those early days all over again. I cried almost non-stop on Monday and Tuesday at work. I had several letters and e-mails about the service saying how special it was, how memorable it was and in some cases how it changed people's lives. Paul Burgess, a colleague from London, was very impressed and said how much he appreciated the music. Here are a few of the messages that came.

Dear Mick, Barbara and family,

I would just like to say thank you for including us in the celebration of Sarah's life.

It meant a lot to me (and I'm sure to Chris and Martin) to be included in what was a lovely tribute to Sarah and helped us to understand what made her the person that she was.

It was all very moving but I noticed in particular the quote from Tina Emery saying how grateful she was to her parents that they had given her the confidence to 'fulfil her dreams'. You also gave Sarah that confidence and it was clear how many people loved her because of it.

I meant it when I said that if you want to contact me at any time to talk about the trip I'll be glad to do so and Chris and Martin feel the same.

Thank you again and I hope that Sunday helped you all as well.

Love, Susan

Dear Barbara and Mick,

Thank you for asking us to the memorial day for Sarah. It was so good to see you both and we were just full of admiration for you all, making such a moving, thought-provoking and at times exhilarating occasion for us to remember and think about Sarah. We felt we ended up knowing her better. We were especially moved by Anna and Matthew who were so warm and generous to everyone, despite the continuing shock of it all.

I know you're very busy but if you do get the chance to visit Southampton do come and stay. I'm retiring in December and will have more time to be human, I hope. With much love to all of you.

Lindsay and Sally

I had to stay late on Tuesday as there was a meeting arranged about rehabilitation research. William, the unit director, was there. He came into my room after the meeting to see how I was. Although it was good of him to do so, I knew I would start weeping again. I did and was so exhausted. I left at 5.50. When I arrived home Mick showed me a piece about the memorial service in the *East Anglian* newspaper and there was a short piece on "Look East", the local BBC news programme. Because of the usual need for such programmes to reduce all pieces of news in order to fit them into their programme slot, only Mick's speech was quoted. There was no mention of her mother, her sister or her brother, all of whom were greatly affected by her death. Here are some of the pieces about the service and about Sarah. The last one is from a mountain bike magazine.

Reports from *The Mercury*, Friday October 6th, 2000

WOMAN DIES IN RAFTING HOLIDAY

Tributes have been paid to an adventurer from Suffolk after she drowned in an accident while white-water rafting in the world's largest canyon.

Freelance journalist Sarah Jones, 36, was thrown from the raft and was last seen floating unconscious in the rapidly-flowing river in a remote part of southern Peru. Her body has not been found.

The horrific accident happened less than a week into a six-month action-packed trip in which Sarah, a leading British mountain biker journalist, had hoped to 'reconsider her life'.

It is thought the sports enthusiast was injured and knocked unconscious as her four fellow crew members were plucked to safety.

A guide risked his life by plunging into the water in a desperate attempt to save Sarah but was unable to reach her.

Despite a lengthy air and land search financed by her distraught family, from Flempton, near Bury St Edmunds, Sarah's body has not been recovered.

A single shoe was discovered several weeks later, washed up on a bank.

Peruvian bureaucracy means her family may have to wait two years before a death certificate is issued, and Sarah's affairs are settled.

The tragedy struck on May 12, but her grieving father Mick Wilson spoke publicly for the first time about his daughter's death, calling for the introduction of international safety regulations.

He made his call a day after a memorial service was held in Bury St Edmunds to celebrate Sarah's life.

Sarah had been white-water rafting once before along the Cotahuasi – one of the world's most dangerous rivers.

Mr Wilson, 65, said his daughter, who lived in Pakenham before separating from her husband, would have been aware of the dangers.

"As far as I know there were safety measures in place, such as ropes across the river and boats nearby but you can't guarantee safety in those kinds of rivers.

"If you go scuba-diving you have to pass tests and there are internationally recognised safety procedures.

"My view is there should be some sort of certification to say what types of rivers you have been on and the kind of experience you have."

He said that Sarah had "an enormous zest for life".

Teresa O'Boyle

EMOTIONAL SERVICE REMEMBERS 'BEST PERSON'

Family and friends remembered Sarah Jones at an emotional service which marked her love of life.

It was held in Bury St Edmunds's Athenaeum and included a photographic exhibition put together by her beloved family.

Some of Sarah's favourite songs by artists such as Bob Dylan and The Waterboys were played during the ceremony, and the thoughts of people whose lives Sarah had touched were recorded in a specially designed programme.

Sarah's mother, Barbara Wilson, described her death as the worst thing that had ever happened.

"We are in total despair. She was the best person in the family, always good and kind, fair and just – but a risk-taker," she wrote.

Her father Mick Wilson said: "Sarah was the heart of the family from which all of us drew our strength."

Sarah, 36, took up skate-boarding and was selected for the English team, aged just 14.

She became a leading punk exponent while a teenager, and wrote two plays before taking a sociology degree course at the University of Sussex.

There she became the secretary of the sailing club before developing a love of mountain biking about 15 years ago.

She contributed to specialist magazines including *Mountain Biking UK* and *Global Adventure*, becoming a leading journalist in the sport.

Sarah organised a number of exhibitions and races and was an organiser of mountain bike rides in Thetford Forest.

Her work took her all over the world and she had been to Peru on previous mountain bike expeditions.

Obituary: Sarah Jones

Readers of *Global Adventure* will have appreciated Sarah Jones' descriptions of her mountain biking journeys through Peru and other places. The immensely courageous and fun-loving Sarah was a fine journalist who could bring the spirit of a place alive in her writing. Many people in the mountain biking world were shocked to hear of her death through drowning as a result of a white water rafting accident in Peru on May 12th. Her body has never been found.

Sarah was loved by all who knew her. She was a great organiser of parties and mountain biking rides, who brought light into the lives of others. Her journalism started with the production of a classic fanzine, "Bad News", which combined scurrilous commentary with humour that made you laugh out loud. Always true to herself, in her 36 years Sarah impressed others with her 'live-and-let-live' philosophy, her love of adventure and risk-taking, and her beautiful nature.

Two of Sarah's closest friends, Alison and John, describing a Christmas card they once received from Sarah, wrote: It's a photograph of a young boy cruising down the road on his BMX bike, his head thrown back and his mouth wide with laughter and glee. Inside the card it just says "Joy to the world". Let's take this as her message to all of us.

(Reproduced by permission of *Global Adventure*.)

A card from Chris, the young rafter, arrived on Wednesday 4th. He said he wanted to speak to us more at the service but had found it too difficult. He had been greatly affected by Sarah's death. He told us that the night she died (she had died about midday), there was a huge thunderstorm. This was in an area of the Andes where it hardly ever rained. We had heard about this storm on our trip to Peru from Max and the owner of the travel company. Max also told us they had lit candles for Sarah and a Swiss nun working nearby said a mass for her the following day. Chris told us the guides were surprised at the storm as it was so rare. He went on to say that he was the last to go to bed and was looking at the rain, falling on a tarpaulin put up because of the storm. He saw lights flickering on the tarpaulin. There was no explanation for the lights and he felt it was Sarah saying she was all right.

This is my reply to this distressed young man. He never wrote back.

Dear Chris,

Thank you for your very special card and for coming on Sunday. You, Martin and Susan were indeed very welcome. We wanted people from the trip to be there and really appreciate you writing to us.

We understand how distressing it must have been for you and the others on the trip. What a terrible thing to happen on your trip that was supposed to be so wonderful. Also, we are more kindly disposed to [the owner of the travel company] now. When we got home on Sunday evening there was a warm, kind e-mail from him saying he wished he could be at the service and how sorry he was etc. If only he'd said all that in Peru. I expect it was guilt that made him so withdrawn there.

Chris, we would dearly love to have a copy of your diary for May 12th – even if it doesn't add anything new, it would help us get closer to Sarah.

Also Chris, if you want to talk to us please phone or come to visit. We have had so much support from family and friends and the group for bereaved parents. I doubt you young people have a proper network to turn to in your distress. Mick and I feel close to you, Martin and Susan because you were the last to see our lovely Sarah. And you seem to realise that she was special – as indeed she was.

Please keep in touch – perhaps Sarah *was* communicating with you via the flickering light. It sounds just like the kind of thing she would have done.

With love and best wishes,

Barbara (A. Wilson)

Sarah's mum

◇

CHAPTER SIX

Can you make a phone call if you're dead?

2003

Looking back on Sarah's life, as we frequently do these days in an act of re-living the past, we can pick out various stages of development in which her personality and behaviour seemed to represent fairly lengthy intervals. There was her babyhood, her first year when she was our only child; then her childhood at primary school; her life as a teenager; her rebellion when she became a punk, her student days; and then adulthood when she worked as a publishing assistant for her dad. Thankfully, at all these stages, even the punkdom, Sarah remained in close touch with mum and dad and her brother and sister.

Mick was working in a school in Birchington, Kent, when Sarah was born. We were renting a cottage in St Nicholas at Wade, quite near Canterbury. Unlike her death, which was sudden, her birth was slow and eventually had to be completed by a Caesarean operation. We were of course thrilled at this baby, she was all we had ever wanted, lovely, healthy and alert. We showed her off wherever we went and she rewarded everybody with her winning ways and adorable smile. As members of the 60s generation we thought of ourselves as being pretty liberated and it wasn't long before we were involved in the people, parties and protests of those days, which themselves were stimulated by the music of the Beatles, Stones, and most of all Dylan.

Within three years Anna and Matthew were born, both in Colchester where Mick had returned to teach in a secondary modern school, known as Monkwick County Secondary. Life for Barbara, however, was frustrating as a housewife and it is obvious now that she was not using her intellectual potential in that role. Because of Mick's success at teaching he eventually got a job at a training college for teachers in Reading and we moved there. Barbara, who had pursued various A-levels at evening classes, obtained entry to Reading University to study Psychology, and really she has never looked back career-wise since those days. She obtained a first class honours degree, then her masters degree, and soon followed this with a PhD. There was no stopping her and her subsequent career has been periodically marked by honours of all kinds, including an OBE, publication of over 250 journal articles, 11 books, and countless chapters (so far!).

While Barbara was pursuing her career Mick was in the enviable position of looking after the three children. It was he who got them to school, who was there to meet them after school, who cooked the evening meals. He loved this life and now thanks his lucky stars that he was able to spend so much time with his kids, although it did mean that his own career suffered from lack of commitment. We were a very liberated family and husband and wife shared all the chores. Barbara cooked at weekends and did all the laundry, Mick cleaned the house, cooked on weekdays, and the two of them shopped together. The three children seemed to respond well to this family life. They were happy, never ill, and were lucky enough to be taught at an excellent primary school where creativity and child-centred education flourished. We can see them now, in their colourful and somewhat eccentric, hippy clothes. In fact we were perhaps too far out for most of our neighbours who lived in the suburbs of Reading. In later life Sarah, Anna and Matthew frequently referred to this period as being somewhat difficult for them because they were thought of as outsiders − 'gypsies' as they were sometimes called − and there must have been something wrong with their dad because he cooked and cleaned the house!

Generally, though, family life was idyllic and perhaps best marked by the setting up of the 'Red Fox Gang'. This was a gang consisting of Mick, Sarah, Anna, Matthew, and a couple of Sarah's friends. As we lived opposite the lovely Sulham Woods we would spend much of our time there, playing games of imagination and daring as we walked on to the lovely curve of the River Thames at Pangbourne where we usually had a drink and snack. We still have the sledge we bought for them, named (somewhat in 'Citizen Kane' style) 'Red Fox'. It was hardly ever used as snow seemed to miss Reading every year we were there! Later on, fishing became a part of our lives, especially for Matthew and Mick, and the two of them even used to poach trout from one of the private rivers in that area. One day Matthew fell in the Thames fully clothed. As he bobbed up, Mick grabbed him and pulled him out, and the pair of them ran the mile and a half home to get Matthew into a hot bath.

Sarah responded fully to this life: she loved the world of the imagination and was always telling herself and others magical stories. She was a voracious reader and was always with a book. We often laugh at the way she would be cleaning her teeth with a book she was reading in the other hand or propped up against the washbasin. She played great games of drama with Anna and Matthew, always getting them to put on costumes from old clothes and present plays to others. The three of them were encouraged to write stories and poems and in the early days, even before they could write, Mick was copying their stories in typescript as they spoke them. The type-written pages were then given to the children and they added their own colourful illustrations. In this way several books were made, although none published. We compare those halcyon days of education with the rather monotonous, seemingly dull and uncreative education our grandchildren receive as they pursue the national curriculum, fill in the blanks, and become efficient in spelling and the passing of exams − even at the age of seven, for God's sake!

As teenagers, Sarah, Anna and Matthew got heavily involved in skate-boarding, which was a very long-lasting craze in the seventies. In fact Matthew, like many of his contemporaries, still skate-boards as a relaxing pastime. Sarah was, as always, quite a daredevil and reached a high enough level to be selected for the England girl's team. We have a lovely picture of her with the fashionable long curled hair of those days, holding her skate-board with considerable pride.

Then suddenly Sarah was a punk and changed her image completely. This was a shock to us, as you might imagine. She rapidly entered into the punk way of life and soon moved into a commune. Although she had her own room in our house she preferred to live in a squat about three hundred yards up the road from us. As usual Sarah did not do things in half measures. She not only became a punk but had to be one of the leading punks in the town. So her clothes and hairstyle were even more outrageous than some of the punks who were simply in it for the purpose of being fashionable. Sarah had to take on the punk philosophy, which meant not working at anything that might lead to advancement of a materialistic kind.

Fortunately for us, we always remained in contact with Sarah during this period: she always had a room waiting for her, and we tried as hard as possible not to be critical – although our hearts were bleeding for the daughter who had previously been so involved in her studies. She was no longer interested in her A-levels and pulled out of college. We had some laughs about her friends and way of life and one day Mick gave in to her pleas for him to make an appearance with a punk band, the members of which Sarah knew quite well. Mick had been playing trumpet for a number of years with a jazz band that was quite well known in the Reading area. Sarah wanted him to play just for one session ("Just one number then Dad!") with a punk band in a pub near the railway station on a Sunday night. Mick had resisted for several months but finally gave in and said he would turn up – although he wouldn't guarantee that he'd join the band on stage. On the night in question Mick turned up and was slightly perturbed to discover that the all-male band, a group of fairly tough and somewhat ugly punk types, were all dressed as old-style female nurses. This was odd enough, but the audience was even more strange. It consisted of the most extra-ordinarily dressed punks you can imagine, they were pretty high on booze, and they swayed threateningly towards the stage and even tried to get up on it. In fact the band and the audience were as one, united in their determination to be as loud and outra-geous as possible. However, the most daunting thing for Mick was that he could see some of his academic associates from the University of Reading standing at the back of the hall, obviously having come to view the punk show, perhaps slumming it for the night, or maybe conducting a sociological study?

Mick waited until the last number of the night was called and Sarah came over to remonstrate. So he got up on stage, the band started to play, in what key Mick never found out. He just stood there blasting away and wiggling the trumpet valves as though he were playing "The Flight of the Bumble Bee". The audience thought this was great and screamed their delight. But because of the constant wiggling of the valves one of them became unscrewed and flew out and across the stage. Mick made a dive for it and ended up scrabbling amongst the feet of the 'nurses' until he found the missing spring and valve head. The audience thought all of this was great, and indeed one tall punk male came up to Mick at the finish of the number and said, "That was great when your instrument came apart. You must keep that in the act!"

Well, Mick took some stick back at work on Monday but as far as the punks were concerned he was a hero, and for the first time in many years his eldest daughter showered him with approval.

Sarah's life in the squat, and her interest in the punk way of life lasted for one or two years more but then she gave it all up in order to become a student once more. She broke free from the punk philosophy by writing two short plays about their life of drugs and booze and anarchy. We still have the plays and maybe one day they will be produced on stage? They are both extremely funny, and one in particular is based on a real life experience which involved the punks in the squat going to the Royal Berkshire Hospital to raid the fruit and drinks machine there. It ends up with the punks in all their splendour, boots, chains and Mohican hair styles, being chased through the hospital by doctors in white uniforms.

At about this time Sarah was introduced to sailing and typically she took to the riskiness of it. She managed also to get into Sussex University to study Sociology. At university she became an ardent sailor and spent all her spare time at sea. Nothing worried her, not even sailing in a Force 8 across the Channel. By this time Mick had taken up publishing and ran a small company. Sarah, lacking any real ambition to be a sociologist or teacher or whatever at this time, fell into Mick's business and became a manager. It was great for us because we saw her every day. She married Gerard and this we thought was a real love match. Sarah was very happy in these days. She and Gez had taken up the sport of mountain biking. They loved getting away at weekends to attend mountain biking rallies and races and they made strong friends with a group of committed bikers, some of whom worked as journalists. Both took up journalism on an amateur basis and contributed a number of articles to magazines. They even started up their own mountain biking fanzine, which achieved some notoriety in the mountain biking world. Sarah was always a good writer and showed real talent for journalism. She also helped her husband overcome his problems with dyslexia so that he, too, was able to contribute articles to the fanzine. They were, to all intents and purposes, a happily married couple. They lived with us for a few years and then began to rent properties in the Suffolk area where we now lived. Unfortunately, their marriage went wrong and for the last two years of her life Sarah lived on her own. She continued to work with Mick and the family saw her most days. She travelled with Barbara and the two became wonderful friends as a result of their journeys.

But Sarah had been to Peru and fell in love with the country. She was unhappy as a result of the failure of her marriage, and she was growing bored with her work as a publisher. She decided to go to Peru again and intended to continue her journalism while there. We both thought this was the best thing for her to do. She needed to make a clean break from her previous work and needed the challenge of a new start. We helped all we could to prepare for Peru and her new life there. Fortunately for us, she lived with us again for the last five months. Her love filled our house for that short time before we said our goodbyes and Mick took her to Stansted Airport and to what was to be her last flight from England.

The rest of October 2000

My sleep pattern began to return to normal. I continued to work efficiently at the academic things but had still seen only one patient. On Sunday October 8th, Mick and I drove to London for a Neurological Rehabilitation Conference. The conference started Monday morning. I was the first speaker as I had been the year before when Sarah was also at the conference. This was the first time I had used PowerPoint and I felt some concern because I had seen so many PowerPoint presentations break down. Agnes and Julia had checked everything with me, Julia had e-mailed everything to the organisers and both Agnes and Julia reassured me that all would be well. It was not. The machine was wrong, the disc was wrong, the lead from my own laptop did not fit and so forth. The staff managed at last to get everything working and we started 15 minutes late. I did not like the stress but I would have been a great deal more stressed before Sarah's death. The main change in my attitude since Sarah's death, and one that persists, is being less bothered by anything other than real problems.

For most of Monday I coped well with no tears. Mick was exhibiting his company's products and he also coped well. There were a few sad moments 'seeing' Sarah as she had been – in the exhibition hall last year.

On Tuesday afternoon our friend Jennie Ponsford from Australia gave a keynote address. She showed a video; part of it was the husband of a woman who had a severe head injury. He talked about the waves of grief washing over him. I broke down silently sobbing into my handkerchief. I knew so well what he meant. Later a colleague from Brazil, working in London, came to me and said her ex-husband was Peruvian. He had links with the government and might be able to help us. I was sobbing again. I did not want to hear this (although I know she was doing it with the best of motives). I had heard enough about offers of help. The lawyers in Lima and Bury St Edmunds would have to sort it out. It was all too exhausting for me.

The conference finished on Wednesday afternoon. We both thought it was good. Just before we left, a South African colleague came up to talk to me. She had met Sarah in South Africa the year before. I cried talking to her but they were my only tears that day. We went home and took Anna, Rosie and Francesca to Café Uno for dinner. Waiting for us was an e-mail from a man who had been at the memorial service.

Hi Mick,

This is Dean, I'm the one with the broken shoulder at Sarah's memorial. Just a note to say how moved I was by the whole experience. I'm 32 and, hard as it is to believe, Sarah is the closest person to me that has died. Like many of the people there I had a tear in my eyes through the ceremony and a smile at the choice of records played, we were allies when it came to music on Trailbreak weekends!

I am a guide for Trailbreak and that is where I first met Sarah, on the weekends that they run. Last year I did a ride in the Elan Valley. Half-way round in a short steep climb that previously no-one had got up, I passed Sarah on my first attempt but only managed half-way up and turned round for another go. On this second run Sarah stopped at the mid-way point and shouted at me all the way to the top, giving encouragement all the way. Last month I did the same hill again, after three goes I still hadn't cracked it. On the fourth run I thought of Sarah and her shouting. Didn't quite make it to the top but I got my best run in. All the weekends have points on them that remind me of Sarah, where I think of her and the laughs we had.

My girlfriend Annie, was going to meet Sarah in Peru and go on a Mountain Bike trip with her. Sarah died before Annie went over and I think it hit her quite hard, she certainly thought a lot about her whilst she was out there, even visiting the gorge where the accident happened. She sends her regards and thoughts.

Thank you for inviting us to honour Sarah's memory, as long as I Mountain Bike I will remember Sarah and the fun we had.

Dean & Annie

Back to Cambridge on Thursday with more tears reading e-mails and talking to colleagues. Mick and I had a very low day. Sarah's death was so final and bleak I desperately wanted to see her again. Her loss was so hard to bear. I kept thinking of the song "Sometimes my burden is so hard to bear, so hard to bear."

I had a call from a London psychologist, Shelley Channon, on Friday 13th. She said how sorry she was about Sarah and then went on to say that I was a role-model for clinical neuropsychologists as I did research, academic and clinical work. I started to cry saying I was no longer a clinician and I would give up all my achievements if I could have Sarah back. I am sure Shelley was not expecting such an outburst when she was just trying to be nice. I realise I hardly ever do that kind of thing now. I keep my grief to myself much more. I had another dream about Sarah that night — it was hard to remember, but we were simply looking through photographs together in a comradely way. At about this time Mick wrote a poem about Sarah.

SARAH

"She died doing what she loved doing"
say those who want to comfort,
missing the irony,

> suggesting she loved pursuing
> death as if it were a chase,
> a hunt, even fun!
> Rather she died doing what she had to do
> in the circumstances:
> fighting against the fear of it,
> the awful finality of
> losing all sense of life.
> She would have known
> what she stood to lose:
> never experiencing her friends
> and family again.
> never laughing, never crying,
> never moving to dance,
> never hearing songs,
> never thrilling to the rhythm
> that pulsates through all of us
> left here.

Our holiday in Egypt was approaching and there was trouble in the Middle East. Ariel Sharon had walked into a mosque, which caused uproar amongst the Palestinians. We wondered if we would be able to travel to Egypt. Two schoolgirls from Yorkshire had been swept away recently on a school trip and drowned. One girl's body was found but the other had not been found. I thought I should write to the parents as I would have wanted to hear from someone in a similar situation when Sarah died. Julia found the address of the school on the internet and I wrote to the parents. I put the letter in an unsealed envelope and put this in with a letter to the headmaster explaining why I was writing. I wanted him to know I was not a crank. I never heard back from the headmaster or the parents and do not know if the letter was forwarded on to them. Hannah's body was found some weeks later. I hope the finding of the body helped the parents a little. For us though, the lack of a body is not the worst thing. Sarah's loss is worse. Having no body is eventually accepted. One has to deal with whatever cards are dealt. Sarah would have found the idea of being lost in some remote valley romantic. I remember once when we were watching the television programme "Meet the Ancestors", Sarah said, "I like the thought of someone finding my body in several hundred years and trying to work out what happened to me."

Jon Evans and I had the launch of our new paging service in Ely on the 20th — with considerable media coverage. I was involved with interviews and talks. Jon heard he had won an award that I had recommended him for, Mick had won an Anglo-Dutch small business award and I had been nominated by the British Psychological Society as one of six people who had made "a distinguished contribution to professional psychology". So on the work front things were going well. On the personal front we had many days where we felt depressed and bereft. We also had calm days and we did not cry so often. I remember saying to Agnes that every so often I had to give myself a short holiday from grieving as it was too exhausting to keep it up all the time. I would also hear Sarah's voice saying, "Oh, mum, it's all right, you get on with your life." My birthday came. The main present was the trip to Egypt. I checked the internet to find out what advice the Foreign Office had to offer for tourists to Egypt. There was no reason not to go, dress modestly, avoid crowds and be aware that the situation could change, was the main advice. We were travelling with Bales and I trusted the company to look after their clients.

My second patient was seen on my birthday. Another man I had known for a few years. He had Huntington's disease. I saw him at his home. His wife, a sociable woman, asked how I was, had I had a good year, how was the family and so on. I had decided very firmly that I would not say anything but I could not bring myself to lie so had to tell her Sarah had died. I did not break down although my eyes filled up. We talked about the woman's state of health too. She had been through a bad time but I really felt unable to deal with her troubles. I was polite enough I think but inside I was saying to myself, "Please don't tell me any more."

We left for Egypt on Wednesday October 25th. I did not keep a journal but we loved the trip, the country, the temples, the tombs, the museums and the Nile cruise. We hardly cried at first and did not tell any of our companions. Then one night on the cruise, in the bar, we were with the oldest woman in our group. She was very pleasant and over a drink said to us, "Who will be waiting for you when you get home?" An innocent remark but one that had Mick and me in tears. I cried quietly and told her there should be three children and two grandchildren but one daughter had died. She coped well and encouraged us to talk. The next day, on deck, Mick told a group of people and came to find me as I had a copy of the memorial programme in my bag and he wanted to show it to people. Soon everyone knew and we were talking and crying more. It did not spoil Egypt though – an astonishing country that I hope to return to one day. I decided that whenever I was asked the question, "How many children do you have?" or "Do you have children?", I would always say, "Three." I do have three. I have been asked since and I say, "Three." Sometimes, depending on the person, the circumstances and my mood, I say, "and one died in a rafting accident in Peru." Sometimes I leave it at "Three." I often talk about Sarah as if she is alive, particularly to people who do not know our circumstances. I might say, "My daughter's like that." More often though I talk of Anna as "my surviving daughter". We returned home on Thursday November 2nd. Waiting for us were several letters including one from Janet and David. We had sent them a programme along with several other people. This is their letter.

Dear Barbara and Mick,

Thank you so much for sending us a copy of the service you had to celebrate the life of your dear Sarah. We were so touched to receive it. As

I write, I gaze at the beautiful photograph of Sarah on the front of the programme – showing her so full of life and hope... It is almost beyond belief when I think about what happened.

Having read the programme, and the writings of so many people who knew Sarah, I think it must have been a wonderful tribute to her, and a wonderful occasion, though agonisingly sad, to come together with so many who loved her and shared her life, to honour her.

I can well imagine how you would have gone down again after it was over. But that is the nature of grief – stumbling along, one step forward, two steps back, another step forward and so on.

We trust you will continue to be supported and accompanied as you go on in the coming weeks and months.

We would very much like to come and see you in Suffolk sometime. I saw an article in a magazine recently showing gorgeous photographs of Southwold. It looked so picturesque.

We'll let you know if and when there is a possibility.

Meanwhile, take care of yourselves, and keep in touch.

With our continued compassionate thoughts and love from,

Janet and David

November 2000

A quiet month. There had been a nasty train accident at Hatfield with resulting delays to all services. I had to go by train to London on several occasions. The first time was to give a talk at University College London on the morning of November 6th and at the Institute of Psychiatry in the afternoon. I had lunch with Shelley Channon and Paul Burgess. Previously, my relationship with Paul had been difficult, we were not always on the same wavelength, but Sarah's death changed all that. He was so sympathetic and positive about the memorial service that I felt quite differently about him. I remember he had telephoned me at home one evening a few weeks after Sarah died. He kept saying, "It's so terrible, it's so terrible." He wept and spoke to me for ages. Paul is a keen surfer and I remember meeting him at a conference in Hawaii when he had almost drowned in a surfing accident and seemed to be in a state of shock. I believe his father had also died the previous year so, one way and another, Paul and I seemed to be drawn together now.

I went to the Institute of Psychiatry where I had trained as a clinical psychologist over 20 years earlier. I spoke to three old colleagues, two of whom did not know about Sarah. I told them and remembered another dream I had about Sarah in Egypt. In the dream I knew Sarah was dead but she was with us all. She told me she needed to make a phone call. I turned to some woman and said, "Can you make a phone call if you're dead?" "Oh yes," said the woman. I looked at Sarah's muscly legs and thought, "Those legs will never get old." At one point in the dream, Sarah was sitting next to me and I said to her, "Sarah, I don't mind you being dead if you can be here with us like this." The strangest part of the dream, though, was a scene in which a Japanese colleague was selling paintings including a painting of a bike that the colleague had done herself. People were fighting over it. An unknown woman bought it and gave it to us in memory of Sarah.

The following evening I managed to attend my first talk at the main unit in Cambridge. In term time we have a lunchtime talk every Wednesday. I had not been since May and I found going to the main unit in Chaucer Road was so difficult – but I struggled in on Wednesday November 8th. The speaker was Tim Dalgleish on "Mood changes in memory". It was a good talk even though I fell asleep for about 10 minutes at one point (something I was now prone to frequently). The talk was about negative thoughts which made me think about Sarah. I wept to myself. I wept earlier that morning too. The grief kept coming back. I asked William, my boss, by e-mail, if I could have compassionate leave to go to Peru. He e-mailed back, "Of course." Like most acts of kindness that set me weeping once more. I cried at home in the evening when Anna came round. It was coming up for six months since Sarah had died. I wanted to see her. It was too long to be without my darling, darling girl.

I wept the next day too. Fergus, my previous trainee, had gone to South America in between qualifying as a clinical psychologist and taking up a post at the Oliver Zangwill Centre in January 2001. Fergus knew Anna. She was a clinical tutor on his course. When Anna knew Fergus was going to Peru she asked him to leave some flowers for Sarah in any beautiful place he chose. Fergus had e-mailed Anna the day before. He had not yet reached Peru but was in Chile on the 'Day of the Dead' so he thought he would leave some flowers for Sarah. Both Anna and I were very moved by this.

I observed Agnes testing a patient for a research study and I fell asleep while she was testing him. This was not the old me, falling asleep all the time. It must have been because grief is so exhausting. I dreamt of Sarah again that night. It was a variation on the 'she isn't really dead' theme. Sarah was due back in England on November 23rd. In the dream she turned up on November 23rd and just had not bothered to get in touch with us. I was not at all sure I liked these dreams. Although they were great at the time, I wanted the feeling of relief to last for more than the split second after waking.

Anna and I had a weekend in London together. I wanted to give Anna a treat. She had been so supportive of me in the past six months. We shopped before going first to a Thai restaurant in Trafalgar Square and then to see "Stones in his Pocket" at the Duke of York. It was a clever, funny Irish play. Mick and Paul looked after the girls and when we arrived home on Sunday, we were told they had been good.

Paul (our ex-son-in-law, who had been married to Anna, and was Rosie's dad) was now living with us. He heard his closest brother had died in Portugal. I bought him a ticket to go to Faro for the funeral. Rosie was upset. She knew her Uncle Stan and had already lost one family member recently. Mick was ill in bed with a respiratory infection. He had not been really well in months. Sarah's death had aged him more than it had me. Paul was crying over Stan. I felt some sympathy, but mostly felt it was not so awful as Sarah's death. Mick went to Frankfurt, Paul went to Portugal and I went to London.

Sarah was to have been due home on November 23rd and I found myself very sad and weepy again the few days before she was due back. We kept thinking how excited we would have been. I was going to take a day off work to go to meet her at Stansted. I saw my third patient that week. It was not so bad. This patient did not know about Sarah and did not ask me about my family so it was easier to be with her. I kept thinking, I should be going to the airport tomorrow to meet Sarah. I would have bought champagne. We would have had a celebratory dinner. It was hard to believe that Sarah was not going to come waltzing through the door saying, "Hi, mum!" or phone me and say, "How are things?" I thought, "You just have to keep going." I wanted to put everything right, I'm a problem solver, I get over difficulties. This problem I could not put right. I wondered if life would ever be easy?

I survived November 23rd better than I expected, although it was such a terribly sad thing to have lived through. Carol telephoned in the evening. She had not realised the significance of the day. We both cried together over the phone. I telephoned Matt in Los Angeles. He was low. The next day we went to dinner with Carol's crowd at Hintlesham Hall. Waves of grief washed over us. I had a meeting in London on Saturday 26th. Several people at the meeting commiserated about Sarah, making me cry again. How could this terrible thing happen to our successful, competent family? It seemed so unbelievable.

On Monday 27th I met my colleague German Berrios in the concourse at Addenbrooke's. He asked how I was, so I began weeping again. This public weeping seemed to go on and on, yet I was almost over that stage. Most days I left work early. I still did most of the cooking. This was one job I could do. With so many things I found that my heart was not in it. On November 29th I was an external examiner for a PhD. I managed that – it was another first. I realised I could cope with most aspects of work. I was not sure that I wanted to remain working and I considered early retirement but decided I might as well do what I was doing and get paid for it for the time being at least.

On November 30th Carol, Anna, Mick and I drove to London. It was the day of the awards for the Anglo-Dutch businesses. Mick and I arranged to stay overnight at the Tower Bridge Thistle where the awards were being held. We checked in and had a wonderful view of Tower Bridge from our room. We had a table for Mick's company. There were 12 of us altogether. The food was not very good but the occasion was enjoyable. There were four awards for enterprise and four runners-up for four sections: small British business, small Dutch business, large British business and large Dutch business. Mick's company won the small British award, and it was presented to Mick by Richard Caborn, the Minister for Trade.

We finished at 3.00 p.m. Sarah should have been there of course. She worked for Mick for years. That night we went to see *Long Day's Journey into Night* by Eugene

O'Neill. Jessica Lange played the mother. She was brilliant! Although the play and the performance were both superb it was painful for us because of the grief that permeated the dysfunctional family.

December 2000

We knew this month would be hard as it was our first Christmas without Sarah. She was such a fan of Christmas. She bought tons of presents. Everything had to be a secret as she wanted to surprise everyone. She was a child in many ways – always looking for excitement and adventure.

On December 6th I saw my first new patient who had been referred by the service for people with visual impairments. The question for me was, "Are his difficulties due to poor eyesight or visuo-perceptual problems?" I spent the morning testing him and thought it was more than simply poor acuity. This was also the day of the Oliver Zangwill Centre's fourth birthday party. A large group of people came, including ex-clients. Fiona, our manager, gave a good speech. Jon and I both received compliments on our awards from the British Psychological Society. I met up with others later in the afternoon to discuss the man I had seen in the morning to make suggestions and offer advice. Every one was listening intently to me. I thought, "Oh my god, I am not an expert, I am just trying to find my way through the fog." I hate being seen as an expert when I feel I am struggling along just like most people.

Rosie wanted me to help with her Christmas shopping on Saturday December 9th. I obliged. This had always been Sarah's job. Soon after Sarah died Rosie said to the family, "Who is going to help me with my Christmas shopping?" I said, "Well, I suppose it will have to be me." Rosie just nodded. Most of Saturday was spent on that. I am sure Sarah would have enjoyed it more than I did.

We received a report from Pepe Lopez on Wednesday 13th. He was the guide who had tried to retrieve Sarah's body from the river. He said that when Sarah was first seen in the water she appeared to be conscious but unable to help herself. (I thought that might be because of the broken neck.) It made me very tearful. We had to send yet more money and more documents to Peru to try to get the death certificate. I wanted Sarah so much, my beautiful, darling girl.

Friday December 15th would have been my mother's 92nd birthday. I drove to Agnes's house in Newmarket and left my car there as Agnes was driving us both to Southampton for Lindsay McLellan's Festschrift. Lindsay McLellan was a professor of rehabilitation and a former boss of mine and the Festschrift was a special event to celebrate his life and work. I was giving one of the talks in his honour. Everyone felt affection for Lindsay who was there. The day felt good. I spoke to several people over lunch including some who did not know about Sarah so I am afraid I became tearful yet again. Nevertheless, it was on the decrease overall. I arrived at Agnes's house at 7.35 p.m. and then drove to Ely for the staff Christmas dinner. I found it hard work and left early. My socialising skills were still rather weak.

I spoke to Matt on the phone. He had a flight back from New York for Christmas. As he was in Los Angeles he bought a ticket for a Greyhound bus to New York. I was worried as I knew that there were some bad storms in parts of the USA.

Mick and I drove to Cambridge to take the train to Kings Cross and the London Conference of the British Psychological Society where I was to receive my award for distinguished contributions to applied psychology. The ceremony was low-key, but pleasant enough. The award winners were then taken to have a special photograph taken. This was to appear in 2001 in the National Portrait Gallery as part of an exhibition to celebrate the 100th birthday of the British Psychological Society. That evening was yet another Christmas dinner – this time for Mick's company. Matt had phoned to say the Greyhound bus was stuck in Denver and was diverting to Phoenix. It looked as if he would not get his flight from New York to London. A later call told us he was back in Los Angeles. The Greyhound bus people said they could get him to New York on Thursday evening via Dallas and Memphis but he would miss his flight.

I managed to get Matthew on a British Airways flight to London. It cost Matthew a lot and he was cross he had not been able to arrange to get to New York on time but I thought he had to be home for Christmas and we were all due to go to Peter Island in the British Virgin Islands, on Boxing Day.

My next patient, the fifth since Sarah died, was seen on December 20th. This was another person I had known for years. This visit was relatively easy. I felt low though, partly because of Matthew. In addition I had several Christmas cards arriving from people who did not know about Sarah, so that made me cry, and from people who did know and said something kind, so that made me cry too. I wrote in my diary for that day, "What a terrible thing Sarah has done to us, all for the sake of some stupid thrill on a river." I went home early as I had to go to the solicitor with Mick. We had been a few times; we had to sign documents and pay money on more than one occasion.

Matthew arrived home on Friday December 22nd. I arrived home from work in Ely to find Mick, Matt and Anna in the midst of a nasty argument. Matt had terrible toothache and jet lag. I assumed this was part of the explanation for the row. All was resolved finally but this was our first big family row since Sarah's death. Yet another 'first'.

We were expecting Christmas to be difficult as so many people told us it would be. Sarah always loved Christmas. She put considerable energy into choosing presents and every one had to be surprised. We had to keep our presents to Sarah a surprise too. As Christmas Day was Rosie's birthday, we had a tradition of Christmas in the morning and birthday in the afternoon. This year, for the second consecutive time, Carol had invited us to her house for Christmas dinner. The year before, the first time this happened, Rosie had explained to Carol that we had to have her birthday presents and birthday cake in the afternoon. Carol, of course, obliged.

As we were eating our Christmas dinner I had a strong sense that Sarah was sitting at the end of the table. We toasted her and wept a little but managed to get through Christmas and Rosie's birthday with less anguish than we had expected.

On Boxing Day, Mick, Matt, Anna, Francesca and I left early for Heathrow and our trip to Peter Island. Rosie and Paul were going to Euro Disney in Paris and then to friends in Brighton. We flew to Antigua, then had to hang around the small airport there for our delayed plane to Tortola (the main island of the British Virgin Islands). We were feeling tired and sticky, but on arrival in Tortola things started to look up. Our luggage was transported and we were taken to a yacht for our transfer to Peter Island. We went on the upper deck to watch a lovely starlit sky and mountains. One of the crew brought us drinks and we were taken in luxury to Peter Island for a 10-day holiday. We knew then that this promised to be a special holiday – and so it proved. New Year's Eve was a mixture of sadness and laughter. The previous New Year we had all been together on Mauritius and now we had to survive without Sarah. A whole new year would go by with no Sarah in it.

January 2001

Peter Island was everything we hoped for. Beautiful scenery, wonderful food, excellent service, good swimming. We did not argue and were all relaxed. Matt's toothache became unbearable and we had to go to Tortola one day for emergency treatment. My Brazilian friend, Anita, was staying with her boyfriend Pascal, who lives on St Barts. They arranged for a private plane to collect us on Wednesday January 3rd to take us to St Barts and spend two nights with them. It was exciting climbing on to the little plane. Francesca took it all in her stride as if she was well used to private planes. We had wonderful views flying to St Barts and a spectacular view landing on the airfield. We had not met Pascal before but he was very easy to get on with and proved to be exceptionally good with Francesca. We went out for a superb lunch the day we arrived. Francesca and Pascal pretended to steal food from one another's plates, both laughing uproariously. The visit was mostly full of laughter, eating, sunbathing and walking. Pascal had donkeys, rabbits and chickens at his house. Francesca spent a great deal of time feeding the donkeys and chickens and trying to stroke the rabbits. I had a big crying session on the beach one day when I was talking to Anita about Sarah who should have been there.

We returned to Peter Island on Friday 5th. We were glad to be back but sad to leave Anita and Pascal who had given us such a good time. On Peter Island there was one resort and the average space for each guest was six acres! That was more our style. We loved it so much that we arranged to go for next Christmas and New Year, making sure we would take Rosie this time.

We arrived home on January 8th and went back to the usual things. I was still writing chapters and doing the academic work and still leaving work early, mostly about 4.30 p.m. I still did most of the cooking as Mick did not feel up to this chore yet. It was also my excuse for leaving work early. And I was still going to the gym or swimming almost every day. I felt sure the exercise was helping me to keep sane. Mick told me frequently that he felt it was a kind of yoga for me. On January 11th I noted in my diary that I usually had two or three short weeps a day and there were times I desperately wanted to hug Sarah, but I was not in such excruciating pain as I had been in the early days and weeks. On January 12th I spent a long time arranging more travel for later in the year. We were going to the International Neuropsychological Society conference in Brazil in July and to the Brain Injury Conference in Australia in May. We decided to go to Peru from Australia and trek to the site of Sarah's death with the help of Pepe Lopez. I was advised by Trailfinders (the firm I telephoned to book the tickets) not to go to Peru via Australia. I said it was a personal matter and we had no choice. The travel was finally sorted out with a reasonable itinerary. Later that day a visiting Argentinian doctor came to talk to me to ask if I would be a consultant to a new rehabilitation centre to be opened in Buenos Aires. I agreed. He then asked about Sarah and as usual, I talked about her at great length and naturally cried a great deal too. To this day I talk about Sarah every day. From the first days I had people saying to me, "If you need someone to talk to, I'm here." The problem for us was *not* talking.

By this stage I was able to work at the weekends once more. This was mostly writing and preparing talks. The weekend of January 13th/14th I managed 5$\frac{1}{4}$ hours. On January 16th I arrived home to find a letter from Jan and Betsy, the Dutch couple from The Compassionate Friends. It was a lovely letter that had Mick and me both sobbing. I replied the following day – still crying. I felt so washed out with crying that I seemed to be working in slow motion. Anything would start us crying – plays, films, music, and news where, if there was anything in the least bit sad, we wept.

The following weekend I had a sore throat. I was not ill but I was in pain. This was unlike me – apart from the mild cold I had picked up in Peru in May, I had not been unwell for years. I would have thought that all the crying and grief would have made me vulnerable to all sorts of infections but this was not the case. Maybe all the exercising I did protected me in some way? I dosed up with Nurofen to get through the days.

On January 24th I went to a meeting on memory at the Royal Society in London. I met a colleague from work whose wife had died unexpectedly from a rare form of cancer just over a year before Sarah died. I said to him, "We have both lost somebody too soon." He said on the journey to the Royal Society something reminded him of his wife. He wept and I wept, united by this painful bond. I talked to more people over lunch. Some knew about Sarah, some did not. Most were kind, gentle and sensitive. I realised how many people I knew cared about me and about Sarah and the family. One colleague said she was at a Baha'i shrine recently and prayed for Sarah. Another colleague cried with me over the loss.

I went to the morning talks of the second day at the Royal Society. It was still hard for me to listen to too many talks, though, so I skipped the afternoon. My throat was better and I decided to risk the gym once I arrived home. I felt better for the exercise. I returned to swimming the following day. I always thought of Sarah at the gym and at the pool. Her death had not made me fear swimming, although I would never take risks in the sea. I could now go for longer periods without thinking about her. From constant thoughts I progressed to several minutes without her coming into my mind and by January I could probably go, at least on some occasions, for as long as half an hour. The only times I managed longer without thinking about her were when I gave a talk. She did not come into my mind then. On January 26th I went to the leaving lunch of a colleague who had been working for me on some short-term research money. I managed, but the only social occasions where I felt comfortable were meals out with the family. On Sunday, Carol, Peter, Simon, Jo, Cameron and Molly joined us for Sunday lunch and that was a successful occasion.

I gave another talk on Monday 29th at Peterborough General Hospital. Once again, I felt it went well, but my heart was not in it. I wanted Sarah back. I was tired of grief and tired of trying to be normal.

On January 31st, Carol and I set off for three days in Carcassonne. This was my Christmas present to Carol to thank her for her strength and support following Sarah's death.

February 2001

Carol and I enjoyed Carcassonne. It was cold but bright. We were in a good hotel. We ate well, drank well and walked a great deal. One evening we had dinner in a restaurant that prided itself on wonderful French cuisine. At the next table were a British couple we recognised from the hotel. They demanded fish and chips and would not consider anything on the menu. The chef came up to them and said that if they wanted fish and chips they would have to leave. Eventually he pointed imperiously towards the door and said, "Go!" We felt like applauding.

Work continued in much the same way except that I was now able to stay until about 5.00 p.m. I usually arrived round about 7.00 a.m. but swam first when I was at Addenbrooke's. If I was working in Ely I went to the gym when they opened at 7.00 a.m. before going to work.

Matt returned to Los Angeles on Friday February 2nd and telephoned me on the 6th to say he had had to have emergency dental treatment following an extremely bad toothache. He had seen a dentist in Tortola during our New Year's holiday – apparently a swab had been left in the tooth. His whole lower jaw was infected, he had two teeth removed and several stitches in his gum. He sounded in a bad way. I had to phone the dentist and pay the bill by credit card. Since Sarah's death we seemed to pay out money constantly.

I was still receiving letters from people who had only just heard about Sarah. They still led to tears about my poor, sweet, lovely girl. One interesting e-mail arrived from the National Portrait Gallery asking if I would give a public lecture in July on "Studying the Brain" as part of the celebration for the centenary year of the British Psychological Society. My portrait was to be shown in an exhibition of British psychologists from May to September 2001. This was also part of the centenary year. I agreed to do the talk, which I did in July, beyond the time frame of this book. The talk went well with a good audience and many questions. I was busy writing papers and chapters. For some reason the writing seemed easy. It was as if I had stopped fretting about what to say. Grief had made me freer in putting pen to paper. I have always written and published academic books, chapters and papers but never so much and so easily as I was now able to do. Seeing patients was altogether different and, to this day, I see far fewer than I used to. Two a week is my maximum, whereas before I would average about five a week. (Much later, in the year 2003, Mick and I were to see a wonderful film about bereavement, called *The Son's Room*. This Italian film tells the story of the loss of a grown-up son in a drowning accident and the effects on his immediate family. The father is a psychiatrist and the film explores his inability to help his patients in the face of his grief for his son. I was particularly struck by the emotional echoes it held for me in a similar situation. Mick and I concluded that the director must have been advised by someone who had experienced the loss of a child. The film won the top award at the 2001 Cannes film festival.)

On Wednesday February 13th, Mick and I left for Chicago and the North American International Neuropsychological Conference. This conference was much easier for us, especially for Mick. I was tearful at times particularly when I had to tell people who did not know. For the first time though, I did not feel obliged to tell everyone who said, "How are you?" What had happened to me? This keeping quiet about our tragedy, at least some of the time, was a step forwards. On Friday I had lunch with Audrey Holland whose son Ben had been beaten to death. We cried together. I met Jim Becker who had sent me my favourite book on grief, *A Broken Heart Still Beats*. He had sent Audrey the same book. One day I met a neuropsychologist from Mexico. I did not know her well but I once wrote a chapter for a book she edited. She saw me crying so I told her about Sarah. She then told me that she had lost her two-year-old daughter very unexpectedly six years ago. She took me for coffee with a friend of hers who cried even more than either of the bereaved mothers! I cried too. The friend had known the daughter. There are so many more bereaved parents around than one realises. We arrived home on Monday February 19th. Apart from work and exercise nothing much happened for the rest of February. The tickets for Mali arrived on February 28th.

March 2001

In my journal, I noted on March 1st that I was coping better. I felt Chicago had moved me forward again. I had had two dreams where Sarah was around – just being herself. These were normal dreams not the "Oh, you're not really dead then?" dreams. I still wept on occasion, usually for a brief period, and I felt she was around somehow. I either felt her presence in the room or I felt she was just away travelling. It was almost as if she was not really dead at all.

Work was going much the same. I was still writing, still seeing very few patients, still exercising every day. I was an adviser for a documentary film on amnesia and met with the film makers and some patients on March 3rd. The following day (Mick's 66th birthday) I left for my holiday in Mali. We had had Mick's birthday dinner early. I was slightly nervous about my trip. We would be trekking for five days in Dogon country. I hoped I would be fit enough. Like Sarawak, this was to be another trip for Sarah. She would probably have come with me had she been alive.

On the morning of March 4th Mick took me to Heathrow where we said goodbye. The group of travellers finally arrived in Bamako at 8.55 p.m. and, after more hanging around, met James, our tour guide. We reached the Hotel Mandé, on the banks of the river, at 10.10 p.m. – too late for dinner. There were 16 in the group including one married couple. I found myself sharing with a woman from Norfolk who worked at the University of East Anglia. Initially, I was not sure about her. She enthused about things in a rather loud voice. By the end of the trip though I was very fond of her. We had very similar political views which helped. At 10.30 p.m. we all met for a briefing and a beer. By the time all the paperwork was done it was 12.15 and it was 12.30 when we went to bed. We were called at 6.30 a.m. – so it was a tiring day.

Bamako was bustling, lively and very African. We left by bus and our first stop was in Segou, where we had lunch and wandered around a highly colourful and extremely busy market. It was quite unlike anything I had seen before. At another stop along the road, I bought a Bozo statue for Mick, the Bozo are fishermen. We were heading for Djenné which has the largest mud mosque in the world. Everything was exciting and busy. We reached the encampment (like a hostel) at 6.40 p.m. We had cold showers and went over to dinner. Michael Palin and a TV crew were staying at the same place and were making a programme about Mali. I thought I would not say anything to anyone in the group about Sarah, but realised it depended on the topics that came up, the people I was with and the mood I was in.

The next morning after breakfast we set off on a walking tour of Djenné which is a UNESCO world heritage site. Djenné is quite a place. The whole village is made of mud in a traditional style. Most of the men and boys were setting off to pray (Mali is mostly Moslem). Because the day we were there was a festival day, the men and boys were in their finery and looking absolutely splendid. Some of the women were also dressed up and looking gorgeous, although many of the girls were working, mostly fetching water from the wells. There were sheep and goats everywhere. Many were being killed that day for the festival. We were told that if a man had one wife he was supposed to kill one sheep, if he had two wives, it was two sheep and so on.

We went into a place that sold mud paintings called bogolons. These are done by women on cloth and are typical of everyday scenes. I bought one for Anna of Bambara women working in the fields. On the way back the men and boys were returning along with the chief of the area who looked extremely magnificent. I was sold on Mali. I thought what I had seen so far was great and I was looking forward to the rest of the trip. Sarah would have loved it.

That afternoon we set off in horse-drawn carts for Djenné-Djeno (old Djenné). It was quite an adventure charging through the crowded streets in the incredibly bumpy carts. We saw the museum and the archaeological site with thousands of pieces of pottery lying around.

A group of us braved the post office the next morning to buy stamps for our postcards. It took ages, but even that seemed like an adventure. I bought a pretty chameleon box for Rosie (the previous evening I bought myself some blue glass beads). Back on the bus and a drive to Sangha, a large Dogon village where we were to begin our trek.

Thursday March 8th was the first day of our trek into the Dogon country. The Dogon are famous for their wooden carvings and their wooden carved doors. The chance to see some of their work was one of the reasons I chose this trip. We left our main luggage in Sangha, packed a rucksack to be carried by the porters and just carried a small day sack for ourselves. We each had to carry three litres of water, along with sun screen, camera, snacks and any other odds and ends we needed. We left at 7.05 a.m. with our Dogon guide, Dao. He was a tall, splendid, beautiful man dressed in immaculate white, traditional cotton Dogon clothing and hat. The walking was pretty straightforward, the countryside somewhat harsh and barren. It was mostly rock with some patches of dry grass and a few trees. Every now and again we had a stunning view over the Bandiagarra escarpment which was quite high. Then we saw great stretches of yellow sand dotted with green trees. I hung around with the "three old ladies", Eiley (my room-mate) – 56, Jan – 57, and me – 59. Lis who was 50 wanted to be in our gang but as she was younger we said she could be a trainee. I was certainly as fit as the best of them – despite being the oldest in the entire group.

After lunch and a siesta, we set off at 3.00 p.m. and walked down a very rocky path for most of the way. I was helped by a little lad about 11 years old called Simon. Every time we came to a rock or a difficult section, a little black hand would stretch out to help. We each had a little boy watching us – they were so courteous, charming and polite. I accepted Simon's helping hand each time it was offered. I had bought a book of drawings from him in the morning – for about 50 pence. We had to be careful giving money. We had to check with Dao, who often chased the children away. He did not want us to give them much as they will then earn more than their fathers which is not right.

We reached a village later in the afternoon. It was just what I'd hoped for. The Dogon have kept their old traditions. They welcomed us with a cold drink and we were escorted to an area to watch a Dogon masked dance. It was fantastic. Afterwards Dao explained the different masks to us and we took photographs. The masks were very beautiful and the people so welcoming and likeable. I bought some Dogon statues for Mick – and we moved on to the camp. We had little two-person tents set in a sandy open space, a long dining table and smelly toilets. There were no showers but we were each given a small bowl of water to wash in.

By now I had told Eiley about Sarah. I became tearful the day before when Lis asked me about my family. I was having to lie quite a few times because I didn't want to tell anyone. Eiley was fine and sympathetic. I did cry but quietly and softly. That night I did not sleep well, dogs, donkeys and cockerels were making noises all night.

Next morning we reached a village and were taken into the school − into a class of 66 children who sang us two songs with great gusto. I was crying along with one or two others. We left money for the school. On to another village where we saw one of the special meeting houses, only for men and boys. I thought watching village life was the most interesting spectacle. We had another good lunch before lazing under the trees for our siesta. The locals all watched us and we watched them. The young girls, about 12 years old, were doing the washing, the boys were watering the donkeys and cattle. Some locals were selling crafts. They came up to show us things while we were lying on our mattresses. It was amusing and pleasant. We set off at 3.30 p.m. and walked until 5.00 p.m. Arrived at camp and were given our basins of water. I had a strip wash in the tent while Eiley was out (and later she did the same). I was coping with the trekking, so were most of the others. The walking was easier than I had expected.

On Saturday March 10th we went to several villages and had lunch at a swish encampment with showers, toilets and flowers. We found it very up-market for Mali. Just after we arrived, Dao poured water over our heads, legs and feet. It felt wonderful and we felt high. That day had been the hardest trekking. We still had help from local lads, though. We gave them between 20 and 50 pence at the end of the day − with Dao's approval.

We reached the camp at 5.30 and I had a beer. While we were drinking, villagers arrived to be patched up by James and Jan, who both had good medical kits. There was a woman with a sore arm, a boy with a nasty, horrible wound on his leg and two little boys with eye infections. That was a sad part of the trip − the helplessness of the Dogon in face of illness or injury. We were seeing the real village life of Africa. We had not seen a road since we left Sangha and had seen only two four-wheel drive vehicles and three little motorcycles.

The hardest walk was on Sunday March 11th. We had a steep climb up the escarpment which was beautiful and exhilarating. The rocks were firm and not slippery so it was not too bad. The first village where we stopped was interesting, although the children looked very poor and dirty. They were mostly beautiful, but so many had hernias, runny noses, bad eyes and coughs. We passed one poor woman with obvious toothache and a horrible swollen face. Jan and James did what they could and Jan frequently dished out money and instructions to see a doctor.

We continued walking high on the plateau with vast black rocks and amazing views. We passed some 14th century Tellem buildings in the rocks, climbed through gorges and felt pleased with ourselves. I felt I was in a piece of unspoilt, rural Africa and couldn't quite believe I was there. We saw scenes that etched themselves in my memory: a lone man sitting under a tree contemplating the view; three women in colourful costumes with water buckets on their heads and babies on their backs; regular sightings of donkeys, goats, sheep and cattle. The Dogon have an elaborate greeting ceremony that takes several seconds to complete. It starts with "Ago po" (hello) then "Sayon" (how are your children?), "Sayon" (fine), then "how is your husband/wife?" "Fine." "How're your parents?" "Fine." Then the second person has to go through the process. Finally, both say, "Thank you, thank you, thank you." It's quite a thing to see it especially when it is between Dao and the chief of the village.

James and Jan treated a woman with a wounded leg on our way to the campsite for that evening. We stopped at the edge of the nearby village while James and Dao talked to the head man — the Hogon — who asked us through Dao if we could donate anything for a village school. We did. At 6.15 we reached the campsite. It was in a beautiful setting with rocky outcrops all around. The scene was peaceful. We sat down exhausted. After a cold drink I was off to the tent for a wash and change. We had dinner under a lovely starlit sky and I started to think about Sarah and that she should have been there. Jan asked how I was. I replied, "Sad," and she asked me why so I told her and Lis (who was nearby). I ended up sobbing and the whole table could see me.

As that was our last evening on the trek, the porters had decided to give us 'a feast'. We had contributed some money the day before for them to buy a sheep. The sheep travelled with the porters, who led it by a rope all day. It was killed and roasting on a spit before we reached the camp. We had onion soup to start, then some traditional Dogon food — ground millet and a sauce made of baobab leaves. The millet was bearable but nobody liked the slimy, nauseating sauce. Then came the roast lamb which was delicious. I had one beer (my daily limit) and felt exhausted. What with the demanding walk and all the crying over Sarah (it was 10 months to the day since she died) I went to bed. I lay in the tent listening to the Dogon people singing, dancing and drumming outside. I fell asleep to the rhythmic, soothing music.

On Tuesday March 13th we set off after breakfast for a walking tour of Mopti. Our two local guides were Ali and Baba! I told Ali I needed a football shirt from Mali for Matthew who has a collection of such shirts from all over the world. Ali went off, came back later with the shirt and shorts and charged me £12. I once paid £75 for a shirt in Kyoto so thought that this was very reasonable. The town was busy and interesting. We went to an area where the Bela people herd animals. They keep them in large corrals and let them out during the day.

Next we all went to the market. Like Segou it was incredibly busy and colourful. We were woken at 5.00 a.m. on March 14th and left at 6.00 a.m. after breakfast. We were on an open boat, a long one with six rows each of four seats and a little bench in front of each row. The roof was thatched, the sides were open. Around the sides was a plank about one foot wide. This we used to walk on to get to the toilet at the back. The toilet had an open roof and a hole straight through to the water. It was not too smelly and, indeed, was one of the best toilets outside of the hotels. We had a man at the front, the pilot, and one at the back in charge of the engine. Amaga, the cook, was also on board together with a little lad about 12 years old who appeared to be with the pilot. Amaga had a little charcoal fire and an area to prepare food. We were allowed to climb up on the roof but there were to be no more than three people at a time up there.

We passed villages, boats, birds and a group of hippopotami. Again, it was exciting and thrilling. Amaga passed round biscuits and herbal tea at one point. We stopped at 10.45 to walk into the village of Kataka – a village with a mosque. We had not been allowed to enter the mosque in Djenné but were allowed in this one, for a fee. The whole place was very dusty. We were followed everywhere by children and some adults. It was obviously an event when people like us came. Everyone was friendly. All called out, "Ça va?" and many wanted to shake our hands. Back to the boat and more travelling. Amaga served lunch on the boat. Plates of green beans were topped with sardines, tuna, tomatoes, cucumber and eggs. We passed the plates down the boat and the whole system worked well.

The people along the river were Bozo, one of the smallest tribes in Mali and all fisherfolk. There are about 17,000 of them. The Dogon comprise about five per cent of the Malian population (there are around 500,000 Dogon). The Dogon and the Bozo are great friends. We also saw more Bela and Peuhl people that afternoon. Everyone seemed excited to see us. We pitched camp just before 6.00 p.m. in a rather desolate and bleak campsite. We were all hot and sweaty and could only have the most measly of washes. Dinner was great – excellent fresh grilled fish with couscous and sauce. I was woken many times during the night by croaking frogs, which made a change from the braying donkeys we had heard earlier on the trek. Our wake up call on March 15th was at 5.30 a.m. It was hard getting ready in the dark with so little space. We had to roll up our sleeping bags, take down our mosquito nets and so forth. Eiley was always the last of the group to be ready and I was always nearly last. At home – and before Sarah died – I was always so quick and speedy. The boat left at 6.05 a.m. Once under way, we were given a bowl of water to wash our face and hands. Breakfast followed consisting of bread, spread and a hot drink. We soon reached Lake Debo and were on the lake all day.

Next day we docked at 4.35 p.m. in the port of Koroumé, 19 kilometres from the fabled city of Timbuktu. The unloading took place among the usual hustle and bustle. We made our goodbyes and thankyous to Amago and the boatman. There were three jeeps waiting for us. We had to stop at the "Welcome to Timbuktu" sign so that everyone could take photographs.

On Saturday March 17th we set off for a walking tour of Timbuktu. The city was different from other Malian towns we had seen. The main group of people here was the Tuareg, who are lighter in colour than other Malians. The Bela were also present and appeared to be very poor. The Bela here did not have any animals as they all died in a drought several years ago. The streets were very sandy and dusty and the buildings were grey, but the town was enlivened by the brightly coloured clothes people wore. A group of boys accompanied us. They all spoke some English, unlike other towns, where French was spoken along with local languages. Our guide also spoke English but was hard to hear because he kept his blue Tuareg scarf over his face. After visiting the Great Mosque, we were shown various historic houses where earlier explorers had lived and another mosque that had been a big, Islamic university until the 16th century. Some of us went to a Tuareg 'house' – a tent – where we were given tea and hassled like mad by merchants. Several of us visited the markets in the afternoon before going on a four-wheel drive into the Sahara desert to visit a Tuareg camp. The scenery was beautiful and the camp in the desert seemed unspoilt with no tourist traps or merchants – just a few tents, a school and some wells.

We had seen traditional Timbuktu. On the walking tour we went to a workshop that made doors. Timbuktu is famous for them; but only one family is allowed to make doors and has been doing so since the 14th century.

On Sunday March 18th we flew to Bamako in the morning, then spent several hours at the Hotel Mandé where we were allowed some day rooms to share. I swam, sunbathed, had lunch and went for a tour of Bamako. That evening our flight was five hours late in leaving and I just missed the connection in Paris to London. Mick had already left for Heathrow to meet me but I managed to contact him on his mobile phone. At least I arrived home in one piece. Before Sarah died I know I would have felt far more distressed over missing the connection. Since then, I realise that this is not one of life's most important things.

I arrived home on March 19th, Francesca's fifth birthday. We called in to see Anna, Rosie and Francesca on the way home from Heathrow, to wish Francesca happy birthday and to give them all their presents from Mali.

I went back to work the next day and later in the week had my annual appraisal with William. That went without problems but I found myself weepy again about Sarah. I had not done that at work for quite a while. Most of the time I still felt she was not really dead, she was out there in the world somewhere. At other times I missed her desperately, I wanted to see her, talk to her, hug her, laugh with her and tell her things. I wanted her to go to Mali and see the wonderful places I had been to.

On Saturday March 24th Francesca had a birthday party at her house and on Sunday we all went to Carol's for a Mother's Day 'do'. Although both events were good, Mick and I were both feeling low at that time. I did an interview for *BBC News 24* on our NeuroPage project and I was still advising Jacqui Spector for the Channel 5 documentary on "Amnesia". On the way home from work one night I heard Dylan's "Forever Young" on the radio and wept. It made me feel depressed for several hours.

Rosie had lost two other people since Sarah's death. Her Uncle Stan, her father's brother and the father of her favourite cousin, had died in Portugal in November. Then in March, her father's close friend, Justine, had died at the age of 32 from complications arising from diabetes. Justine had a daughter, Leah. She died on Leah's sixth birthday. Rosie knew Justine well and was upset. At the age of 13 she had seen three people die in 10 months. Francesca had met Justine and Leah although she did not know them well. When she heard she said to Anna, "But mums don't die." "Sometimes they do," said Anna, "but not very often." "But they don't die on your birthday," said Francesca. She talked about death frequently and in a matter-of-fact way, saying things like, "When I'm grown up will grandma be dead?" Rosie still talked very little about Sarah. Anna told her that if she wanted to talk about Sarah it was OK. Rosie said she did not talk about her because she did not want to upset herself and she did not want to upset us. After Justine's death she said on one occasion that she was cursed as other children her age did not have three people die in 10 months.

April 2001

By this time I was more or less doing a full day at work, staying until 5.30 or so. I was also working well at the weekends. Occasionally I thought about retiring, but mostly felt comfortable with the way things were – not too many patients, although I was seeing one or two a week. A colleague from Bristol telephoned on April 4th and at first we spoke about Mali and I was jolly. Then he asked how Mick was. I felt the grief wash over me again – that too familiar feeling – and cried once more. I suppose that will always happen, albeit less frequently. I also felt Mick had aged since Sarah's death, more than I had. He was still angry with her for being so stupid as to go on the trip. He said that when he was Sarah's age, with three children, he had no idea about all the things he was to do and achieve in the next 30 years and Sarah would never do anything else. We both knew, however, that she had packed a lot into her 36 years.

Matthew was 35 years old on April 6th. We spoke on the phone. He was in Los Angeles and seemed in a good mood although he still cried readily when he thought about Sarah.

On the same day I heard that I had been elected to the Academy of Medical Sciences which is considered to be quite an honour. The British Psychological Society asked if I would be willing for them to put my name forward for another society, The Academy of Learned Societies in the Social Sciences. I was elected to that society later in the year. On April 9th I watched a programme about high-risk surfers. They had personalities like Sarah's. She would have enjoyed the programme. I kept thinking about their families and how they would feel if anything happened.

David and Janet from Belgium came to visit on April 11th. David had a meeting in Suffolk. They talked about the memorial service they had held on the tenth anniversary of their daughter, Eleanor's, death. I thought, "I don't want it to be 10 years since Sarah's death. It's too long. She will be too far away".

By mid-April I was preparing for my talks in Australia in May and our forthcoming trip to Peru. I felt stressed by the organisation involved and the knowledge that the first anniversary was approaching. It was Easter time. I remembered that last Easter I was in Brazil and had to plan my return trip so that I could get home in time for Sarah's farewell dinner. She was alive then and should still be alive now.

Both Mick and I were feeling depressed. We talked a great deal about Sarah and both knew that the first anniversary would be a bad time. I was also worried about being jet-lagged when we set off on our trek in Peru. As usual when I was miserable I thought about another trip. 'Explore' had just sent information about a new trip they were starting in the autumn. This was to be a lowland gorilla search in Gabon. I checked my leave situation and my diary, realised I could just fit in that nine-day trip and sent my form off on April 19th for a trip in November. In the event, it was not as good as the Mali trip, but I did get through the whole holiday without saying anything about Sarah's death. I talked about her as if she were alive. Someone asked how old she was and I said "38". That is how old she would be now. I felt I had moved forward, though, as previously, I felt compelled to tell people about losing her.

We had also booked for the next weekend meeting of The Compassionate Friends to be held in Glasgow in May, shortly before our trip to Australia. Anna decided to join us this time. Cindy and her partner, Eleanor, were coming to look after Rosie and Francesca. Mick and I put "Forever Young" on to an audiotape to take for the music session and both ended up sobbing. I also drafted a short piece about Sarah for The Compassionate Friends meeting to go along with her photograph in the 'portrait' section. I got a lump in my throat but did not cry because I was at work and expecting a patient any minute. It was nearly always possible now to control such things if one had to. There was simply this terrible sadness inside. I thanked 'God' or whatever for my grandchildren. At first I thought I could have borne their loss more easily than Sarah's, but not now. They were our future. When Anna and the girls came to dinner on Sunday 29th, as they did most Sundays, I wanted Sarah there, I wanted to lay a place for her and put out a chair.

May 2001

The first week in May was a sad week for all of us. May 3rd was the anniversary of the last day I saw Sarah, then there was the last day I spoke to her on the phone, the last e-mail I received and so on. Matt, Anna, Mick and Rosie all had their 'last times they saw her' occasions too. I think Anna felt worse than anyone. What a sad, terrible thing, though, that Sarah was no longer there. Marilyn Monroe was 36 when she died, so was Diana and so was my lovely Sarah. I was busy going through the slides for Australia and getting ready for The Compassionate Friends meeting. The main thing Mick and I noticed about the meeting was how much better we were than last time. We had moved on. We were beginning to support people more newly bereaved — or who were coping less well. There were, however, some people whose children had died before Sarah but who were still more distressed than us. Once again we heard awful stories and were confirmed in our view that Sarah's death was not so bad as it might have been — the manner of her death, that is. The sense of loss was just as bad as anyone's.

As in the previous year, we attended the session where people took tapes of songs that had been important for them or their dead children. We played "Forever Young" and wept of course. We also went to the poetry and prose session. I read out part of *Letter to a Younger Son* and Anna read out part of her speech. Patricia Lloyd who organised the session along with her husband, read a poem she had written called "Being Lucky". It struck a chord with me. Here is the poem.

BEING LUCKY

by Patricia Lloyd

"Think how lucky you are
That *all* your children are not dead."

"Nowadays we are so lucky –
It used to be touch and go
Whether children survived their childhood."

"How lucky we are not to live in a country
Where thousands die
In earthquakes and floods."

It comes as a surprise to learn of my "luck"
Through comments on the lips
Of some I call friends.
But I realise their need to avoid
Pain's stark reality:
And I know that in self-protection
They are addressing their own agenda.

Others are prepared to
Enter the harsh desert
Of those facing loss,
The place of pain and exposure
Where the protective
Bright canopy of hope is ripped away.

These are the ones who know well
That suffering cannot be measured
By numbers of dead, or size of disaster.
The mother finding her infant dead in the cot
Feels the self-same anguish as
The father weeping over his son's body,
Crushed in the earthquake's devastation.
Each loss is intensely personal.

Dear friends, can you not realise
My daughter's death

Defines my world?
I no longer belong to yours
In the same way that I did.
It is irrelevant to speak of luck
When the loss of one dear, irreplaceable girl
Leaves me desolate.

We arrived home safely. Matt also came home from America looking well.

I cried more that week than I had for a while and left early from work again. I felt sure this was because the first anniversary was approaching. I went to the National Portrait Gallery for the preview of the exhibition of "Faces in mind: A hundred years of British psychology". My photograph was there along with the other five award winners of the distinguished contributions to professional psychology – and other psychologists. It was a pleasant enough occasion but these awards and accolades meant so much less since Sarah died. I would give them all up if I could get her back. On Friday May 11th I thought about Sarah and how, this time last year, she was still alive. I wanted to get the trek to Peru out of the way.

We went out to Maison Bleu for a belated birthday meal for Matthew. On Friday afternoon Mick and I had to see our solicitor about the death certificate. The three of us then went to a notary public to sort out a power of attorney for the Peruvian lawyer. The notary public was unpleasant. He did not smile or shake our hands or greet us in any way except to say, "Peru, eh?" and, "Are you happy?" He knew what it was about. His behaviour was insensitive and crass. I was not happy. I signed the document but was appalled at this man who charged £50 for his signature that took a second to complete.

We survived May 12th without too much distress. Carol had organised the anniversary event in her garden. We talked about Sarah and cried and watched Cameron and Francesca playing in the sandpit. We were leaving at 8.00 a.m. the next day for Australia and then our trek to Peru to get to the site of Sarah's death. Most of our packing had been completed on the Saturday and Matthew offered to take us to the airport on Sunday morning.

At the airport, Mick was looking at the *Sunday Telegraph* and showed me an article written by Nigel Starmer-Smith who had lost two children to cancer. I found the piece heart-wrenching and wanted to write to Nigel Starmer-Smith. I never did at that time, and even later when I wrote to ask his permission to quote this piece, I could not get in touch with him. However the *Sunday Telegraph* gave me permission to quote this wonderfully brave and inspiring article.

TWICE THE HEARTBREAK

Nine years ago Nigel Starmer-Smith lost his daughter Charlotte to a rare disease. A fortnight ago, his 19-year-old son Julian died of cancer. Here he tells their story.

There are not words. Oh, but there are. Words that can distil something of the essence of the boy – or was he already a man? I can only try to convey the pain of the hurt, the pride of the parent, the disbelief over repeated tragedy – the loss of a daughter and now, a son. But my wife Rosamund and I do believe, as Plato first declared, that there is a Heaven beyond our consciousness, and that Charlotte and Julian are together in some immortal form – a pretty wonderful combination.

There is a terrace on the third floor of the John Radcliffe Hospital, Oxford. I must have spent quite a few hours there during the last weeks of Julian's illness, sometimes with Ros, sometimes with a friend, sometimes alone. Hour by hour, night by day, my wife and our other son, Charles, maintained a mask of hopefulness by Julian's bedside. On the terrace, I – the weakest of the three of us – could slip off that mask for brief moments.

From the terrace there's a striking vista across the leafy Thames Valley, a few Oxford spires upstanding, enclosed by the hills of Cumnor Hinksey and Beckley. In the midst, so clear at sunrise, stands the tower of St Nicholas' Church, Old Marston, close by the home of my 92-year-old father. In this landscape are locked all my childhood years, school, university, and lots of family happiness. In those desolate hours and days, as I stood and stared out, so many memories returned to me, while I tried to pierce the mental numbness, searching my soul to make some sense of the senseless.

My 19-year-old treasured son lay close by, two floors above, fighting to stay alive as T-cell lymphoma, a rare form of cancer, ravaged his young body. Julian – Jules, as he preferred it – so full of life, athleticism and fun. Surely life could not desert him?

It had all been so sudden. Late last August Julian had returned from a mission to south-west India, where he and several school friends had spent weeks barrowing concrete and carting bricks to build a simple house for a local family. A week later he was in the Infectious Diseases unit at the Churchill Hospital, Oxford, with a high fever. Whatever it was left him as quickly as it came. All was well and life returned to normal. We can only reflect now on whether this brief illness might have been the catalyst for something more serious.

Seven months later, newly qualified as an advanced skiing instructor after the second epic trip of his gap year to the snow caps of Quebec, Julian's high fever returned. He flew into Heathrow; within 48 hours he had been readmitted to hospital with soaring temperatures and intolerable sweats sapping the energy of his fit young body.

The painstaking search by specialists to identify the cause began. As each analysis of blood, liver and bone-marrow tissue eliminated possible diseases, our fears grew. Finally the lymph node biopsy revealed that cancer was invading his blood. He was transferred to John Radcliffe and it was there, on Good Friday, that Ros and I were gently told the worst possible news. That this was a variant of T-cell lymphoma; that his chances of survival were slim. Rightly, Julian was told, too, but not that he had little chance of recovery.

Nine-and-a-half years ago, Julian's sister Charlotte died on Remembrance Day, aged 16, of haemophagocytic anaemia, another rare disease. Charlotte's illness had exhibited similar characteristics, but there was no diagnostic connection. In her case glandular fever had been the trigger of a rare type of blood disorder which, like Julian's, was to take her from unbounded vitality to death in just five weeks.

Charlotte's death left Ros, Charlie, Julian and me broken-hearted and bemused. For almost 10 years, scarcely a day had passed without some memory of her infectious laughter, her sparkling eyes and carefree style. What joy she brought us; what a loss to bear.

I could not stop thinking of Charlotte as I paced the hospital terrace, Julian's condition becoming ever more desperate, the consultants more troubled and rightly short on reassurance. But no, this could never be repeated in one family. Please God, please, spare my wonderful child. But there was to be no answer, no consolation, no prayed-for miracle.

Throughout this agonising time there was Ros, ministering with such courage and love to her son, coping so gently with the horrific side-effects of two weeks of chemotherapy. Her words to me on Charlotte's death came to mind; words first conveyed to her by the Great Ormond Street chaplain when, as a staff nurse, she had been deeply hurt by the loss of a particular child patient. "You must remember, children are a gift from God, they are only lent to us." So, once again, was our brief tenure of loan about to expire?

It would be easy to say that the second time round we were better prepared, and to an extent we were. We could anticipate the physical and psychological agonies we would be forced to confront. But in truth, we never allowed ourselves to believe that history was repeating itself.

And then there was Charles. As the days and nights passed and merged into one, Ros and I worried desperately for our other son, now 22, a young man who had lost his adored elder sister, and had now to look as the life, but not the spirit, of his brother ebbed slowly away. Charles was everything to Julian; his role model, his confidant, his best friend. And Charles reciprocated in kind. Julian's hair had been lost through chemotherapy; Charles shaved his head, too, in an unspoken pact of fraternal loyalty. Even when Julian's voice had left him, he would mouth, "I want Charlie." And Charles he had, hour by hour, at his bedside, holding, caressing, gently talking.

Each of us, on our own with Julian at a different time in those last few days, received a truly powerful hug from a frail, once so athletic boy, and those whispered words, "I love you."

Supporting our small family group was a medical team beyond reproach. Dr Chris Hatton, his fellow consultants, registrars and doctors did everything possible in their fight to save Julian, as far-flung consultations and transatlantic advice was to no avail. Throughout, the nursing team on Ward 5E gave Julian every loving care.

We never allowed ourselves to consider that within days we would be burying Julian alongside Charlotte in the country churchyard at Rotherfield Peppard. To do otherwise would have been a threat to our sanity. We let our instincts for self-preservation take over; we clung on to hope, however remote, to the very end.

Now we can only see with our eyes shut, that affectionate, athletic young man who has touched the lives of so many. For his mum and me, there's the lad at Radley College, his unembarrassed hug and kiss when we came to pick him up for Sunday lunch. There were myriad phone-calls – whether he was at school or away on his travels – his first enquiry of us always, "Are you all right?" So it had been ever since Charlotte died.

Home and abroad we see him, generous to a fault, at the hub of the social scene, blond highlights in his hair, dyed latterly to a shock of ice blue. He's there, too, at BBC 5 Live, working as he did to save money for his travels, telephonist, office-boy, friend to all. There's the proud car owner. How he loved his car, he funded it himself; all the latest gadgets, and the inevitable go-faster stripes. And this time we're on the touchline at Radley College or Henley RFC, watching the scrum-half with the most devastating break off the back of the scrum I ever saw, the smallest, but fastest, player on the field. A modest smile, as always, but never a boast.

As with Charlotte, it's no use to dwell on what might have been. For Ros and me there are positive things we can cling to, not just the memories. We've gained an understanding, through all our children, of the depth and quality of friendship, intimacy and mutual support that exists between so many boys and girls of today, as the awkwardness and formality of a generation ago has been swept by the board.

The offer of Radley College to stage his funeral last Thursday was a generous and loving testimony. A thousand people were in the college chapel, where Julian was carried to his rest and read to by some of his closest friends, giving comfort to us all, and making us, his parents, proud for ever.

When Charlotte died, we established a charity fund which raised nearly half a million pounds. The Isolation Unit at the Royal Berkshire Hospital, Reading, stands to her name. This time donations will go towards the establishment of Research Fellowships at Oxford University in Julian's name. These will be set up under the guidance of Dr Chris

Hatton, head of the medical team which fought so hard to save our son. It will help, we hope, to unearth the causes and, God willing, a cure for this particular aggressive form of cancer which, though still rare, is increasing in young men at an alarming rate.

In the final analysis, it seems we have a choice. As Dylan Thomas put it, we could "Rage, rage against the dying of the light," or, as we prefer, follow the words of a close friend of Charles who sent this poem to him the other day:

> You can remember him and only
> that he is gone,
>
> Or you can cherish his memory and
> let it live on,
>
> You can cry and close your mind,
> Be empty and turn your back,
>
> You can do what he'd want, smile,
> open your eyes, love and go on.

You see, then, why there is in fact no choice. For Jules' sake, buoyed up by his radiant smile and his exemplary care for others, we turn our faces to the wind. For me, for Ros and Charlie, these are the only words we need.

I started this book about the first year on the 12-hour flight from Amsterdam to Singapore on May 13th. We wanted to buy a good, digital video to film the trek in Peru and a Walkman to play the songs from Sarah's memorial service. We had speakers already that were packed in Mick's flight bag. We decided to buy the camera and Walkman in Singapore at the duty-free shop. We had one hour between flights. Fortunately, the people in duty-free were very efficient. We were shown the video we wanted. Matt had done his homework previously and told us what to buy. The credit card was authorised and we were sent to another shop much further away for the Walkman. We rushed down and explained we were in a hurry. One person checked the card and another wrapped the Walkman and we made our flight on to Sydney. We landed at 6.00 p.m. local time on May 14th. We stayed at the Observatory Hotel, a very good and famous Sydney location. After a shower, supper and some delicious chilled white wine, we went to bed and slept for 12 hours.

Even though the next day, May 15th, was the first anniversary of the day we heard the terrible news, we felt fine. I was met at 11.30 and taken to the Sydney Children's Hospital where I gave my first talk on memory. It went down well.

At 7.00 a.m. on May 16th, we left the hotel at 7.00 a.m. to travel to the conference of the Australian Society for the Study of Brain Injury that was being held on

Magnetic Island, which has a beautiful volcanic landscape. At breakfast on May 17th we met up with two friends from New Zealand, Kay and Tommy Farrar. They knew Sarah, who had been fond of them both, and had promised to visit them in New Zealand. They were both at the meeting in South Africa the summer before Sarah died and I have a lovely photo of the three of them together. We also met Jennie Ponsford, the colleague who had sent such good letters after Sarah's death.

We went out to dinner with Jennie, Kay and Tommy, to an open-air restaurant on the beach surrounded by delightful possums. We talked a great deal about Sarah and I think everyone was in tears.

In the morning I ran a three-hour workshop that was a shortened version of the one Agnes and I had run in London earlier in the month. I felt it had gone reasonably well, but I had a rather small audience of 36 people as, unlike memory, reduced states of awareness is not a field where many psychologists work.

I gave my keynote address the following day entitled "Rehabilitation of the Dysexecutive Syndrome: A Goal-Planning Approach". It seemed to be well received. Kay said it was worth coming to the conference for that and some others said it was "brilliant". Well, it was not brilliant but I felt happy with it. Swam and went to the beach with Kay and Tommy that afternoon. Mick went for a walk up the mountainside. We all went to the conference dinner that evening.

We left Australia on Thursday May 24th. The flight to LA took 13 hours. I slept well. Mick did not. We landed, only 25 minutes late, at 1.55 p.m. and arrived at the hotel at 3.00 p.m. It was still Thursday. We swam, showered, had dinner and went to bed early. We were leaving for Peru the following morning, Friday May 25th, at 9.00 a.m.

❧

CHAPTER SEVEN

We kiss the joy as it flies

2003

So far we have not spoken much about the actual white-water rafting venture itself and how we felt about Sarah's participation in such a dangerous sport. Neither, for reasons connected with the laws of libel, have we mentioned the name of the company that organised the rafting expedition and whose crew, guides, and leaders were responsible for the safety and protection of the excursionists who volunteered to participate in the rafting of what was a grade 5 series of rapids. It was originally our intention to name the company and we had sought their permission in the understanding that there would be no criticisms of their organisation and safety measures. However, because of their procrastination and doubts it was decided by the publishers not to name the company in this book.

So what is it we wish to say now that we have had three years to reflect on our impressions, based on accounts of the accident given to us by members of the expedition, some of whom organised the rafting and others who were fellow-adventurers of Sarah's, attracted by the thrills of the sport? First of all we would want to point out to would-be rafters that they should think very carefully about their own abilities to fight against dangerous rapids in the event of there being an accident that leads to them being pitched into the water; they should also be aware of the dangers connected with a combination of rocks, rapids, and freezing cold waters. They should ask themselves how good are they in the water, how well can they swim, are they strong enough to withstand extreme pressures of currents, rapids and hydraulic holes? Above all, however, they should find out how experienced and qualified are the people organising their rafting expedition, and how well they are prepared for unforeseen accidents that might occur. What safety measures are available to the company in the form of ropes and accompanying watercraft capable of fast movement in water – sufficient to catch up with anyone being dragged away by extremely fast-running rapids? They should check the grading of the river at the time they are to enter and ask themselves whether they are sufficiently experienced and strong enough to enter a high-graded rapid.

What we are saying here is not offered as a criticism of the actual company involved in the expedition that led to our daughter's death. As far as we can ascertain from the company members, those volunteers who participated in the venture, and subsequent 'experts' who reviewed the expedition, all safety measures were in place and the volunteers were fully knowledgeable of the risks they were taking. Nevertheless, five of the volunteers were pitched into a grade 5 river and one of them was killed. There should be no deaths, and we know that the expedition leaders recognise this as well as anybody. We have also wondered ourselves whether a single kayak and a possibly cumbersome cataraft were sufficient to be able to cope with five people in the water. Was such a boat as the latter capable of chasing *and reaching* any one or more of the crew who were pitched into the rapids? While it is true that the kayak was able to reach and rescue one or two in the water, was it not insufficient to reach others who might flow by in the meantime? It seems that most members of the expedition thought, after the event, that Sarah was incapable of helping herself; she could not grab the safety ropes. This implies she was hurt in such a way that she could not react physically to help herself. To us this means that organisers of future expeditions must recognise that people can get hurt so badly by rocks or whatever that they become helpless and need people in fast craft in sufficient numbers to give chase downriver at speed.

Since the death of our daughter we have witnessed several scenes of water rafting on television holiday programmes and we have usually been appalled at the lackadaisical approach to rafting exhibited by the presenters and holiday-makers. Whitewater rafting is treated as a bit of a laugh, a joy-ride, something akin to funfair amusement rides. Our daughter Anna has even seen a mother and her two little children participate in rafting while on a surprise holiday offered by a television programme. Such scenes and attitudes appal us and we would appeal to television holiday presenters to think more seriously about what they might be encouraging relatively unfit people and maybe poor swimmers to participate in when they so glibly throw the not-so-fit holiday-makers into white-water rafting. We would also appeal to the organisers of rafting expeditions to consider very carefully how well prepared their volunteers might be for such hazardous ventures. We would like to see some form of certification introduced whereby would-be rafters have to provide evidence as to how experienced they are in white-water rafting, how fit they are, and how good they are at swimming. After all, those holiday-makers who participate in scuba diving have to provide evidence of their abilities, their training and their experience before they are taken out by diving schools. Something similar should be put in place for would-be rafters. We are not talking about mountain biking, hiking or walking tours here: we are talking about a sport that is equal in danger to rock-climbing, and we believe that no respectable holiday company in the world would allow holiday-makers to climb dangerous rocks or mountains without some evidence of previous experience and ability.

As a footnote to the above questions we would like to report on a phone conversation Mick had recently with the organiser of Sarah's fatal expedition, who pointed out that he had not been able to run a white water-rafting expedition for some considerable time because of his feelings over Sarah's death; not in fact until about a "year ago" when he returned to the area where Sarah was killed. He proudly told Mick that they had, since Sarah's expedition, introduced "lots of new safety measures" and, although these were all small in themselves, he believed they made his rafting expeditions that much safer. Mick's first thought was, "Why were those safety measures not in place when our daughter fell into the icy rapids of the Cotahuasi River in the year 2000?" His second thought was, "Would they have made all the difference and led to Sarah's rescue?" Mick did not ask these questions of the organiser, who, he sensed over the telephone, could have bitten off his own tongue immediately he blurted out, with pride, the news of the improvements. Continuing these reflections a little longer, we would ask would-be rafters to check the safety regulations and procedures operated by the company organising their expedition, and most particularly ask what would happen if a crew member became incapacitated in the river? Would there be a sufficient number of fast-running craft to catch up with them?

Looking back at Chapter Six it is obvious to us both that we were changing even during that first year, although we were not always aware of the changes at the time. Reading Barbara's description of Mali it is noticeable that the trip – the exciting adventure of the expedition to a variety of extraordinary places and the meeting up with exotic people – had an effect on Barbara's daily thinking. Although Sarah was not out of her mind for long, Barbara was able to cope with many of her interactions with other people without grief breaking through. What was in fact happening was a kind of preview of later years when grief does not hit so frequently or indeed sharply. Mick, too, was coping better on the trip to Australia. In fact he spent much of the time on Magnetic Island getting very fit in preparation for the trek through the mountainous region of the Cotahuasi Valley that was shortly to follow.

What advice can we give to people who might face a similar bereavement? The thing is not to sit around doing nothing. Even when one's concentration is poor it is better to be involved in something such as work or getting fit or travelling – if this is possible. Going out to meals with family and friends was a good way to indulge oneself. Keep saying, "Life goes on!" Keep your loved and lost one in mind, yes of course, you can hardly let go anyway; but aim to experience other things.

Activities of daily living cannot be avoided, however hard you might want to stop the bus and get off! And don't feel guilty at enjoying yourself. Sometimes you are brought up terribly short, just as Wordsworth was in one of his poems, where he catches himself smiling at something and at that moment he is brought back to the reality of the loss of a loved one. This happens frequently in grief. We sometimes wondered what people were thinking when they saw us laughing and joking around. Their feelings were probably a mixture of uncertainty and relief. We did enjoy ourselves, even in that first year, but if we ever felt guilty we would remind ourselves that Sarah would have wanted us to be happy or at peace. In fact we constantly referred to Sarah's blessing on such occasions and could hear her say, "You go on, enjoy yourselves, don't be unhappy because of me."

Two weeks ago we attended the annual meeting of the Scottish branch of TCF. Although we are not Scots ourselves, the meeting is open to any member of TCF so we thought we would attend as it was so close to the third anniversary of Sarah's death. It was a most impressive and helpful meeting for us both. The organising committee, led by Hugh and Maureen McAninch, of the Scottish branch did a wonderful job. All meetings and events that we attended were impressively organised and we came away feeling inspired and at peace with ourselves. In our jobs, we are highly experienced attendees of both national and international conferences, but there's nothing to compare with TCF for providing a thorough examination of the human spirit! Here is a club whose members did not choose to join but who are irreversibly bound in their shared sorrows. What does this club do for us and what has it done for us in the past three years?

For a start, Barbara has described how we arrived at our first meeting only eight weeks after Sarah's death. We were in a terrible state and were given considerable support from the other members. We were desperately clinging on to any advice given and were given scope to share our grief with others in a similar plight. At the Perth conference, however, we found ourselves in the role of 'old hands'. There were 23 new members, all needing solace, explanations, and the opportunity to articulate the awful tragedies they had recently experienced. So what do we get out of TCF now?

It is true that a burden shared is a burden halved as it were. Being with people who have had similar terrible experiences allows you to see the generality of tragic events and thus takes you outside yourselves to some extent. We are able to cry not only *with* others but also *for* others at TCF meetings. What is more we are now in a position to commiserate with parents whose pain is more recent and sharper than ours. Sometimes we say to ourselves, "How lucky we are!" Which is very strange. But there are lots of things that are strange about the workings of grief.

Another thing we are always saying at TCF meetings is that the way in which we lost Sarah is not as bad as some of the ways others have lost their children. Sarah did not die after a lengthy period of illness and pain, she did not kill herself, she was not killed by someone else. But we have met parents – and met them at the Perth meeting – whose children have died in these circumstances. The main speaker at Perth was Mick North, a father of one of the 16 five-year-olds and their teacher killed in the Dunblane massacre in 1996. Two years before this terrible event Mick lost his wife from breast cancer so was bringing up his daughter Sophie alone. Mick gave an excellent, measured description of the Dunblane parents' efforts to come to terms with the atrocity and how they organised themselves to cope with media attention, legal concerns and all the complications that followed in the wake of the atrocity. There are no words we can write here that can stand in for or measure up to Mick North's own book, *Dunblane: Never Forget*. All we can do is to thoroughly and unwaveringly recommend it to the reader, and also remind him or her that one of the main achievements brought about by pressure from the Dunblane parents was a welcome change in the British gun laws.

One of the sessions Mick attended at the Perth meeting was for fathers only. Although it started somewhat hesitatingly it progressed to being a session that proved to be quite inspiring in its own quiet way. On the previous night we had met the parents of a son who had killed himself by hanging in his own house. The tragic event had happened only weeks earlier and both parents were obviously totally devastated and crying out for help. Mick was glad to see the father at the session and to note how bravely he spoke about the loss of his son. There was also a very tough-looking, large Scot whose son had died five months earlier who was finding it very difficult to come to terms with the group of grieving fathers, and was fighting against even being in their company. But even he eventually spoke about the event of his son's death and also told the group that another son had lost two stones in weight since his brother's death.

The group talked about the difficulties men seem to face when showing emotions or actually crying and the general feeling was that men should learn to cry more easily because of the emotional release that it can bring. After most of us had described how we lost our child a man who, up until then, had not spoken much and who Mick had mistakenly thought of as being cynical (in fact he has a very dry sense of humour) began to tell the group how his son had also killed himself in their family home. He said that he drew some comfort from the fact that his boy had not gone to a strange place to end his life but had felt secure enough in the family home to do this act. In the pause that followed Mick began to cry and this was done with no embarrassment whatsoever. After the session the two men who had lost sons in the same way could be seen in a huddle, talking about whatever they needed to talk about.

One thing we think we should stress about TCF meetings is that they run the whole gamut of emotions. They are not entirely sombre occasions where one sees only sad faces and hears only the sobs of the bereaved. At times the meetings are quite the contrary and laughter can ring round the room or the bar or breakfast hall. We would have to call the meetings inspiring and for much of the time people are happy to be talking to each other about their loved children. However, they do allow for tears and regrets and nobody feels out of place when this happens. The bar is one of the favourite places for many people and late into the Saturday night much laughter can be heard as old friends swap stories. We remember particularly the 2001 gathering, held in a hotel in Glasgow, which was also hosting many barber shop quartets as there was a festival of this mode of singing in Glasgow at the time. Late in the night it soon became clear that the barber shop quartets and many of the TCF members were singing songs together. The singers confided in us that they were at first very apprehensive about sharing the hotel with the TCF but were very much relieved to find that we were human after all!

Another group of parents attending TCF meetings are those who have lost an only child. We often think of them because of their particularly painful loss and the emptiness they must feel in their daily lives without their special loved one. Again we think of ourselves as being lucky. We haven't spent much time talking about Anna and Matthew because our time has been taken up with the tragic loss of their sister. This book is for her. However, it is also for the family and we have been helped a great deal by Anna and Matthew's advice. They have felt Sarah's loss terribly also. They are, in their own ways, just as special as Sarah and we don't want to let her loss get in the way of our relationships with them. Anna is a good woman, a hard-working woman who did not take the risks nor the worrying alternative paths that Sarah took. Anna has brought up two wonderful daughters of her own and we as grandparents are, yes we say it again, lucky to be able to see them almost every day. When we are with our grandchildren it is like starting all over again. More lives to treasure.

Matthew, too, has been a strength to us in his way although he has perhaps been hit hardest by Sarah's death. He telephones us nearly every day to see how we are and he keeps us posted as to how he is getting on in his work and social life. Like Sarah, he has many friends who love him, and again we are thankful that we see him often. Both our remaining kids have acted as a great audience for their parents, we can confide in them and share our bereavement with them. Yes, we think we are a better family now but this has not happened automatically through grief. We have to work at it just as hard as anybody else. But we do have the luxury of being able to think of our angel Sarah and remind ourselves of how unselfish, spirited, honest and beautiful she was. We kiss the joy as it flies!

CHAPTER EIGHT

The final goodbye: "Forever Young"

Peru May/June 2001

We left Los Angeles on Friday May 25th and went first to Dallas. I phoned Anna from the airport. She was well. Rosie was in France on a water sports holiday (she promised us she would not go white-water rafting). Francesca spoke to me and said she had a dream about a lady in Peru (this was probably her old dream about a lady going in the river). We landed in Lima at 11.26 p.m.

The following morning we caught the plane to Arequipa, which is in a beautiful location. There are stunning, white-topped mountains all around. Pepe Lopez was there to meet us. We found it easy to relate to him. He seemed straight and honest, and his English was good. We went to La Hosteria, the pretty hotel we stayed in last year where the woman held me and remembered Sarah. She was still working there. Pepe talked to us for a while about the trip and then left us for the afternoon. After unpacking, we went into the city centre, had a good lunch and then sat in the Plaza d'Armas watching people and pigeons. It is (or was) a picturesque square (just after we returned home we heard about a bad earthquake that damaged the city centre of Arequipa).

We met Pepe for dinner and he talked about the next few days. I said, "We want the truth even if it is painful". He said he would tell us the truth. I mentioned that we had heard slightly different versions of Sarah's last minutes and were hoping Pepe could provide the definitive version. He thought the different versions were due to the fact that people had seen the accident from different perspectives. Earlier that day Pepe said he had followed Sarah down the river for about 20 minutes. This worried Mick who thought she might have been struggling in terror and pain for that time. I thought it meant that Pepe had followed her body for 20 minutes.

On Sunday May 27th, we left Arequipa in a minibus with a driver called Edwin and a cook called Raoul, neither of whom spoke English. Raoul turned out to be a very good cook. The journey, mostly on dirt roads, to Cotahuasi town was pretty awful. We thought it was even worse than last year. Pepe said they had had more rain in the rainy season this year. The scenery near Arequipa was harsh and barren with no vegetation at all in some areas. As we pushed on, however, the scenery became more beautiful and dramatic. The snow-capped peaks with their brilliant blue backgrounds are lovely. Because of the altitude, it was cold. As we neared Cota-huasi town we had to reverse for over a mile because a bus was coming from the town and there was only room for one vehicle at a time on the road. Since leaving Arequipa we had seen hardly any traffic. The area was very remote, empty, beautiful and dangerous. Pepe showed us a photocopied journal article about the first people to kayak down the River Cotahuasi. The article was frightening as it showed how dangerous the river was even for experienced people – and Sarah was not experienced. Mick said that if Sarah had seen the report she would not have gone on the trip. I was not sure as she was foolish about her sporting activities. Here is the article.

RIO COTAHUASI: THE WORLD'S DEEPEST CANYON – REALLY!
by John Foss

Should she haul the kayak 100 metres back to camp, or take on the tumul-tuous cascade? She decides to go for it. Shoving off, she successfully navigates the top section, then drops into a turbulent, river-wide hole at the bottom. Ejected violently out of the hole, she recovers quickly by executing an Eskimo roll.

Downstream, I toss out a rope. "Eva!" I yell. "Your helmet's gone!"

Panic subsides when, to everybody's relief, her helmet surfaces fifty meters downstream. Eva calmly paddles over, grabs it, and heads to shore. Relaxing in camp that night, we christen the rapid "Casi Desastre" (Almost Disaster).

It's been non-stop Class V whitewater for two days. Eva, Jon, and I are in the depths of a magnificent canyon formed by the Rio Marán, the major tributary of the Rio Cotahuasi. Here, on the west side of the Andes in southwestern Peru, the Cotahuasi watershed is one of the great concentrations of precipitous canyons on earth. It's an amazing part of the world – to the east lie the headwaters of the Amazon; to the west the Pacific Ocean; to the north, the Altiplano; and to the south, the Valley of Volcanoes and Colca canyon. Cartographers at Peru's Instituto Geográfico National (IGN) in Lima recently concluded that Cotahuasi canyon is actually deeper than Colca canyon, which has long been billed by the National Geographic Society as the deepest canyon in the world (*National Geographic*, January, 1993).

Is Cotahuasi canyon, in fact, the deepest? Well, it's all a matter of defi-nition. The American Geological Institute defines "canyon" as ". . . a long, deep, relatively narrow; steep-sided valley confined between lofty and precipitous walls in a plateau or mountainous area, often with a stream at the bottom where downcutting greatly exceeds weathering." Alas, there is no agreement among geographers on quantitative criteria – minimum width-to-depth ratio, whether to calculate depth from the highest point, the lowest point, or the average elevation above the river, or even and, perhaps most importantly, the maximum allowable distance between the two opposite points of measurements. Thus, claims that 'canyons' in the Himalayas such as Namche Barwa on the Tsango River in Tibet (known as the Brahmaputra River in India) and Nepal's Kali Grandaki River are deeper than the Cotahuasi may be incorrect, as the distances vary from the river bottom to its measured points.

The Cotahuasi basin ranges from 14.5–16.5 degrees South latitude straddling the west side of the continental divide. The headwaters drain the roof of South America, a series of 5,000-metre peaks that include Cerro Supramarca (5,240 m), Cerro Alcabalusa (5,224 m), Cerro Chancahuana (5,105 m), Cerro Chacacomo (5,250 m), Cerro Condomarca (5,168 m), and Cerro Quillo (5,038 m), that shape the divide between the Cotahuasi and Rio Apurimac to the north.

From these pinnacles, the Rio Huarcaya, a tiny rivulet, flows south through a series of open boulder-strewn canyons. It tumbles out of the high Andes, later merging with Rio Pampamarca in the narrow depths of the Aimaña gorge to form the Rio Cotahuasi. From here, the river roars 80 kilometers downstream to empty into the Pacific Ocean. On its 200-kilometer journey to the sea, the river drops over 3,800 meters – a phenomenal average gradient of 19 m/km (100 ft/mile). In its headlong descent, the river had carved a magnificent canyon, exposing multiple layers ranging in age and lithology from Quaternary volcanic ash to ancient Precambrian basement rock.

We first heard of the Cotahuasi canyon on an expedition down the Rio Colca in 1993. A Peruvian friend, Dr Fredy Revilla, a fellow boater, told us about the river, and showed a home video. Impressed, we returned to Peru in 1994, and again in 1995. In all, we have completed three expeditions to the Cotahuasi with an international group of Peruvian, Chilean, and American paddlers. The team included kayakers, Jon Barker, Dave Black, Kurt Casey, Franz Helfenstein, Greg Moore, Eva Luna Ramirez de Arellano, Duilio and Gian Marco Vellutino, myself and rafters Aldo Chiappe, Fico Gallese, Pepé Lopez, and Pepé Negro.

Despite claims by locals that it couldn't be done, last year's expedition proved that the Cotahuasi can be run to the sea. Thanks to generous sponsorship by Malden Mills-Polartec, REI, and other equipment manufacturers, we got II Expedición Peruano-Norteamericana al Cañon de Cotahuasi underway. The expedition had three objectives: (1) to descend the Rio Marán, a spectacular canyon that rivals in profile the nearby Colca canyon; (2) to paddle the upper reaches of the Cotahuasi, including the difficult Aimaña gorge we bypassed earlier; and (3) to map and photograph an ancient Huari site that we'd come across before, but not had time to explore.

Jon Barker and I arrive in Lima first to get ready for the Río Marán trip. Two days later, Eva flies in from Cuzco. Then, it's a 28-hour bus ride down the coast and out to the Altiplano. When we finally get to Marcabamba, it looks like the entire population has turned out to greet us. We get a warm welcome from the mayor, but local fishermen repeatedly warn of dangerous rapids, "unrunnable" waterfalls, and the certainty of our collective deaths, should we attempt to run the river. While not unduly alarmed, they do convince us to put in further downstream than we originally planned – near the village of Lampa. This way, we bypass a long, "unrunnable" stretch of river.

We get a late start. The trail is too steep for burros. With the help of two villagers, we carry our heavy kayaks filled with our gear, video and camera equipment and 10 days' worth of food. Each kayak weighs at least 35 kilograms. It takes us three hours of strenuous boat-hauling to reach a place to camp high above the river. It's dark before we get there. Totally exhausted, we bid farewell to our Peruvian friends, and under star-studded skies in the stark, moonlit desert, bed down for the night.

The next morning, we trek to the river. Two hundred meters below, we can hear the raging whitewater. Sweating profusely in the hot desert sun, we haul our gear around the long, "unrunnable" section the locals warned us about. Then, after a couple of 20-meter boat rappels, we reach the water's edge. It's midday.

In the water and approaching the canyon, I'm thinking maybe the locals are right. Downstream are vertical walls and boulder-choked Class V rapids as far as the eye can see. Maybe we're in over our heads. Using 1:50,000 scale topographic maps, we've been counting on an average gradient of 50 m/km around the Pampa de Lampa immediately below the put-in. We're lucky to find an easy flow of 25–35 m³/sec – perfect for an unknown, exploratory first descent.

Over the first five days, our progress is erratic. We run only one kilometre the first day. The next day three, then eight, three again, and two. It's slow going. We have to scout ahead, portage, and run drop after drop, threading our way down the narrow, limestone gorge. The Marán has all the challenges of a great Class V run: waterfalls and explosive ramps requiring continuous technical maneuvering through a narrow, boulder-choked course. We try not to think about the ultimate nightmare – Class VI rapids and vertical cliffs with no portage possible – a scenario that would mean a long, arduous bailout from the canyon.

One rapid stands out. Eva names it, "Aprieta los cachets!" (Tighten Your Butt!), and it gets our blood pumping. Towering and curvaceous limestone walls enclose a roaring maelstrom. There is no direct route except a blind entry on the far left. We climb the vertical walls on both sides of the river, but the view offers little solace. All we see is an entry two meters wide that leads to a tight, 90-degree turn immediately below. The middle section of the rapid boils with the deafening sound of raging water.

After agonizing for an hour or so, we decide to go ahead. We'll run the drop – blind. It may have been possible to portage high on the cliff to the left, but that would have required a gruelling, roped climb out of the inner gorge, and a subsequent rappel back to the river. In the end, we decide to stagger our runs at 10-second intervals. This way, we'll avoid a pile up if there's a 'keeper hole' ahead, i.e. a breaking wave with escape impossible. I go first and slip through the narrow slot. I make a quick draw stroke to correct for the sharp turn, then accelerate down a ramp, crash through a big hole, wash up on a pillow rock, and make the final left turn into a welcome flat-water pool. Eva and Jon follow with similar runs, the three of us howling and happy to be safely through "Tighten Your Butt". A little further on, with dusk falling, we make camp.

The next day, the bedrock geology changes from ancient Mesozoic limestone to Quaternary gravels. Accordingly, paddling is easier. We weave our way leisurely along the Rio Marán, enjoying some thirty kilometres of continuous Class IV rapids all the way to the Rio Cotahuasi. After that, we have many kilometres of romping in Class III rapids, on the way down to Iquipi, some fifty kilometers upstream from the Pacific. Here we take out.

With such a great warm-up, we are ready when the time comes to join our paddling pals. We meet in Cotahuasi, high in the Andes. It's a beautiful village 14 hours by bus north of Arequipa, a village with centuries-old Spanish architecture. Here, llamas saunter along winding cobblestone streets, and the faces of villagers conjure up visions of an earlier time, when their ancestors clashed with Spanish conquistadors. We receive a warm and emotional welcome from villagers who remember us from last year's expedition.

Bullet holes pock-mark the police station, a grim reminder of Peru's recent battle with terrorists. It's tranquil now in Cotahuasi, and indeed in most outlying areas of Peru. Peru's popular president, Alberto Fujimori, arrived in town the week before. It is believed that all the publicity surrounding the IGN's findings (Cotahuasi canyon being deeper than the Colca) might have been behind the presidential visit.

Duilio, Dave, and Kurt get to Cotahuasi before our crew. While waiting for us, they get things ready, scout downriver, and successfully complete a first descent of the spectacular, horseshoe-shaped Aimaña gorge. This canyon, along with the entire upper Cotahuasi, is layered with volcanic ash deposited during a series of volcanic eruptions. The river has rapidly (in geological time) cut through the loose sediment to form a deep chasm around the Pampa de Aimaña gorge.

Located directly below the village, the Aimaña gorge presents a formidable challenge. A Class VI cascade at the entrance necessitates a portage at the top of the canyon. Last year, we found this section so intimidating we bypassed it altogether.

Over three days, Duilio, Dave, and Kurt make two descents of this precipitous canyon using burros to transport the kayaks. To portage out of the inner canyon, they use a steel cable suspension bridge, and return to the river via steep switchbacks.

We are all together for the second run – Mungui Rapid. It gets its name from a small village on the north side of the river, and turns out to be the toughest drop in the gorge. First, there's a long, complicated entry. Tight, technical moves are called for in the middle, and the rapid culminates with some very big reversals. Eva's performance provides the most exciting theatrics. Midway in the rapid she tips over, floats through a boulder sieve upside down, and finally rolls right side up just above a big hole at the bottom.

The Cataracts of Sipia, just below the Aimaña gorge are, arguably, the most spectacular part of the river. Here, the water plunges over a series of three 50-meter drops that cut a magnificent gash through a massive block of tilted Mesozoic limestone. We spend most of the day and night next to the raging cataracts. The walls are bathed in the silvery iridescence of a full moon. Camped on the ledges, I feel as though we are sleeping next to an out-of-control freight train roaring over the abyss!

As we ready our equipment for the portage, our logistics maestro, Rene, organizes his burros for our trek around the waterfalls. When not helping us, Rene lives a peaceful life in paradise, one kilometre upstream from the cataracts. A resourceful and happy-go-lucky fellow, he is our main man on the Cotahuasi. After some problems last year, we know full-well that his sometimes ornery pack-animals are key to the success of our expedition.

"What do you think about us running the river that flows by your house?" I ask him.

He smiles warmly. "Increíble . . . super hermoso!" he replies.

Leaving the river behind, we follow Rene single-file as he patiently leads the burros carrying the kayaks up the steep switchbacks in the meter-wide trail. Our colourful plastic kayaks contrast jarringly – almost a visible clash of cultures – with these timeless beasts of burden. In this airy realm, we stare down on condors, those magnificent raptors, soaring above the narrow cleft.

It's five hours into the trek. We are on a terrace overlooking the inner gorge. Rather than portage to the river at Chaupo, a small village three hours away, we take a 'short cut' – a rappel into the inner gorge just below the cascades. Villagers tell us that there's a fishermen's trail down below that leads to the river. Unfortunately, we underestimate the time it takes to descend. As it turns dark, we are still making our way down the vertical cliffs of boulder-packed mud. We need flashlights, as we hastily stow our boating gear underneath an overhang, 200 meters above the river. Then, exhausted, hungry and dehydrated, we make our way down to the river. It's 11 p.m.

The next morning, Kurt and I climb up the cliff to finish the job of rappelling the boats. It takes an hour of rope work to get our boats back on the river – one of the most spectacular, demanding portages in memory.

Back in the canyon, we easily hike upstream along the shore to the base of the cataracts. We are rewarded with stunning, misty views of the lowest cascade crashing into the tranquil pool below. The pool is a favourite with local fishermen. With their jury-rigged tackle attached to tin can reels, they are quite adept at catching the big trout that lurk in the depths.

There are rumors that the river below Chaupo is flat. It is . . . for about 500 meters. A massive debris flow at the mouth of the Quebrada Andamayo has choked the river to form a pool. This marks the beginning of days of non-stop whitewater. We name the first long, complicated rapid "Barro Rojo" (Red Mud), but we call the whole gorge "Flatwater Canyon," to commemorate the spectacularly erroneous information we receive from the locals.

The Quebrada Andamayo debris flow has deposited millions of tons of house-sized boulders, mud, and silt into the river. As we paddle downstream, I feel as though we are heading back in time. We enter the Cañon de Marpa. Dike-veined walls of billion-year-old Precambrian rock enclose Huari ruins of the pre-Inca culture that dominated central Peru from 400–1200 AD. Cotahuasi in Quechua means, "House on the Hill." It undoubtedly refers to the superb agricultural terraces and stone foundations on the steep slopes overlooking the river. The Huari built sophisticated gravity-fed irrigation systems that delivered water from springs high above. Cavities in the canyon walls entomb human skeletons and clothing that provide clues to their burial rites. We marvel at the ruins of this ancient civilization.

Some archaeologists believe that the Huari civilization developed about the same time as the Tiahuanaco culture on the shores of Lake Titicaca. Some theories suggest a relationship whereby the Huari functioned as a strategic military outpost, with Taihuanaco as the political and ceremonial center. Gazing upon cantilevered walkways, stone-inlaid roads, and the terraces lining the river corridor, it is easy to imagine the remote Cotahuasi canyon forming an impenetrable fortress.

There is archaeological evidence to suggest that ancient people, accustomed to the harsh life on the Altiplano, used the canyon for agriculture. Staple crops such as maize, tubers (potatoes, yuccas), and local grains (quinoa) probably grew better there. They still do. Yet, most of the terraces have been abandoned throughout the Andes. It's not clear why. One explanation points to fluctuations in rainfall. Less rainfall would lower the water table and reduce the supply of water for irrigation. On the other hand, evaporation may have led to a harmful accumulation of salts and minerals in the soil in this arid climate. Finally, Huari culture was already in decline by the 1200s, and many have been peacefully assimilated by the Incas when they consolidated their empire. In any case, European diseases – particularly influenza, smallpox, and measles – ravaged the indigenous populations in the Andes, as they did throughout the New World. This too, might account for the terraces falling into disuse.

After returning to Arequipa, we hear a rumor that engineers have been eyeing the Cataracts of Sipia. Already, they've gone over the site with a view to developing its hydroelectric potential.

Cotahuasi canyon, the Río Marán, and the Valley of the Volcanoes are unique and magnificent. True, nations have a need to develop hydroelectric and other forms of energy. But these natural wonders surely transcend such immediate concerns. In a very real sense, Cotahuasi canyon, the Río Marán, and the Valley of the Volcanoes belong to the people of Peru, now and for generations to come. It took millennia to create these works of nature. Only by creating a national park can their preservation be guaranteed.

We hope to present the case for preservation to President Fujimori. We'd appreciate any suggestions, ideas, and support on how to proceed. We'd especially like to hear from those with experience in establishing a national park in South America.

(Reproduced from *South American Explorer*, Spring 1996)

(Unfortunately, there is a very sad and extraordinarily coincidental follow-up to our inclusion of this extract from John Foss's article, and it has left us unable to come to terms with its tragic consequences. As with all the other quotations we have used in this book it was necessary to seek permission for such use from the publisher of the journal, in this case the *South American Explorer* as well as the author. We wrote in March 2004 to the publisher of the journal first of all, saying,

We wonder if you can help us? Our daughter Sarah was killed in a whitewater rafting accident in the year 2000. We have written a book about Sarah and our family's bereavement, which includes our own expedition to the site where Sarah was last seen . . . The book is to be published later this year and specifically, we want to quote a passage from a journal entitled 'South American Explorer', written by John Foss, who describes the River Cotahuasi most brilliantly in his article. Do you know how we might be able to contact John Foss – or the editorial board of the journal? We would be most grateful if you can provide us with any relevant information.

Michael and Barbara Wilson

Don from *South American Explorer* e-mailed us back the following message:

John Foss died in a white water accident some years ago. I've tried to contact any relatives he might have in Placerville, CO. But, no one was available today. Maybe tomorrow. I'll let you know. For our part, we have no objections to you using whatever you wish, and for the record, I doubt anybody else does either. So if you don't hear from anybody soon to the contrary, go ahead.
   Hope this helps.

All the best,

Don

All we want to say, and it is now only hours after we received Don's message, is that we shall try to think of John and Sarah as being linked forever by their love of the Cotahuasi, their spirit of adventure, and their similar departures from the beauty and excitement of the river valleys of the South American continent.)

I slept for several hours on and off in the van, perhaps because of the altitude. For much of the time we were travelling at around 5,000 metres (16,400 feet). We arrived at the hostel in Cotahuasi town exactly 12 hours after leaving Arequipa. This was the same hostel the five of us stayed in last year, with the flooded court-yard. There was no flooding this time. The owner remembered us and was friendly and welcoming. The food was better than last year because Raoul cooked it. We slept well.
   The weather on the following day was glorious, bright, crisp and clear showing the magnificent mountains nearby at their best. While Pepe, Edwin and Raoul were loading the van, Mick and I set off for a quick walk around the town, which still seemed in a time warp. We filmed the blacksmith shoeing a horse (a good scene), but we also saw a little girl, possibly aged about eight years, who was looking after two drunken or drugged parents (not a good scene). Earlier, Mick had seen the man lying

with his back against a wall, with his hat pulled down over his eyes – "Looking like a scene out of a Clint Eastwood film." Mick ran back to get his camera but when he returned the man was rolling in the road in torment, his wife was on the pavement in a stupor, and the little girl was trying to get her father to sit up. She looked at Mick with embarrassment as she vainly pulled at her father's sleeve. Mick turned away in respect for the little girl. Later we were to talk about this incident and Mick compared the wonderfully happy but short life of Sarah with what must be going on in the little girl's life. We knew that Sarah had had an almost idyllic childhood in comparison and wondered what lay in store for the little girl.

We set off to collect the mules and donkeys at a lower level in the valley. There was a considerable amount of unloading of the van and loading of the pack animals, so Mick and I went off for a walk. Pepe had hired a father and son to look after the animals. There were three donkeys that carried most of the luggage, tents and provisions plus two mules that carried a few things and one horse that did not carry anything (the load distribution did not seem fair to me). At first we followed the same track that we had taken last year. By 1.00 p.m. we were near the Sipia falls, close to the place where we held last year's ceremony. We did not feel the need to go to the falls again so pushed on.

The next part of the trail, part of an old Inca trail, was steep, so Pepe suggested we ride. I was given the horse and Mick one of the mules. After 20 minutes Mick said he wanted to walk as he did not feel in control. I was enjoying the ride and felt the horse was probably more sure-footed than me on the steep, shale-like, path. Mick is always more nervous of animals than me. He said he was petrified! He walked the rest of the way while I did a mixture of walking and riding. I had to dismount for the steep downhill parts and rode going uphill. Eventually, however, I just walked as I needed to stretch my legs.

The scenery was spectacular with wonderful mountains, colours and shapes. I found it extraordinarily beautiful, the most beautiful scenery I had ever seen. I know Sarah would have loved it and I was glad she had experienced such beauty before she died. On the other hand, neither she nor I would have known about this place if she had not gone on the trip and, of course, I would prefer never to have seen this beauty if it meant having Sarah back. We reached Chaupo, our camping spot, at 3.50 p.m. It was an oasis of green in the rocky surroundings. The place was a farm and Sarah had stayed there too on her way to the rafting part of the trip.

The animals had a good drink in a stream and Pepe talked about the accident. He said that Sarah was conscious at first, and had looked directly at him from the water as it swept her past him. She was the last of the five to come out of the 'hole'. The raft had not turned over as we had thought but had upended, so the guide had remained on the raft. We had always wondered why he did not go in the water too. So five people went in the water and Sarah was the last to emerge from this whirlpool-type place. Pepe thought she might have broken her neck just as we were told at the memorial service. At first she was choking and in the correct position but soon after there was another rapid. When she emerged from that she was completely lifeless and just tossed about. Pepe followed her by boat, and on foot, for about 20 minutes but she was floating very very quickly. It was so, so sad. My poor, lovely, beautiful girl. I wanted her back so very much.

We walked to the tents that had been pitched in a field owned by the farmer. Again, it was so beautiful there with the steep mountains, the lush meadow, the tethered pack animals and the farmer's cows and dogs. Our animals had a good feed from the tall grass around. Earlier in the day we had seen a herd of llamas. They looked as if they had been dyed as their coats were a mixture of rust and white. However, Pepe told us these were old Inca colours and quite natural. We had seen lots of llamas grazing over the past two days, but this morning's group were being herded. We had also seen an eagle and several hawks but very few people and no tourists of course. Raoul provided a good meal that we ate under the stars. We had soup, beef curry and rice together with a bottle of Chilean wine. We went to bed surrounded by the tethered donkeys, mules, horses, cows and sheep.

On May 29th, we enjoyed a breakfast of hot French toast. Our 'showers' were pretty basic, we were given a basin of water each just like in Mali. We trudged across the field to find a toilet spot and became covered in burrs so spent ages de-burring ourselves. I was not completely successful and kept finding burrs for days afterwards. Some even turned up back in England. Pepe, Mick and I left at 8.30. I found a stick that helped me up and down the steep parts of the trail. Some of the paths were tricky being shingle and shale on precipitous cliffs and narrow paths so we had to go very slowly in some places.

At this point we are presenting Sarah's diary of the last five days of her life before the fatal day of May 12th. She describes the scenery we have been covering in this final chapter. The diary was among her belongings and we found it extremely painful to read — just once and then it was put away until now, when we begin typing from her handwritten script . . .

Sunday 7th May

Woke up early, toothache easier. Stuff all ready — checked out but took key with me! No problems with flight except got there early boring wait with no café. Met at Arequipa by Cachimira(?), went to hotel which is very nice. Met rest of group briefly and went straight for tour of monastery — v. beautiful in places. Ate wonderful meal — excellent cow's heart and local freshwater shrimp. Some people went for siesta, but others went to shops (no whiskey!). On Place des Armes, local girls went crazy for gringo men. Chris (good-looking one) kept getting his photo taken. Group seems really nice. N. [the owner of the travel company] turned up 7.30, six of us went for food and beer at German pub. All the guides turned up and stayed late, but us punters went back for an early night.

Monday 8ᵗʰ May

6.00 start–7.00 departure. Straight to airport for Sue's luggage. Hung around for a while, nearly bought cheap local rum but found whiskey just in time. Bus is brand new and *really* luxurious – all it needs is a toilet and N. coming round with tea and biscuits on a tray. First half (distance-wise) is on easy tarmac – then last half on terrible roads but absolutely <u>awesome</u> scenery. Frequently changing, started as desert, boulder fields... then climbed high into mountains – dramatic, snowy peaks. Saw vicuana (3 groups), a rabbit-like animal called a vicachi (?), and, late in the day, a bob-cat. V. rare to see these – had large, bushy, stripy tail. Roadworks at one point due to landslide, took advantage of break to have lunch. Other truck coming up whilst diggers throwing rocks down. Max shouted down 'Fucking idiots' (in Spanish). They reached us and got out carrying huge gun. Said it was for shooting chinchillas, but looked like it was for show. Chris and Geoff suffered badly from altitude sickness (the 2 smokers!) – Geoff especially looked really ill. I felt fine. Reached Cotahuasi late – desperate to find somewhere to eat. Hostel not too bad – but wouldn't risk the bed clothes! Found little dive to eat in. OK, good hot sauce. Bit of a shock for some of the others though.

Tuesday 9ᵗʰ May

Drove out of town for 1 hour to end of road. Pretty exciting drive – had to get out once. Most walked last bit – just N., Max, Sue and I stayed in. Some great views down the canyon. N. and 2 Pepes took trekkers off, others stayed to load mules. Stunning scenery – bit like Arizona. Amazing red colours. Trekked 2 hours to Sepia falls – real vertigo territory. Bathed, ate lunch, got braver about approaching edge. Set off 2 hrs. later for 3 hour trek – Geoff on a mission – sprinted off into distance. Quite a climb, v. narrow with off camber path on scree slope – scary. Took it easy at back – got to campsite around 4 pm. Waterfall disappointing – managed a bit of a wash. Discovered 2 mules missing – Geoff and Chris's gear has gone, plus some food (all the chocolate!). Reme set off back along route to look for them. Ate mild curry, drank a lot of Chilean red (late start tomorrow), told dirty jokes (especially Max and Nick).

Wednesday 10ᵗʰ May

No sign of mules. We set off – leaving muleteers to wait for Reme. 2 hours trek – through cactus fields – not so much climbing as yesterday but v. narrow, single track. Would be v. technical on a mountain bike. Got to river at 11.15 – that whitewater noise will be our backing track for next 6 days. Camp on beach, but bed-spaces are in short supply. Guys have found a donkey-field but it's a bit of a scramble to get to. Had lunch, tried bathing but the river is freezing. Also, they were right – the rapids are 'continuous'. Had a siesta – mules very late. Eventually turn up at 3.00 pm., with <u>most</u> of missing stuff, but no food or safety ropes. N. will leave, with Reme – local muleteer leader to find the thief. (Mules were stolen (!) at start of trek, thief had buried stuff along route to his house. Reme tracked mules back to house, which was locked.) We will stay here – if N. is back by 12.00 tomorrow we will set off in afternoon. Evening – some people walked to village but couldn't get wine – they will bring it tomorrow. I went with Sue, Peter, Martin and Cashimira to hot springs. About 1 km. walk – at a real fast pace along beach, small pool of warm water. Had a wonderful bath, then got hot and sweaty walking back in the dark. Ate, had a little whiskey. More bad, filthy jokes.

Thursday 11ᵗʰ May

Slept till 7.00 (a lie-in) – could have slept longer, but too worried I would miss breakfast! 2 big bowls porridge later. Set off for another session at hot springs with Pepe Lopez, Chris, Nick, Geoff and Sue. Shaved my legs! And Nick had a shave. Max arrived too late to take pictures. Came back, sunbathed for a couple of hours. Edgar arrived back with mule and all the gear except the food – what a hero! N. has gone to Cotahuasi to buy more food – we will leave tomorrow. In the meantime, it is time for swimming/rescue lesson. Feeling very nervous, but it turns out quite easy. In the end we all go in, although Sue and I are the only ones sensible enough to wear wetsuits. Max nearly didn't go in, but got so much abuse he was forced to, and quite enjoyed it after all.

We saw the accident site first from above. Pepe told us that two mules had been stolen from the trip with Sarah, and that one of these had been carrying all the safety gear so the group had to wait two days for replacement safety gear. He said that if the gear had arrived one day later, the whole trip would have been aborted. That made us feel very bad. Just one more day and they would never have started that wretched rafting! We indulged in more 'if onlys' then. "If only the gear had arrived one day later," or "If only the gear had not been stolen and they had left two days earlier, the river would not have been so high, and they might never have been upended." It seemed as if everything had conspired against Sarah.

Before reaching the place where we could see the accident site, we had walked through the cactus forest where Max Milligan had taken a picture of the group striking funny poses among the cacti. This was also the spot where the last known photograph of Sarah was taken – the one where she looked so happy. Pepe took a photograph of Mick and me in the same spot. I wept there and wept when we saw the river from above. We reached the river bank at 1.30 and from then on, we kept stopping and starting for Mick to film everything and for Pepe to give us the narrative on film. "This is where the boat got stuck." "This is where they were all swimming." "This is where Sarah was floating down with no control going over the other rapid." "This is where I last saw her." "This is where we think she is." And so on.

I was appalled that anyone could go into this terrible, churning water with so many rocks to be injured by. Yet Pepe said that the water was less fierce this year. It was now considered a grade 4 whereas last year it was a grade 5. How could the organisers have let people go in and how could the people agree? If I had been Sarah I would have flatly refused to enter the water.

Throughout the day we had seen only one man with three donkeys, two men with a mule and some donkeys and two lone men hiking. The place was truly remote and isolated. We had found the trekking physically demanding and emotionally painful even though part of us appreciated the beauty and wildness of this part of the Peruvian Andes. We reached the camp site that was in a beautiful valley just below the scene of the accident, feeling tired. We enjoyed a salad, Coca Cola and pineapple juice and watched four torrent ducks playing and swimming in the raging waters of the river. Pepe said it was unusual to see two pairs of these birds together and not common to see even one pair. We watched these fragile birds for a long time, enjoying their ability to swim against the turbulent waters. We felt they were a sign from Sarah, saying, "Be happy." Even though in my heart I did not believe in such signs, we watched out for them during the trip. Pepe believed in such signs and Mick said the birds were a sign for him that Sarah was in this place. At the very least, these playful, entertaining birds seemed like a symbol of hope. We decided to have the ceremony just above this spot the next day. Before dinner we walked among the Inca and pre-Inca ruins nearby. There were impressive acres of walled terraces. We could feel the spirit of these old civilisations and felt it was a good place for Sarah to be. If she had to die then she would have appreciated resting forever in this remote, wild, beautiful valley with the spirits of the Incas all around. That night we saw the Southern Cross above the river. This is Mick's favourite constellation. Again it seemed to be another sign that Sarah was there, especially when we saw a shooting star flash in front of the four points of the cross. It was a brilliant night lit by stars we felt we could touch. They would shine down on Sarah night after night forever.

Two years later Mick was to write the following poem that was inspired by this starry night by the river. We also include an interesting footnote to the occasion of the writing.

> I can talk to you Sarah
> Although you're not here
> I know where you were

When you were last seen
Face down in the water.

Dead stones as if amazed watching
Your progress to a fast death.

You always wanted the passion of speed and grace
And mindlessness
As in a supreme sport
Though in fact you were
Uncoordinated to be truthful.

You got what you always wanted
In that last journey,
Fast, furious, delirious.
Supremely sporting could one say?

A year later
We take our time
In the river valley
Filled with life and growth.

At night it has the brightest stars
You will ever see!

Are you watching
My lovely daughter
Now that you are part of this valley,
This land, this continent, this revolving planet?

Do you feel the speed
Of the universe?

Look, my star is moving with all the others!
Faster than anything!

Make room for me when my time comes.

(I had just completed this poem late on Thursday October 16th and went out into the garden to look at the stars. Almost immediately a shooting star shot rapidly across the low sky from east to west. It was not one of those faint stars high above, like a scratch on a blackboard but a reddish and very obvious slash, almost comet-like, leaving a fading trace in its wake. I went back into the house. Fifteen minutes later I said to myself, "I'll go into the garden again and if I see another shooting star I'll take it as a sign" (even though I am a non-believer in such things). As I opened the door, and before I got out into the garden, another star, even brighter than the first shot across the sky from west to east.)

In the morning Mick picked a safe place in the river to bathe. The water was icy cold and took his breath away. He thought of Sarah's body being trapped, maybe a couple of hundred metres higher up the valley, and wondered whether any atom of her was in the water in which he bathed.

Mick and I set off with Pepe the next morning. We took the CD memorial tape, the Walkman and speakers together with some 'presents' to throw into the river for Sarah. The place we decided to hold the ceremony was the spot where Sarah was presumed to be dead or at least unconscious before being pulled down into the depths. Pepe moved away, Mick set up the speakers on some rocks and we began.

First I told her about the memorial service in October and threw in a copy of the programme. Before we played the first song, "Don't Think Twice, It's Alright", I said that Matthew had chosen the songs for the memorial service. We were overcome and held each other, both of us were crying. I then told Sarah about a book I had just read called, *It's not about the Bike*, by Lance Armstrong, the American cyclist who over-came cancer and won the Tour de France on three occasions. I knew Sarah would have liked the book so I threw my copy into the river for her. We played song number two beginning, "I always flirt with death". A copy of Anna's speech was thrown in next. I told Sarah that this was the best speech of the service. I read the last paragraph aloud before throwing it in the river. The third song, "Just like Fred Astaire", came next. Simon, Jo, Cameron and Molly had given us a card and a photograph to go into the river so these went in along with a short piece I had written for The Compassionate Friends newsletter. "Fisherman's Blues" was played and then Mick made a little speech for Sarah. He threw in a pen from his publishing company where Sarah had worked for 14 years and a postcard of Heron Island where Sarah had always wanted to go. Finally, we played the song I now always associate with Sarah, "Forever Young". During the ceremony there was one lonely swallow flying above and one beautiful yellow butterfly skimming the water. Once again, these appeared to be signs that Sarah was there and at peace. Pepe came up and hugged us saying how sorry he was. We felt it had been a good service but emotion-ally exhausting.

By this time the others had loaded up the animals and we left. The first part of the route was fairly easy, but then we had to wade across a fast-flowing stream. Pepe took our backpacks across first, then he led me and then Mick. It was not easy finding our footing and keeping upright. This was only a stream, yet we were made aware of the power of the water. Before lunch, Pepe took us into the house of a farmer he knew. The farm was by the riverbank. There had been a landslide there 20 days earlier and the farmer had lost land and fruit trees. He gave us wine and made us welcome. I realised he was talking, in Spanish, to Pepe about Sarah. Of course everyone along the river knew about her and about the reward for her body. As we left he said in Spanish, "You are welcome here at any time." I cried at this kindness.

Next morning, Mick wanted to film and take photographs. We walked until noon with a few brief stops. We had crossed the most frightening path – a ridge a few inches wide across a steep, shale slope. This was the path I had travelled on horseback on the way out. This time we walked across with Pepe, one at a time. I thought, "Don't think about the drop, just go slowly, just put one foot in front of the other." It is a good thing I am not of a nervous disposition as this particular path would have made me very nervous.

Back in Cotahuasi town, we returned to the Hostal Chavez. We phoned Anna. She was pleased to hear from us. I think people at home had been anxious about the trip. They were not sure we would cope.

Just before 5.00 p.m. we set off with the owner of the hostel, his wife and daughter to drive to the thermal baths. Sarah had been there in May 2000 and we had all been there the year before when Rosie had been the centre of attention. If white tourists were unusual, white children were particularly unusual. We swam there, although the high temperature made it difficult to swim for very long.

On Friday June 1st we set off for the long journey back to Arequipa. We had breakfast in a spectacular spot high in the mountains. Later we saw chinchilla, vicuna and a vulture. We reached the hotel in the evening. Mick and I took Pepe, Edwin and Raoul to dinner at Leonides, where we enjoyed the meal. A friend of Pepe's came in, a kayaker and guide. We discussed Sarah and her trip. Pepe said Sarah was not just a client but a journalist who was writing an article about the trip. He implied that she was allowed to go, despite her relative inexperience, because she was a journalist. I was sceptical, thinking the travel company she had gone with, and other companies of course, would take anyone who could pay. We knew that young Chris, the last to be rescued from the raft Sarah was on, had no rafting experience at all.

I wanted to be home. We set off for Lima on June 3rd and for home on the 4th, but we were delayed in Miami. Forty minutes into the British Airways flight to London, we were told we had to return to Miami as one engine had overheated. We flew around jettisoning fuel. Some people were frightened. I was not as I believed it was possible to fly with only one engine functioning. We spent the night at a good hotel in Miami, care of British Airways. Next day we flew home safely and were met by Matthew at Heathrow.

So we had survived the first year and the trek. Some people said to us, "Did it bring you peace?" or "Did it help you achieve closure?", a meaningless term to me. We did not achieve peace or closure. At the time we achieved emotional turmoil and physical exhaustion. The trip was something we felt we had to do. In retrospect, it was helpful to see what Sarah would have seen during her last days. We were pleased that, given she had to die, she was in such a beautiful place. We liked the valley and the ruins around. We felt her presence there, although that may well have been wishful thinking. We continue to miss her, yearn for her, think about her and talk about her. We are still angry with her for going on the trip and causing us this anguish. We are sad that her nieces are left without their wonderful auntie. Rosie will always remember her but Francesca will have nothing but the most fragmentary memories. We still have not been successful in getting a death certificate. We continue to be less bothered by the unimportant things in life, like missing a train or losing a belonging, and we still feel an immediate bond with any other parents who tell us they have lost a child.

We thought our hearts were broken when we lost our firstborn child. Our hearts have healed, or at least the open wound has become a scar. We cry very readily. The disaster in the United States on September 11th 2001 affected almost all the world, but we felt particularly affected as we knew how parents losing adult children would feel, especially those who did not have a body to bury. Yet we felt their situation was worse than ours for men had caused the deaths of the people in New York, Washington and Pennsylvania. Sarah chose her white-water rafting trip and was not the victim of brutality or terror. At times her death seems inevitable, at times we cannot really believe she is dead. We can laugh, enjoy ourselves, work, play, sleep, eat, despite this wound. The first year is hard, but as all bereaved parents say, "You learn to live with it". This is a cliché but it is also true. Sarah, we miss you, we love you, we will never forget you. You were our joy, our treasure, our precious gift and we will try to live our lives better because of you.

Epilogue

LAST WORD FROM SARAH (AS IT WERE)

I've been talking to you, Sarah,
For four years now
Since you died,
And I'm sorry to say this
But I feel as though I've been talking to myself.
You certainly don't answer me
And I have to fill in all the gaps
Where your words ought to be.
So, I'm going to ask you now,
Here is your chance:
I want you to take over
And speak to me.

I'll say this dad
I didn't want to die on that day
And in fact I didn't think I would.
OK, I was scared
As we all were
But I thought I would be alright.
We had practised all the safety procedures
And although the river looked terrifying
I felt secure with my mates.
And then there were all the others
Waiting down river to rescue anyone who might fall in.

It happened straight away.
I just made a joke to the others standing on the bank,
We pushed off
And immediately the boat was sucked round, and
Try as we might we could not right it;
And soon it reared up and we were in the rapid.
Christ almighty Dad!

Turmoil, pressure, biting cold,
Pain.
You name it
It was all there.
Panic!
I couldn't breathe and I couldn't help myself!
Was it my head, my neck, my back?
Why couldn't I move?
I was moving alright!
At a huge pace
As the rapid sucked me on and down
And up and down again.

Breathing was so bloody difficult,
Choking as the rescuers flashed by!
I was swept along past peaceful inlets,
Between vast rocks.

Viewed from above
I was a stick someone's thrown into fast running water,
Except that it wasn't at all jolly
Bobbing up and down, believe me!

Yes, the would-be rescuers were right,
I did at one point put up a bit of a fight
And got into the right position
But that was not enough
Because I couldn't control my body
To get to a bank.
Just speeding down and up and sometimes round
And sometimes into a rock
Or scraping on gravel.

Well, you know me dad.
I can take so much
And then I have to say 'Sod it!'
I can't go on.
And so I stopped struggling and drifted
With the rapid
And looked up at the lovely blue sky
And the lovely high mountains
And the hot sun
And I let myself become part of it.

Don't worry about it Dad
It was peaceful in the end.
The pain had gone
And the fear.
It was a relief really,
No more silly anger
Or ambition
Or fear
Or regrets.
Just me and the sky and the mountains and sun,
And rocks and, as I rolled over for the last time,
The river.

ৡ

References

Allende, I. (1995) *Paula*. Translated by Margaret Sayers Peden. New York: HarperCollins.

Armstrong, Lance & Jenkins, S. (2000) *It's not about the Bike*. New York: Putnam.

Byatt, A. S. (1998) *The July Ghost*. In S. Dziemianowicz, D. Little & R. Weinberg (eds), *Mistresses of the Dark: 25 Macabre Tales by Master Storytellers*. New York: Barnes & Noble.

Finkbeiner, A. K. (1996) *After the Death of a Child: Living with Loss through the Years*. Baltimore: Johns Hopkins University Press.

Gibran, K. (1923) *The Prophet*. New York: Knopf.

Kettering, T. (1989) The Elephant in the Room. *Bereavement Magazine*. Colorado Springs: Bereavement Publishing Inc., October.

Kübler-Ross, E. (1997) *On Death and Dying*. New York: Touchstone.

Kushner, H. (1981) *When Bad Things Happen to Good People*. New York: Schocken Books.

Leach, C. (1981) *Letter to a Younger Son*. New York: Harcourt Brace Jovanovich.

McCracken, A. & Semel, M. (eds) (1998) *A Broken Heart Still Beats: After Your Child Dies*. Center City, MN: Hazelden.

Mirren, Ena (ed.) & The Compassionate Friends (1996) *Our Children: Coming to Terms with the Loss of a Child: Parents' Own Stories*. London: Hodder & Stoughton.

Murray Parkes, C. (1998) *Bereavement: Studies of Grief in Adult Life*. London: Penguin.

North, M. (2000) *Dunblane: Never Forget*. Edinburgh: Mainstream Publishing.

Pizer, M. (1984) The Existence of Love. In Marjorie Pizer's *Selected Poems, 1963–1983* (p. 78). Sydney, NSW: Pinchgut Press.

Rapoport, N. (1994) *A Woman's Book of Grieving*. New York: William Morrow.

Sarnoff Schiff, H. (1979) *The Bereaved Parent*. London: Souvenir Press.

Tatelbaum, J. (1990) *The Courage to Grieve*. London: Heinemann.

Whitaker, A. (ed.) (1984) *All in the End is Harvest: An Anthology for Those Who Grieve*. London: Darton, Longman & Todd.